Also by G. R. Berridge

BRITISH DIPLOMACY IN TURKEY, 1583 TO THE PRESENT:
  A Study in the Evolution of the Resident Embassy

THE COUNTER-REVOLUTION IN DIPLOMACY and Other Essays

DIPLOMACY: Theory and Practice, Sixth Edition

DIPLOMACY AT THE UN (co-editor with A. Jennings)

DIPLOMATIC CLASSICS: Selected Texts from Commynes to Vattel

DIPLOMATIC THEORY FROM MACHIAVELLI TO KISSINGER
  (with Maurice Keens-Soper and T. G. Otte)

A DIPLOMATIC WHISTLEBLOWER IN THE VICTORIAN ERA:
  The Life and Writings of E. C. Grenville-Murray

ECONOMIC POWER IN ANGLO-SOUTH AFRICAN DIPLOMACY:
  Simonstown, Sharpeville and After

EMBASSIES IN ARMED CONFLICT

GERALD FITZMAURICE (1865–1939), CHIEF DRAGOMAN OF THE
  BRITISH EMBASSY IN TURKEY

INTERNATIONAL POLITICS:
  States, Power and Conflict since 1945, Third Edition

AN INTRODUCTION TO INTERNATIONAL RELATIONS (with D. Heater)

OUTPOSTS OF DIPLOMACY: A History of the Embassy

THE PALGRAVE MACMILLAN DICTIONARY OF DIPLOMACY:
  Third Edition (with Lorna Lloyd)

THE POLITICS OF THE SOUTH AFRICA RUN:
  European Shipping and Pretoria

RETURN TO THE UN:
  UN Diplomacy in Regional Conflicts

SOUTH AFRICA, THE COLONIAL POWERS AND 'AFRICAN DEFENCE':
  The Rise and Fall of the White Entente, 1948–60

TALKING TO THE ENEMY:
  How States without 'Diplomatic Relations' Communicate

TILKIDOM AND THE OTTOMAN EMPIRE:
  The Letters of Gerald Fitzmaurice to George Lloyd

Ambassadors, Journalists and Spies
From ancient Greece to the present day

G. R. Berridge

Emeritus Professor of International Politics,
University of Leicester, UK
and
Senior Fellow, DiploFoundation

www.diplomacy.edu

ISBN: 979-8-9898028-5-2

Contents

Preface

I should begin by saying that I am grateful to publisher and polymath, Prabhu Guptara, for introducing me to the idea of an omnibus publication; that is, one that contains several of an author's previously published works. I had actually never heard of such a thing before, and always assumed that this nineteenth century term signified only a road vehicle carrying many passengers ('bus' being its modern contraction). Anyway, I was attracted to the notion because I had some short works that might be included in a book of this sort, and even more so when I read in the *Oxford English Dictionary*, citing the *Times Literary Supplement*, 5 January 1933, that 'For the author the possibility of becoming popular enough in his lifetime to be omnibused or to omnibus himself with profit may be looked on as a new prize in the race for fame.'

Three of my previously published books are the passengers on this omnibus, presented in chronological order. The first one, *The Diplomacy of Ancient Greece: A short introduction*, is reproduced here as it appeared on the ISSUU platform under the imprint of DiploFoundation, with just minor tweaks and a few corrections. It is chiefly a work of critical synthesis of secondary sources. By marked contrast, the second one, *Diplomacy, Satire and the Victorians: The life and writings of E. C. Grenville-Murray*, is based on a great deal of work on primary sources and was previously published in paperback by The Isis Press under the different main title, *A Diplomatic Whistleblower in the Victorian Era* (Istanbul, 2017). Too broad in girth in its original form even for a double seat on the omnibus, this book has been abridged to an extent enabling it to squeeze in quite comfortably. I have done this by distilling most of the footnotes into a 'Note on Sources' in the end matter, summarising wherever advantageous to clarity, and deleting a few passages of marginal value. I am grateful to Sinan Kuneralp of The Isis Press for giving his blessing to publication of this abridgement. *Diplomacy and Secret Service: A short introduction*, having run to jump on the bus, is the final passenger. This is equally a work chiefly of critical synthesis, and has also appeared previously only on the ISSUU platform courtesy of DiploFoundation. This one takes us into the twentieth and twenty-first centuries and, unlike the one on the ancient Greeks, has been substantially updated.

With one or two exceptions, URLs are not provided for references accessible on the Web because they are often very long and sometimes die. Instead, an *asterisk against a title indicates that, at the time of writing, it can easily be found online, usually without a paywall.

Each book retains its original preface and other prelims.

Finally, I must express my warmest gratitude to Dina Hrecak, Mina Mudrić and Sanja Marić for helping me with the Index, as also to Viktor Mijatović and Aleksandar Nedeljkov for their design and pre-press work.

G. R. B., Leicester, December 2025

The Diplomacy of Ancient Greece
A Short Introduction

G. R. Berridge

Emeritus Professor of International Politics,
University of Leicester, UK
and
Senior Fellow, DiploFoundation

Contents

Preface

This brief introduction to the diplomacy of ancient Greece was originally drafted as a chapter for a book that many years ago I planned to write with Professor John W. Young of the University of Nottingham; we proposed to call this 'A History of Diplomacy'. Unfortunately, because of more urgent priorities we both came to realise that we lacked the time to complete it. But it seemed a shame simply to cast aside the chapter I had written, the more so since the only other general treatment of its subject, *Diplomacy in Ancient Greece* (1975) by Sir Frank Adcock and D. J. Mosley, while quite accessible and still immensely valuable, has a rather awkward structure and no maps; furthermore, much valuable work on the subject, not least on proxeny by William Mack, has been produced since their book was published over 40 years ago. When, therefore, the opportunity to publish my draft on the ISSUU platform presented itself, I jumped at it. At first I thought simply to refresh it here and there and provide some illustrations, but as I came to grips with the subject once more I discovered many weaknesses in my draft. As a result, I have revised it extensively and produced a work double its original length.

I am not an ancient historian, although I have published one piece on the diplomacy of the ancient Near East: 'Amarna diplomacy: a fully-fledged diplomatic system?', in R. Cohen and R. Westbrook (eds), *Amarna Diplomacy: The Beginnings of International Relations* (Johns Hopkins University Press, Baltimore, 2000). Nor do I read Greek. There is in consequence no original research in this book. I have certainly gone back to translations of some of the most important primary sources, notably Herodotus, Thucydides, Xenophon, Plutarch, Diodorus the Sicilian, Isocrates, and the speeches of Demosthenes and Aeschines. But this book is essentially a work of synthesis of existing scholarship designed for the student of diplomacy with no prior knowledge of the subject, as well as for the general reader.

To avoid over-cluttering the pages, as a rule I have restricted the footnotes to parenthetical notes not worthy of highlighting in a box, and to sources for quotations and statements that might otherwise raise an eyebrow. The 'References' in the endmatter provides a complete list of works on which I have drawn.

There have been 11 translations of Thucydides' indispensable history of the Peloponnesian War, which by most accounts is virtually untranslatable. I have used my old copy of the Rex Warner translation, first published by Penguin Books in 1954. However, I recommend as the most accessible version for students the Landmark reprint of Richard Crawley's 1866 translation, edited by Robert Strassler (see *Liz Crawley's piece in *The Oxonian Review*). For those who prefer to read online, the same translation is used in the excellent Perseus Digital Library (in which where available I also cite translations of other important ancient texts). Where I cite Thucydides in the footnotes, I use the page numbers from the Penguin edition but, to ease their discovery in the Crawley translations or any others, I add in square brackets the conventional referencing for such works, e.g. 'pp. 113-14 [2.29.1]', the latter meaning Book 2, Chapter 29, Section 1.

The focus of this book is almost entirely on what modern scholars call the 'Classical' period of ancient Greek history, which corresponds roughly to the fifth and fourth centuries BCE (Before the Common Era). Except where otherwise indicated, dates in the text are BCE.

I am grateful to John W. Young for his encouraging remarks on an early draft, and to Hannah Slavik and Mina Mudric of DiploFoundation for supporting the launch of the book.

G. R. B., Leicester, October 2018

List of boxes

List of maps

Introduction

An extraordinary civilization flourished in 'ancient Greece', the name commonly given to that region in the four centuries prior to the Roman conquest in 30BCE. Despite this, war is also frequently said to have been the hallmark of the relations between its cities. This is an exaggeration: diplomacy had more than a walk-on part in these relationships. And the reason is that, as in the Italian peninsula in the late fifteenth century AD, a minimum recognition of common interests by numerous armed political entities existed alongside a shared culture and means of communication adequate to the geography of the region. Diplomacy was possible and acknowledged to be needed.

These shared circumstances, which included the attitude of the Greeks to political life in general, gave their diplomacy a particular shape and flavour. How were the city-states – for such was the nature of their armed political entities – represented abroad? In other words, who were their diplomats, what tasks were they given, and how did they conduct themselves? Why was the style of their negotiations unusual by modern standards? What role was played by multilateral diplomacy in ancient Greece? Finally, how *effective* were its diplomatic reflexes? These are the chief questions to which the following pages will suggest answers.

The ancient Greek world had over a 1000 city-states (*poleis*, singular *polis*), which made them the components of 'the most densely populated state system in recorded history.'[1] Left at that, this would have militated against a manageable diplomacy: too many conflicts, too many negotiations to conduct simultaneously with the slender resources available. But for long periods many if not most of these small cities were also members of religious leagues and regional federations or confederations such as those of the Boeotians, Achaeans and Aetolians.

---

[1]   Mack, *Proxeny and Polis*, p. vii.

Diplomacy, which requires mutual understanding and certain shared assumptions favourable to the amelioration of conflict, was facilitated in ancient Greece by the culture shared by its people; as the historian Herodotus wrote with the war to resist the Persian invasion in the early fifth century in mind, 'we are all Greeks ... with a common way of life.'[2] Differences on methods of government between democratic, oligarchical and monarchical cities, and ethnic rivalries such as those between Dorians and Ionians, certainly sharpened conflicts; but they were not so deep as to present insuperable obstacles to diplomacy, and were no obstacle at all to diplomacy among their own. The Greeks might fight each other, typically over disputed territory, but in contrast to warring with 'barbarians' (non-Greeks), said the Athenian philosopher, Plato, this was unnatural, fomented by factions, and better regarded as 'civil strife' than 'war'. It was, therefore, to be conducted in a more civilized manner,[3] which made diplomatic reconciliation easier. In any case, more important than their differences were shared religious and other customs, seen most obviously in the great Panhellenic games (see Chapter 3). In addition, there was the 'instinctive love of argument' displayed by the Greeks from earliest times and latterly 'stimulated by the study of rhetoric and philosophy'; to argue from reason is not to fight.[4] To cap their cultural solidarity, the Greeks shared a language. It is true that the country exhibited a bewildering variety of dialects and that the differences between them were quite marked. But as a result of the political, cultural and commercial preponderance of Athens, by the end of the fifth century its own dialect, Attic, had become a common (*koine*) everyday language. When Philip of Macedon made it the official language of his kingdom in the 4th

---

[2] *The Histories*, Book 8.144.

[3] No captured fellow Greeks to be sold into slavery, no gratuitous destruction to be visited on captured territory, and no plundering the corpses of dead soldiers, except for their weapons, Plato, *The Republic*, pp. 227-30 [v. 469-71].

[4] Westlake, 'Diplomacy in Thucydides', p. 227. Compare the radically different arguments of Nicolson, *Evolution of Diplomatic Method*, p. 10 and Grant, 'A note on the tone of Greek diplomacy'. Both maintain that the intensely competitive spirit of the Greeks and their passion for straight talking and love of altercation was fatal to diplomacy. Besides the glaring omissions in Grant's article, I have read far too many despatches sent home by ambassadors boasting of the strong language they used with local ministers to take too seriously the kind of evidence it adduces. Westlake rightly gives it no more than a polite, passing glance and Nicolson's shallow elegance is routinely ignored by historians of ancient Greece.

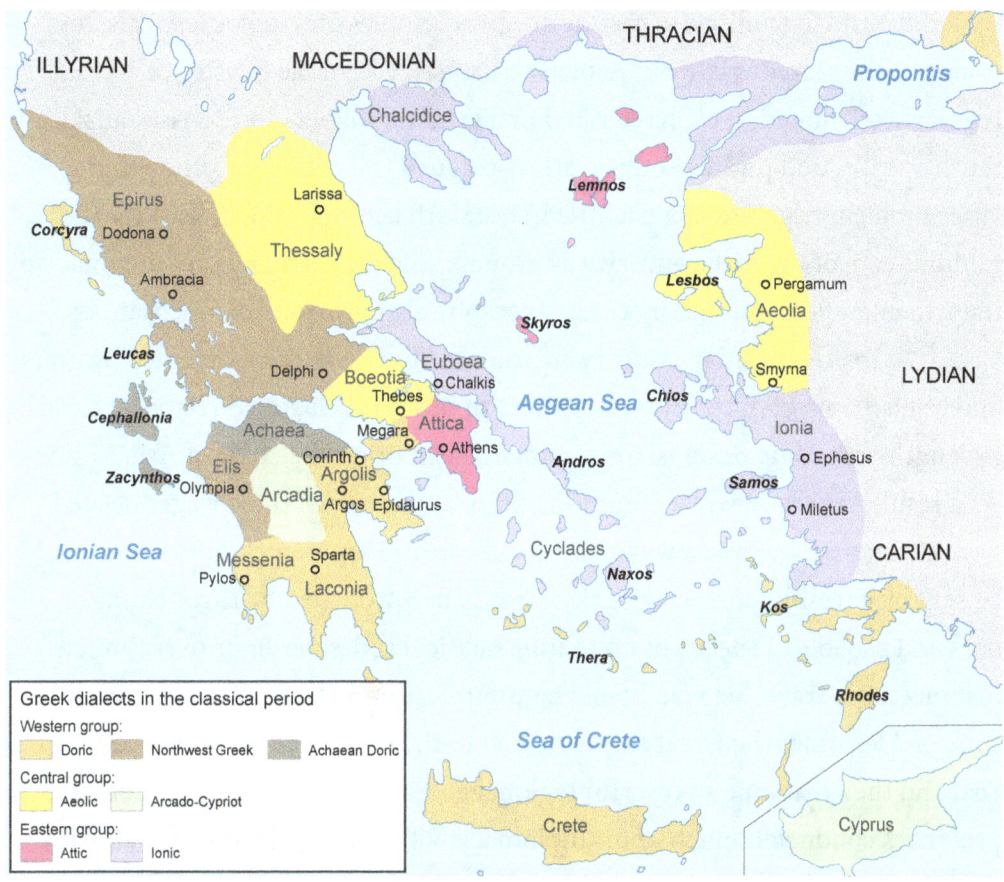

Greek dialects: geographical distribution during the Classical period

century, it was soon the *lingua franca* of the whole Hellenic world (mainland Greece plus its many colonies). Moreover, it was a language with characteristics well suited to the complex and yet clear argument required by diplomacy.

Diplomacy within ancient Greece and between the city-states and neighbouring regions, especially the Achaemenid Empire of Persia, was also facilitated by means of communication adequate to the purposes of common messengers, heralds and ambassadors. Admittedly, telecommunications, whether acoustic or optical (beacon-chains for example), were virtually useless for diplomatic purposes, being capable of little more than transmitting warnings of danger, or news of the outcome of a battle. It is also true that the country was mountainous and the roads bad or non-existent, so that neither wagons, chariots, nor even horses were in general much use. Such roads as did exist served mainly to facilitate access to the great temples and major festivals; for example, the sacred way from Athens to Eleusis, where the 'mysteries' were regularly celebrated (see Chapter 3). Furthermore, robbers were a risk outside the city walls, and pirates and privateers plagued the open sea, although the latter problem began to abate a little in the sixth century and, at least for the middle years of the fifth century was brought under control by the supremacy of the Athenian fleet. But in any case, geography also provided compensations.

Greece is a small country surrounded by the sea and indented by gulfs and inlets, so most of the city-states were to be found clustered relatively close to its lengthy coastline or on islands in the Aegean or off the coast of Asia Minor.[5] As a result, sea travel was a common option and many of the voyages needed were short; passage by sea was also very cheap and an important message could be sent by a freshly-crewed trireme, a war galley propelled by three banks of oars and capable of speeds of up to nine nautical miles per hour over limited distances. Sea travel also facilitated communication with Persia, since until the time of Alexander the Great this extended to the eastern coast of the Aegean Sea, and the great king's powerful regional governors (satraps) in the coastal provinces conducted much of his diplomacy with the Greeks – and dealt with the Greeks on their own behalf when in rebellion against him. The important city of Sardis, only about 70 kilometres inland from the modern Turkish port of Izmir, connected to the king's far-distant residence of Susa via the 'Royal Road'.

Because most overland journeys in Greece were relatively short, these could be undertaken on foot; indeed, when speed was important, runners were invariably employed, couriers on horseback only occasionally. Writing in the late nineteenth century AD but in a vein that would have been equally consoling to a traveller in the fifth century BCE, eminent scholar of ancient geography Henry Fanshawe Tozer remarked that 'the traveller is surprised by the insignificant distances which separate places of world-wide renown.'[6] In sum, while journeying over and around ancient Greece was in general 'neither

---

[5] Settlements *on* the shoreline had traditionally been regarded as too vulnerable to pirate attacks.

[6] Tozer, *Lectures*, p. 4. It is of passing interest that Tozer was brother-in-law to Sir Ernest Satow, whom we shall come across more than once later in this volume.

easy nor particularly pleasant,' it could – except sometimes in deep winter – usually be done relatively quickly.[7] In short, the communications of these centuries did not present a serious obstacle to an active diplomacy. Sometimes it was possible for ambassadors to send messengers home for fresh instructions, or go back themselves and return in time to conclude a vital negotiation, as did the Theban ambassadors at Sparta (the chief settlement of Lacedaemon), where the terms of the resolution of the Corinthian War demanded by the Persian king, Artaxerxes, 'the King's Peace', were accepted by the Greeks in 387.[8]

Thus the existence of the necessary conditions for diplomacy in ancient Greece: a multiplicity of states usually organized into a manageable system of larger units, a shared culture, and adequate communications. What made diplomacy *essential* was that, by definition, among the cities none was so powerful that it could for long hold the rest in thrall. 'As each of the great states in turn – Athens, Sparta, Thebes – attained to a too commanding position,' remarks Tozer, 'a combination was formed amongst the others to put it down.'[9] The principle that operated in Greece as a whole could also be seen in its regions, where a major power such as Sparta in the Peloponese sometimes provoked an alliance of lesser powers against it. At the other extreme, there was pressure to form Hellenic alliances for the purpose of combating extra-Greek powers – Persia, Macedonia, and finally Rome – and then, as also in the much later case of the Italian city-states, there were always those among the Greeks who wished for outside support in their local squabbles. All such manoeuvres, prompted by an interest in security shared by those in fear of the hegemon, required an energetic diplomacy. In the end, the hegemon had to negotiate as well.

And then there was the widespread, if not common interest in trade. Despite the primitive agricultural economy of the time and the isolated locations of most dwelling places, self-sufficiency in essential commodities

---

[7]   Sealey, *Demosthenes*, p. 152. On travelling as 'part of the common Greek consciousness' since the Bronze Age, and its 'pivotal role in the earliest Greek literature', see Pretzler, *Pausanias*, pp. 32-3.
[8]   Xenophon, *Hellenika*, Book 5.1.32-3.
[9]   Tozer, *Lectures*, p. 195.

was not readily attainable. As a result, facilitated by the surrounding sea and many good harbours, ancient Greece saw the development of a considerable trade in such items as corn, wool, dried fish, slaves, and the timber essential for ship-building. Not all states were trading states, it is true; and it is noteworthy that Sparta was not among their number. But Athens, the greatest of the Greek states, was a trading state and was also notoriously dependent for much of its grain – not to mention timber and slaves – on supplies from the Black Sea region.[10] This led Athens to urge a common interest in the security from piracy of the trade routes and take the lead in policing them with its fleet when – for much of the fifth century – it was able to do so. And where trade was active and important, diplomacy readily took root. The mutually beneficial exchange of goods demonstrated the value of bargaining and fostered skill in the activity. It also required a minimum of settled regulation on the handling of disputes between traders and the property rights of a citizen in a foreign state, and demanded at least civil relations with those adjacent to trade routes such as the Hellespont.[11]

What kind of diplomacy was thrown up by these circumstances? The first and quite fundamental point to understand is that diplomacy was not regarded by the ancient Greeks as a distinctive and separate function of government; instead, it was seen simply as an aspect of general political activity. As a result, the city-states had nothing remotely resembling a ministry of foreign affairs or a diplomatic service. Not only in many states was policy fashioned in large councils and assemblies but it was also in such bodies that decisions on diplomatic appointments were made, instructions issued, and ambassadors quizzed on their return. Moreover, those sent abroad were given little public financial support and faced risks. Why, then, did they accept such burdens? The short answer is that, since most were principally politicians, they valued the civic prestige associated with diplomatic duties and also well understood the opportunities provided by them to further their own policies. It is to the

---

[10] According to Demosthenes, this made the Hellespont as vital to Athens as Thermopylae, the narrow coastal passage through which an invading army from the north had to pass, 'On the False Embassy', sec.180.

[11] The modern English name of which is the Dardanelles, in Turkish Çanakkale Boğazı.

personnel who carried out the diplomacy of ancient Greece – among whom the ambassadors were only one group – that we turn next.

1   Personnel

The diplomatic system of ancient Greece employed three main kinds of representative: heralds, ambassadors or envoys, and *proxenoi*. The heralds were very different from the other two and, in light of their responsibility for preparing the way for ambassadors, it would seem natural to take them first. But the *proxenoi* are not only the most interesting of Greek diplomatic agents but also quite possibly made a contribution to such stability as the Greek system enjoyed that was at least equal to that of the ambassadors. It is for these reasons that this chapter begins with the institution of proxeny (*proxenia*).

Proxeny

Diplomatic *proxenoi* were chiefly the resident representatives of one city-state in another, although they were also appointed by other entities, including federations and merchants' associations. They probably first appeared in mainland Greece in the late seventh century, and their subsequent multiplication was in no small part connected with the great increase in international activity – especially commercial activity – before and especially after this juncture. By the middle of the fifth century the institution was firmly rooted in the whole Greek world and survived until its eclipse under the Roman occupation in the first century.

The numbers of *proxenoi* appointed are astonishing. Even very small states had widespread networks of them and, in states with which contact was very frequent, multiple appointments might be made. For example, at one point in the first half of the fourth century, Karthaia, a minor city on the Aegean island of Keos (today Kea), had more than 86 *proxenoi* scattered among other states, fifteen of whom were found in Athens alone. During the Classical period, it is probable that all well-known Athenian politicians held one or more positions as *proxenos*. It has been estimated that over the 500 years or so that

The Greek states at the outbreak of the Peloponnesian War, 431

proxeny flourished, at least 1.2 million grants of *proxenia* in total were made in the Greek world.[12]

A city wishing to name a *proxenos* in another city invariably chose a man with a track record of being well-disposed towards it. This might have been shown by his behaviour in a visiting embassy, as in the case of the Athenian, Cimon, who visited Sparta in this capacity as a young man in 479,[13] or by long familiarity with a resident alien, typically a wealthy merchant such as Heracleides of Salamis, appointed as *proxenos* of Salamis by Athens in 325.[14] It can well be imagined how a state needing an active diplomacy in an emergency

---

[12] Mack, *Proxeny and Polis*, pp. 14-15.

[13] Kagan, *Pericles*, pp. 31-2.

[14] It should be added that, exceptionally, in Sparta it seems that a *proxenos* serving a foreign city was appointed not by that city but by the Spartan king himself.

– as in Athens when its vital grain supply was threatened – would have cared little about the citizenship of a known benefactor willing to serve as a *proxenos*.

City-states appointed so many *proxenoi* in part because they served as a visible statement of their separate identities throughout the Greek world. The choice of a particular man as *proxenos* in a particular city – which choice was often contested by political factions in the nominating city – could also be a way of signalling a particular foreign policy. But these men provided many practical services as well, chief among them being assistance to visitors from the city to which they owed their position; these were private individuals, particularly merchants, as well as public officials, among them ambassadors. Their functions included confirming the identity of the visitors, providing them with advice and local information, opening doors to those with power and authority, and actually speaking on their behalf in law courts and before councils and assemblies in democracies and, where kings ruled, in the milieu of the royal court. In consequence, influential politicians and judges were particularly valued as *proxenoi*. In more disturbed times, they could be called on to assist with the ransom of captives. The *proxenos* was also bound to provide visitors from the city he served with food and shelter in his own house, which was doubly valuable because this surely 'served to strengthen the personal ties of the *proxenos* to leading members of the *polis* he represented'[15] – although hostelries of various kinds were increasingly available to foreigners in ancient Greece and such visitors were particularly welcome in Athens.

Box 1.1   Demosthenes, 384–322

Demosthenes was born into a rich Athenian family but his father died while he was very young and he was defrauded by his guardians of most of his inheritance. Having to earn a living from a trade, he became a professional speech writer for the law courts, and in 355 – although more adept at composing speeches than delivering them – commenced a glittering political career. Demosthenes believed that Athens should be an example of civic virtue and democracy to all Greece and that, because of its special talents, the city should lead the stand against tyranny from within as well as without the Hellenic world – but not impetuously, and via the law and diplomacy, with force as only a last resort. He regarded Philip of Macedon as the most serious external threat, and it was his anger at the deference shown to him by Aeschines that led him to charge his Athenian colleague with treason and cause such bitter and enduring rivalry between them. The Romans, who had read rather than listened to his speeches, 'admired him as a model, an instance of near-perfection in oratory' (Wardman, *Rome's Debt to Greece*, p. 112).

---

15   Mack, *Proxeny and Polis*, p. 70.

As the *proxenos* was the servant of a foreign state who roughly resembled the native dragoman of a European embassy in the much later Ottoman Empire, it should be no surprise that – like the dragoman – he always risked suspicion of disloyalty and sometimes courted danger in his own city. Thus was discomfited the great Athenian orator Demosthenes (Box 1.1) in 343, who was the *proxenos* in Athens for Thebes. At the second trial for treason of Aeschines (Box 1.2), engineered by Demosthenes, his rival had his revenge by describing Demosthenes as 'the paid servant of Thebes and the wickedest man in Hellas.'[16] Occasionally, a *proxenos* was murdered in his home city. Why, then, did prominent citizens accept – even actively seek – the appointment? In Athens they included Cimon, Alcibiades, and Callias as *proxenoi* for Sparta; Nicias for Syracuse; and Thraso as well as Demosthenes for Thebes. In Thessaly, Jason of Pherae, the coming strong man of Greece in the early fourth century, was *proxenos* of Sparta in Thessaly.

> **Box 1.2   Aeschines, 389–314**
> Aeschines was a native of Athens who rose through success both as a soldier and a clerkly servant of the city to be one of the most notable orators and statesmen of the age. He is remembered chiefly for his poisonous legal duels with Demosthenes, from which he eventually emerged the loser. This led to his voluntary exile on the Aegean island of Rhodes, later to that of Samos, where he died. For a short biographical sketch , see *Aeschines (GreekStatesman) , *Encyclopedia Britannica*, vol. 1, 1911 edition.

There were real advantages to receiving a grant of *proxenia*. Most valuable among these was that it highlighted foreign recognition of a citizen's importance and thereby added to his prestige at home. One consequence of this was that a *proxenos* could expect to be listened to with respect on policy towards the state, or states he represented. Eloquent evidence of the prestige attached to the position is the popularity of naming a child 'Proxenos'. But it also brought with it honours and privileges in the appointing city that were in some instances tantamount to the award of citizenship, if they did not – as often happened – provide full citizenship

---

[16]   Aeschines, 'On the Embassy', 2.143.

itself. By encouraging the *proxenos* to visit regularly and develop a stake in the appointing city, these were probably designed to nurture his warm feelings towards it. They typically included the right to own land, freedom from the taxes normally imposed on foreigners, unhindered access to decision-making bodies, a favoured seat at civic ceremonies, and – by no means least – the right of free and safe travel to the city he represented even should a state of war exist with his own. The *proxenos* might also receive valuable gifts of various sorts in gratitude for special services – and be granted asylum should the political situation at home turn ominously against him. As such a valuable asset to a family, it is not surprising that the position of *proxenos* was often passed down through generations of the same family. When Polydamus of Pharsalus arrived in Sparta to ask for military assistance, he began his address by reminding the Spartans that he was their *proxenos* and benefactor – like all his ancestors for as long as could be remembered. A similar opening remark on the same sort of occasion was made to the Spartans by Callias, their *proxenos* in Athens.

Such, then, were the advantages of the position that it was a risk well worth taking. In any case, severe hostility to a *proxenos* in his native city was comparatively rare. This was no doubt partly because so many members of each city-state's political elite were *proxenoi* that countenancing an attack on one would set a precedent that in due course might threaten any number of them. Another reason was that their role was acknowledged to amount to that of a near-genuine *intermediary* between their own state and the one of which they were *proxenos*; and this could become particularly important in war. Unambiguous evidence of this is the routine grant to the *proxenos*, already mentioned, of free and safe travel in peace *and in war*, whereby the appointing state exonerates in advance its *proxenos* from all personal blame for any harm caused to it by his fatherland. And, indeed, there is ample evidence of a *proxenos* being sent by his native city – whether in peace or war (or the more usual Greek position of something in between) – on diplomatic missions to the one he represented. For example, in 451 it was Cimon who negotiated Athens' badly needed Five Years' Peace with Sparta;[17] while Callias, a later Athenian *proxenos* of Sparta in his city, was sent at least three times as ambassador to Sparta;[18] as, it seems likely, was Polydamus of Pharsalus.[19] Further instances are found in the account of the Peloponnesian War by the great historian, Thucydides. Nymphodorus, the *proxenos* for Athens in Thrace during the war, had great influence with its king, Sitalces; he visited Athens and played a key role in bringing over to the Athenians not only this ruler but also the king of Macedonia; while Lichias, *proxenos* of the Argives in Sparta, was sent by the Spartans to Argos with proposals either for war or peace.[20]

But was the *proxenos* a 'true intermediary'? Mack frequently refers to him as 'an intermediary' by way of summing up the numerous services he provided.[21] But when using the term 'true intermediary' after stressing the customary right of safe passage in peace or war provided by appointing states, he is careful to say that it was thus that he was 'cast' in this role.[22] In other words, the appointing state wished the *proxenos* to regard himself in this light – as a man who owed *equal loyalty to both states*. This seems right because this was clearly in the interests of the appointing state. Equally clearly, in most cases it was probably only wishful thinking. Having said that, if anyone came close to being a genuine intermediary in a bilateral relationship – as opposed to an impartial third party introduced into it – it was the *proxenos*.

Was the *proxenos* unique, or was he the prototype – as is commonly suggested – of the modern honorary consul? The case for the latter, which is strong, is that, like the *proxenos*, the honorary consul is usually a citizen of the state where he is appointed to operate (with an equal possibility of having 'dual nationality'), likewise unsalaried, and similarly expected to give much time to assisting visitors, some of whom might have become permanent residents. However, unlike the *proxenos*, who was the only resident representative of a

---

17   Kagan, *Pericles*, pp. 92-3.
18   Xenophon, *Hellenika*, Book 6.3.4; Phillipson, *International Law and Custom*, pp. 153-4.
19   Xenophon, *Hellenika*, Book 6.1.4.
20   Thucydides, *Peloponnesian War*, pp. 113-14 [2.29.1], 354 [5.76.3]. Other examples, particu-larly of *proxenoi* employed in peace negotiations, are provided by Mack, *Proxeny and Polis*, p. 117, n. 109.
21   Mack, *Proxeny and Polis*, p.48, for example.
22   Mack, *Proxeny and Polis*, p. 128.

foreign state extant at the time, few if any honorary consuls have heavy, high-level political responsibilities as well. It is the latter that begin to drag the ancient Greek institution more towards resembling the modern ambassador, and thereby makes the *proxenos* a distinctive type of diplomatic agent: honorary consul, ambassador and lobbyist all rolled into one.

Heralds

Heralds (*kerykes*) were regarded as the offspring of Hermes, the messenger of the gods, and carried a staff (*caduceus*) as the symbol of their office.[23] They were general-purpose messengers and masters of ceremonies, and so needed a powerful voice; among other things, they made announcements at Panhellenic games. And not all of the tasks that took them abroad were of a diplomatic nature; they might, for example, have to serve as a propagandist or transmitter of orders to soldiers on a battlefront. They are not to be confused with messengers pure and simple (*angeloi*), who were probably any trusted and fit citizens who could be enlisted as and when the need arose.[24]

The diplomatic responsibilities of the heralds were heavy and one of these was to serve as a 'truce-bearer' prior to the start of the Panhellenic games (see Chapter 3). More important still was their task of going ahead of ambassadors in order to secure guarantees for their safe reception. Usually working alone, they were able to undertake this dangerous work because they were believed to enjoy divine protection and probably because this and their other duties were more technical than political. Heralds also represented an institution which self-evidently served all cities equally. Nevertheless, they were more at risk when relations were particularly tense, and it was sometimes judged prudent to stipulate in an armistice that their safe conduct should be guaranteed. It has been said that the unusual degree of immunity which they enjoyed applied even to those from non-Greek states such as Persia.[25] They often

---

23 'Caduceus', *EB*.
24 'Barbarian' ambassadors were usually described as mere *angeloi*, Adcock and Mosley, *Diplomacy in Ancient Greece*, p. 152. This is presumably for the same reason that non-Greeks were described as 'barbarians'.
25 Frey and Frey, *The History of Diplomatic Immunity*, p. 16.

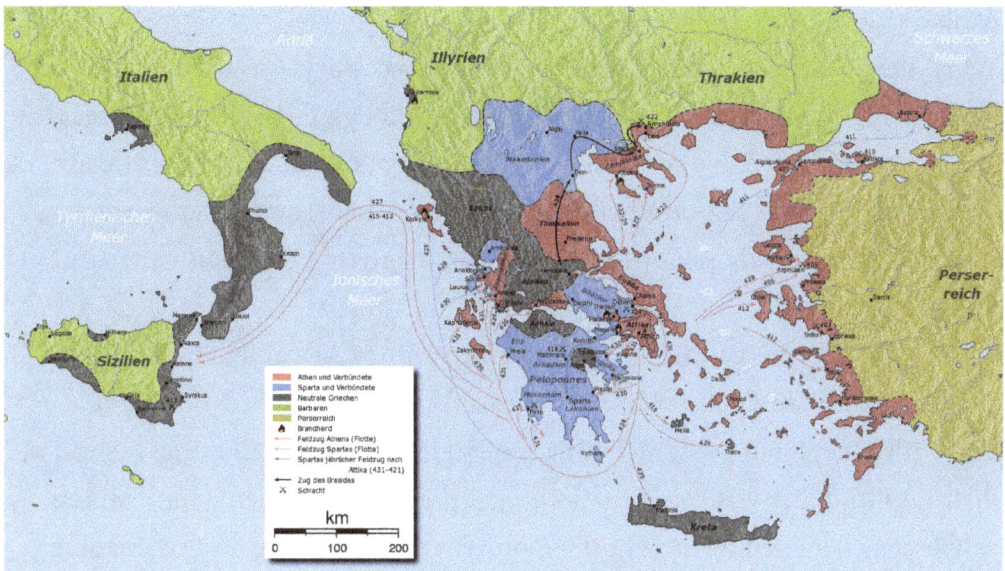

The Peloponnesian War

came from important families which had held the office through generations but despite this, and despite their sanctity, heralds did not *have* to be received, although they usually were. Thucydides says that once a conflict started there was 'no further communication between the two sides except through heralds.'[26] Although this strong statement is contradicted at numerous points by his own history, it seems clear that heralds were certainly the chief mode of communication between the Athenians and the Spartans and their respective allies. In this as in other conflicts, they were responsible not only for issuing ultimatums and declarations of war, and seeking permission for the removal of the dead from a battlefield, but also for conducting dialogues, for example on the proper treatment of consecrated ground following fighting. When their tasks followed a well-understood formula they were probably allowed to rely on memory to convey their messages but when these were more complicated or there was a fear that poor command of language or an inability to resist the temptation to say what they believed would be popular, it is possible that they carried letters.[27]

---

[26] Thucydides, *Peloponnesian War*, p. 97 [2.1.1.].
[27] These were certainly considerations which, according to Thucydides, disposed Nicias, one of the Athenian generals leading the fateful expedition to Sicily late in the fifth century,

Ambassadors

When the need arose and heralds had – where necessary – secured guarantees for their safety, ambassadors were appointed; although if the need was urgent and there was reasonable confidence in their reception, ambassadors already designated might be hot on a herald's heels.[28] In Athens, ambassadors were elected rather than chosen by lot. They were also given credentials to certify their status.

As elsewhere until the late fifteenth century AD, ambassadors in ancient Greece were not sent abroad to establish permanent missions and deal with general business, including general information-gathering. Instead, their responsibility was solely to discharge specific tasks, whereupon – unless deliberately detained by their hosts to prevent them carrying away damaging intelligence[29] – they usually departed promptly for home. It is true that a city of special importance might be visited so often as to make it easy to jump to the conclusion that the envoys had virtually created a resident mission. Such, for example, might be supposed to have been the consequence of the frequent visits of Athenian ambassadors to the Persian city of Susa (modern day Shush near the head of the Persian Gulf) in the late fifth century.[30] But even were these visits to have been frequent and conducted by the same individuals, they could not have produced the local knowledge, contacts, and opportunities for unobtrusive engagement available to a genuine resident mission. At best this was a half-way house towards modern diplomacy. The ambassadors of ancient Greece were what today we would call special envoys, envoys limited in time and function.

Sometimes with full powers to conclude without reference home, the chief task of an ancient Greek embassy was typically one (or sometimes more) of the following: securing a new ruler's friendship on his accession to office; negotiating a treaty, perhaps for an alliance or a peace settlement; giving or

---

to send home 'messengers' with a letter, *Peloponnesian War*, pp. 437-8 [7.8.2]. These men would not have been heralds, but heralds would have presented the same risk.

[28] This, according to Demosthenes, was the case with the first official Athenian embassy to Macedonia, 'On the False Embassy', 19.163.

[29] Xenophon, *Hellenika*, 1.4.4-7.

[30] See Wilamowitz, *Reden und Vorträge*, p. 44, endorsed by both Zimmern, *The Greek Commonwealth*, p. 372, n. 1; Bozeman, *Politics and Culture in International History*, p. 77; and Badian, 'The Peace of Callias', p. 14.

receiving oaths for a treaty already concluded; soliciting agreement to act as an arbitrator; or stiffening the resolve of an imperilled ally or calling on another for urgent help or an explanation of a change of course. The ambassadors of powerful cities were also not above directly interfering in the domestic affairs of another. A case in point is the order to stop work given to the men rebuilding the city walls of Athens by an embassy from Sparta. This was prompted by Sparta's fear of the great rise in the military prestige of Athens that followed the defeat of the Persians by the Hellenes in 480 and the failure of the Spartan embassy to secure the agreement of the Athenian *boule* (council of 500) to issue the order itself.

Greek envoys were usually senior and respected members of the assemblies or more limited membership councils in which foreign policy was shaped; the first term to describe them was the word for elders, *presbeis*. Such was the value attached to the experience and wisdom needed by an envoy that in some states the office had a high minimum age; in Chalcidice, for example, ambassadors had to be at least 50 years old. Some men appointed as ambassadors already held important offices in the state, typically that of general (*strategos*) when it was thought essential to impress a powerful state such as the Persian Empire. Those who had a special interest in foreign policy, such as Callias and Demosthenes in Athens and Antalcidas ('a specialist in Persian diplomacy'[31]) in Sparta, tended to be sent on embassies repeatedly; others might serve on just one or two. However, if a mission did not involve discussion of high policy and was only concerned with a matter such as the reception of oaths, it seems to have been customary to appoint more junior figures.

Perhaps the most significant features of these embassies were the large size and varied composition of their 'diplomatic staff'.[32] Spartan embassies generally employed only three ambassadors but this was unusual. Those of other cities, among them Athens, could despatch embassies with as many as ten or eleven members, the latter number – as in the case of the first official Athenian embassy to Philip of Macedon in 346 – not being rare; this was especially so

---

[31]   Xenophon, *Hellenika*, App. M, p. 398.
[32]   Their suites were also probably large, Phillipson, *International Law and Custom*, pp. 327-8.

when great importance attached to the mission and flattery was a consideration. Furthermore, such large embassies characteristically represented different points of view on policy towards the state for which they were destined.[33] They could also include a representative of an allied state, as one from Tenedos – allied to Athens in the faltering Second Athenian League – was chosen to represent all of the allies on the embassies to Macedon.[34] These embassies were a bilateral variant of the species of multilateral diplomacy that in the early twenty-first century AD it became fashionable to call 'multi-stakeholder diplomacy'. Harold Nicolson called them 'mixed embassies' and deplored the possibility they gave their host of playing off one faction in a mission against another. 'It seems curious to us,' he wrote, 'that intelligent people should have permitted so bad a diplomatic method to survive.'[35]

As it happens, the Greeks were not always so stupid as to send an embassy abroad without giving thought – even if sometimes belated – to the impact of its composition on the outcome sought. For example, in 336 the Athenians sent an embassy to placate Alexander, who had succeeded as ruler of Macedon following the assassination of his father, Philip. Demosthenes, who was well known for his hostility to Macedon, set off as a member of this mission but turned back before it arrived at Alexander's camp. This may have been because of fear, as Aeschines charged, but 'his absence made it easier for Alexander to give the envoys a favorable reply.'[36] Nevertheless, the mixed character of most embassies could indeed be exploited by their hosts. Did it have compensating advantages?

It should be noted to begin with that these Greek embassies were not usually as anarchic as Nicolson implies. For one thing, it was normal for them to have a leader, often the man whose proposal for the embassy led to its appointment. For example:

- Hegesippus, a violent opponent of Macedon, was the acknowledged leader of an Athenian embassy sent in 343 to Pella, the seat of Philip

---

[33] The members of the first official Athenian embassy to Macedon are detailed in Buckler, 'Demosthenes and Aeschines', pp. 119-20, while something of its internal dynamics is revealed in Aeschines, 'On the Embassy'.
[34] Aeschines, 'On the Embassy', 2.20.
[35] Nicolson, *Evolution of Diplomatic Method*, pp. 6-7.
[36] Sealey, *Demosthenes*, p. 202. Aeschines says that he 'came running home – useless in peace and war alike!', 'Against Ctesiphon', 3.161.

II, to demand re-negotiation of a peace settlement of three years earlier (the Peace of Philocrates) which had also allied Athens to his kingdom,[37]

- Demosthenes, then at the height of his influence, was on his own motion sent as 'leader of an embassy to seek an alliance with the Thebans' following the alarming news reaching Athens in late 339 that Philip had taken the Phocian town of Elatea, and

- Demades, similarly appointed on his own motion, in 335 'headed' an Athenian embassy to the Macedonians.[38]

In books 11 to 14 alone of the history of Diodorus the Sicilian, there is mention of five embassies led by one envoy or another. It is true that this is but a fraction of the embassies that flit across his pages like gnats on a summer evening but he reports them in such a matter of fact way as to suggest that this was the norm.[39]

Should a mission prove successful, embassy leadership was commonly signified by attaching the name of the leader to the treaty that issued from it, especially if it were a peace treaty. Notable examples include the Peace of Callias between Athens and Persia (449),[40] the Peace of Nicias between Athens and Sparta (421) (Box 1.3), the Peace of Antalcidas between Sparta and Persia (387),[41] and the Peace of Philocrates between Athens and Macedon (346).[42]

Box 1.3   Nicias, c. 470–414/13

Nicias, an immensely wealthy man, became leader of the aristocratic party in Athens after the death in 429 of the formidable Pericles, with whom he had worked closely and whose style he took great trouble to imitate. He also served as a general during the Peloponnesian War. He was cautious, shrewd, incorruptible, deeply religious, public-spirited and no coward – but he was neither engaging nor charismatic. His qualities served him better

---

[37]   Demosthenes, 'On the False Embassy', 19.331.
[38]   Sealey, *Demosthenes*, pp.196, 203.
[39]   Diodorus Siculus: *The Persian Wars*, pp. 47, 96, 134-5, 210, 293. Two others are named in footnotes by Peter Green, the historian and translator of this edition: pp. 154, 273.
[40]   Assuming this was not a fiction, Powell, *Athens and Sparta*, pp. 49-53.
[41]   Also known as 'the King's Peace'.
[42]   Philocrates had conducted a lengthy campaign in the assembly for negotiations with Philip of Macedon, which eventually led to the despatch of the first official Athenian embassy to Pella in 346. The second embassy, sent to receive Philip's oaths to the treaty, was composed of the same men, Buckler, 'Demosthenes and Aeschines', pp. 117, 119-20, 134; Ryder, 'Demosthenes and Philip II', pp. 58-6.

as a framer of foreign policy and diplomat than as a soldier, although he had some successes even in the latter role. He was *proxenos* for the foremost city-state on the island of Sicily, the Greek city of Syracuse; and an important if eventually unsuccessful check on the imperialist dreamers at Athens. In 421 he played a prominent role in successfully negotiating a one-year truce in the Peloponnesian War with the much-weakened Spartans, and then a peace settlement that bore his name – the Peace of Nicias. When certain important cities refused to enter this agreement, it was expanded into an alliance with the Spartans and, when the war party in Athens revived, Nicias led an embassy to Sparta in an attempt to obtain sufficient concessions to undermine its support; however, in this he failed. It is one of the many ironies of history that the last great adventure of the *proxenos* for Syracuse was his joint command of a major Athenian expedition to Sicily in 415. The major – if unstated – aim of this was to seize Syracuse and thereby control of the whole of that large island. It was also a command that fell to him alone during a period following the loss of his two fellow generals and before he was joined by another. Nicias had, in fact, strongly opposed the whole idea, preferring – as a true conservative – that Athens should enjoy what it had rather than expose itself to a Spartan attack by dividing its forces in the interests of a far-flung enterprise on which the omens were not good. If the Athenian fleet had to be sent at all, he believed, it should simply cruise around the island, and – having put its peoples in awe by what sea powers millennia later would call a 'naval demonstration' – return home. Thucydides reports that this strategy was still much in his mind during the operation, but demoralized his men. In the event, Nicias failed to take decisive action, a Spartan general intervened, and the expedition was a disaster. Nicias was captured and – although some voices urged clemency towards him on the grounds of his previous service to Syracuse, support for peace with Sparta, and opposition to the expedition – he was put to death.

Sources: *Diodorus Siculus*, Book 13.27.3-33.1; *Plutarch's Lives*, vol. 3 ('Nicias'); Powell, *Athens and Sparta*, Ch. 5; Thucydides, *Peloponnesian War*.

It is also likely that some members of an embassy would have had greater age and experience than their fellows (Demosthenes and Aeschines were the youngest members of the first embassy to Philip of Macedon), so they would have carried more weight even if they held no formal leadership position. Unless for some special reason it was agreed otherwise, naturally these elders spoke first in formal encounters with representatives of the city to which they were sent. With a leader, even a mixed embassy would have found it somewhat easier to preserve a show of unity abroad. And a leader had another interest in pressing the embassy's factions to fall into line: his anxiety to have them share the responsibility for its actions when the embassy returned home. This is evident from the attitude of Demosthenes following both the first and second official Athenian embassies to Macedonia.[43]

With or without a leader, the typically mixed character of the Greek embassy was a blessing as well as a curse. Being so obviously representative of the people from whom it had come, it was likely to command respect, especially in a city which also had a democratic constitution. Furthermore, it was more likely to reassure the host government that any agreement made with it would be ratified without serious difficulty – and also ratified by the assemblies of any allies represented on the embassy. A special case of the mixed embassy was the joint embassy of two states needing arbitration of a dispute sent to a third state they hoped to persuade to accept the responsibility.[44] None of the ancient historians and no latter day scholar other than Harold Nicolson seems to have thought the 'mixed' character of the Greek embassies to have been a serious diplomatic handicap.

The unexceptional, essentially political nature of the work of these Greek embassies is further suggested by the fact that, compared to the embassies of Rome and Byzantium, no elaborate protocol marked the occasion of their despatch. Nor could they could expect special treatment on their passage through third states or in their reception at their destinations.

There was no general rule that ambassadors were safe from official molestation in passing through the territory of third parties on their journeys. Indeed, ambassadors themselves could encourage the arrest of ambassadors of an enemy state or alliance, as in the case of the Peloponnesian ambassadors en route to Persia in 430 who were detained in Thrace at the request of two Athenian ambassadors, then taken to Athens where they were all executed.[45] In 397, the Spartans had their revenge, intercepting an embassy en route to Persia

---

[43] Adcock and Mosley, *Diplomacy in Ancient Greece*, pp. 159-60; Sealey, *Demosthenes*, pp. 11-12; Ryder, 'Demosthenes and Philip II', pp. 61-70; Aeschines, 'Against Ctesiphon', 3.63. It is true, however, if Aeschines is to be believed, that at a private meeting of the Athenian ambassadors prior to appearing before Philip (on their second mission) it was agreed that each should speak his own mind to the Macedonian king. He also reported Demosthenes as declaring in his own speech before Philip that the members of the embassy were not all of one mind, 'On the Embassy', 2.107, 2.109.

[44] Tod, *International Arbitration*, p. 83.

[45] Thucydides, *Peloponnesian War*, p. 136 [2.67.1-4].

sponsored by the war party in Athens and executing its members.[46] If a journey was likely to be dangerous, special permission needed to be obtained and on the sea this appears to have been impractical. Ambassadors would generally set off with only the reassurance that – provided their visit was heralded – only their hosts would be required to protect them under the traditional code of hospitality demanded by Zeus, even should they come from an unfriendly city. But this assumed that they behaved themselves as guests: they had no freedom from arrest and punishment for breaking local laws, and thus no diplomatic immunity in the modern sense.

Elaborate protocol no more surrounded the reception than the despatch of ambassadors. Other than a possible dinner or seat at an entertainment, the rules of hospitality did not extend to the provision of food and shelter; for these they generally had to rely on their own resources or those of their *proxenos*. Because of the fear of the use to which the charge of accepting bribes could be put by their political enemies at home, there was also a taboo on the acceptance by ambassadors of gifts – at any rate lavish ones – from their hosts.

In the absence of a foreign ministry and because of the usual paucity of reliable information on foreign states from other sources (see Box 1.4), Greek ambassadors bore heavy responsibilities towards their own cities. Demosthenes said that an envoy was not only responsible for faithfully following his instructions from the assembly and acting in a timely manner because opportunities for pressing an advantage were often fleeting; on his return, he was also responsible for providing an accurate report on his mission and trustworthy advice on policy to be followed in light of its results.[47] Ambassadors sometimes had to return home or send back messengers if they felt the need for new instructions, although at least in the case of Athens they were allowed some discretion in adjusting their negotiations to cope with unforeseen circumstances.[48]

---

[46] Bruce, 'Athenian embassies', pp. 272, 276-7.
[47] Demosthenes alleged that Aeschines, having been bribed by Philip, had fallen down on all four counts, 'On the False Embassy', 19.8.
[48] Aeschines says of the first official Athenian embassy to Macedonia that its 'decree' con-

Box 1.4 Corinth: centre of trade – and foreign intelligence
A significant exception to the general rule that reliable information from abroad was always in short supply to the Greek city states was the wealthy city of Corinth, which lay close to the narrowest section of the neck of land (isthmus) separating the Peloponnese from the northern part of mainland Greece. In about 600, a stone causeway (*diolkos*) was built across this, thus enabling goods and even ships on the east-west route to be hauled from the Gulf of Corinth to the Saronic Gulf instead of having to take the long and dangerous journey around the southern tip of the Peloponnese. In consequence a great centre of transit trade as well as of trade on its own account, Corinth obtained 'excellent access to information and to the ears of leading figures from other states', Kagan, *Pericles*, p. 76. By the time of the outbreak of the Peloponnesian War in 431, Corinth was also second only to Athens as a Greek naval power.

In Athens, ambassadors – like military commanders – were responsible to the law courts and could be charged with criminal behaviour. This might not only be that they had acted treasonously, accepted lavish bribes or pretended to hold their office after it had terminated but also that they had exceeded their instructions, concluded a treaty on unfavourable terms, or even agreed to one that seemed satisfactory at the time but later turned out badly. Such risks probably had more serious consequences for the diplomacy of Athens – and other city-states where similar conditions obtained – than 'mixed embassies'. It probably discouraged some able men from accepting nomination in the first place, sometimes inhibited the negotiations of those who did undertake them, and led to the loss of men unfairly condemned for the manner in which they had conducted a mission. Some were fined, some banished, and some even executed. Philocrates, following the reappraisal by the Athenian assembly of the treaty with Philip of Macedon in 346 which bore his name, fled into exile to avoid facing trial and was condemned to death in his absence.[49] Perhaps only because Aeschines was a brilliant orator was he able to secure his own acquittal in the face of Demosthenes's charges. Nicolson was certainly right to observe that it was 'no sinecure to serve as the ambassador of a Greek City State.'[50]

---

tained the following instruction: 'The ambassadors shall also negotiate concerning any good thing that may be within their power', 'On the Embassy', 2.104.

[49] Earlier in the fourth century (392/1) the peace-minded Athenian envoy to Sparta, Andocides, together with his colleagues, was forced to adopt the same expedient, Adcock and Mosley, *Diplomacy in Ancient Greece*, p. 69.

[50] *Evolution of Diplomatic Method*, p. 6.

2   Bilaterals – private as well as public

How did the ambassadors described in the previous chapter go about pressing their cases on the ruling bodies of other city-states? What, in other words, was the characteristic style of the bilateral diplomacy of the ancient Greeks?

Harold Nicolson hints that there was a significant degree of private negotiation but the common assumption is that the typical embassy of ancient Greece sought agreement to its demands by means of set speeches shaped by the new art of rhetoric and delivered before popular assemblies by each of the mission's members in turn. This accomplished, they retired during the subsequent debate and returned only when it was completed. 'During the period of Greek liberty,' says Nicolson, 'diplomatic negotiations were conducted orally and, at least in theory, with full publicity.'[51] Is it true, therefore, that their task was merely UN General Assembly-style 'open' or 'parliamentary' diplomacy? Whether this is true or not, its public face was certainly the most distinctive feature of the diplomacy of the ancient Greeks and so must be considered first.

Open diplomacy and the art of rhetoric
Undoubtedly the great formal authority and real weight of citizen assemblies in decision-making in most Greek city-states in the classical period obliged visiting embassies to address them openly, and therefore to take particular trouble over their oratory. Public oratory might even be required in city-states, Macedon for one, that were not democracies and so had no popular assembly. Thus Aeschines reports that when the individual members of the second official Athenian embassy to Macedonia addressed Philip they did so in the presence of ambassadors from other cities, among them Thebes, the current military operations of which were at the top of the embassy's agenda. 'All Hellas is watching to see what will happen,' he claims to have privately warned

---

[51]   Nicolson, *Evolution of Diplomatic Method*, p. 7.

his fellow envoys.[52] The quality of oratory was also of great importance to the advocates of rival states making their cases to the arbitral tribunals of third states so numerous in ancient Greece (see Chapter 3), the more so because time limits were placed on their speeches.[53] More and more, therefore, attention had to be given to *rhetoric*, which, it should be added, was as vital to political achievements at home as it was to diplomatic success abroad.

Rhetoric was the name given to the art of winning over a jury or popular assembly by the employment of a variety of debating skills beyond reliance on evidence and logic; in short, the art of winning even with a weak case. The techniques of persuasion included the choice of resonant metaphors, verbal tricks such as appealing to general probability ('Is it really likely that a weak city such as ours would have deliberately broken our treaty with you?'), a tone of delivery (perhaps angry) that appealed to the emotions, and a peroration so crafted as to leave the orator's argument firmly lodged even in the heads of those listeners who had failed to grasp its more subtle components.[54] Sensitivity to rhetoric appeared in the middle of the fifth century and gave birth to a class of professional speech-writers and teachers of rhetoric ('rhetoricians'), among which the Sophists were prominent. The art of rhetoric reached its highest expression in the thought of Aristotle in the middle of the fourth century, although – unlike many rhetoricians – the great philosopher still favoured emphasis on the persuasive power of the truth.

For certain tasks, such as securing agreement in principle to an alliance or calling for help under the terms of an existing treaty, an ambassadorial speech shaped and coloured even by modest gestures to the new art of rhetoric might have been all, or just about all, that was needed. For example, when Sparta sent an envoy to Athens with an urgent plea for assistance against Thebes under a treaty of 371, the assembly 'was swayed by the appeal and voted to send Iphikrates with a force.'[55] It might well be, however, that the significance of

---

52 Aeschines, 'On the Embassy', 2.104 (see also 2.112).
53 Tod, *International Arbitration*, pp. 122–3.
54 A sadly effective modern example, which whipped his 2016 campaign trail audiences into a mindless frenzy, is Donald Trump's 'Let's make America great again' slogan.
55 Sealey, *Demosthenes*, p. 71.

public negotiation in ancient Greece has been exaggerated, probably because the texts of public orations – real or inferred – have survived much more readily than any records of private negotiations and are famously prominent in the history of the Peloponnesian War compiled by the Athenian general, Thucydides, on whom so much reliance is inevitably placed.[56]

Private negotiations

In his biography of legendary Pericles, the dominant figure in Athenian politics in the middle years of the fifth century, Donald Kagan remarks matter-of-factly that as 'a diplomat, he negotiated public treaties and secret agreements …'.[57] And the small states seem to have been particularly fearful of the 'secret diplomacy' of their greater brethren.[58]

There is evidence that some important embassies – even those sent from one democracy to another – were never invited to address a public assembly at all. More importantly, there is also evidence that, even when they were so invited, a great deal of private negotiation also took place between ambassadors and much smaller groups of office holders and influential individuals.[59] This was preliminary to or designed to follow up public debate – or both. In Athens itself the council of five hundred (or its presiding committee) was the first port of call of visiting envoys and it was here that they were interrogated as to the object of their mission and a decision made as to whether they should be permitted to address the assembly; many matters were actually left to the discretion of the council. It is true that set speeches were made before the council as well but it could and sometimes did meet in secret session. At oligarchical Sparta, there was also a citizen assembly but it was much less powerful, and probably even more decisive in private dealings with foreign ambassadors was the role played by the five ephors, the annually elected senior

---

56 On the reasons for this, see Westlake, 'Diplomacy in Thucydides', pp. 227-35.
57 Kagan, *Pericles*, p. 6. It is interesting to muse on what bearing – if any – the well-known 'guest-friendship' (*xenia*) between Pericles and King Archidamus II of Sparta (probably originating in a shared command by their forebears in the Persian Wars) had on the private negotiations between their two states.
58 Aeschines, 'On the Embassy', 2.120.
59 This is the burden of Westlake's valuable 'Diplomacy in Thucydides'.

officers who, together with its two kings, ruled the state; here, personal foreign friendships could be important (see Box 2.1).

> **Box 2.1 Personal friendship and private negotiations**
> Where democracy was at a discount, as in Sparta and Persia, and personal ties with powerful foreigners were close, it seems doubly safe to assume that private negotiations between them were of great importance. A famous case in point is the friendship between the Spartan admiral, Lysander, and the Persian satrap, Cyrus, who had learned to speak Greek. This played an important role in Persia's decision to throw its weight against Athens in the final stage of the Peloponnesian War. It is also interesting to reflect on what bearing – if any – the well-known personal friendship between Pericles and King Archidamus II of Sparta had on the private negotiations between their two states that preceded and sought to prevent this war. Within Greece there were many opportunities for personal friendships to be struck up between leading citizens of different states, among them shared commands in allied military operations (especially against 'barbarians'), Panhellenic public festivals (see Ch. 3), and encounters on embassies. 'Guest-friendships' (*xenia*) thus established were passed on through the generations.

Even in quiet periods, complex questions such as the naval and financial contributions to leagues would probably have been less amenable to settlement by public oratory. But in war and other unsettled times decision-making on all questions – including proposals from foreign ambassadors – could for long periods by-pass altogether not only an assembly but also a council, and devolve to individuals and small, secretive groups.[60] Since officials controlled access to the assembly, it is also a reasonable supposition that when an embassy about which there was special anxiety was allowed to address the people this was because – unless they had simply been forced to permit it by pressure from allied cities – certain understandings about what would be said had already been agreed; in Athens even in normal times the council had the right to frame a resolution to guide discussion of an embassy's business. There were any number of reasons for the increase in secret negotiations at the expense of the popular assembly in wartime and Thucydides provides us with numerous examples from the Peloponnesian War.

For one thing, secret negotiations made it possible to secure a new ally without prematurely arousing the ire of an old one, as in the case of the dealings with embassies from Boeotia and Corinth of certain Spartan ephors opposed

---

[60]   Adcock and Mosley, *Diplomacy in Ancient Greece*, p. 171.

to the peace with Athens and of those on a later occasion of Chios with Sparta, also at the expense of Athens.[61] Secret discussions also made it easier to prevent the sabotage of a policy which was expected to be unpopular at home. Thus, to the disgust of the Athenian envoys, their wartime negotiations on Melos were conducted privately because it suited the Melian 'governing body and the few' to conceal from their people that they intended to take the huge risk – which in the event proved fatal – of refusing absorption into the Athenian empire.[62] For similar reasons, while a privately negotiated understanding between a visiting embassy and an influential individual might not pre-empt an assembly presentation, it could 'fix' the debate and thus have the same effect. Such was the result of the private negotiations between the powerful Athenian, Alcibiades, and the Spartan embassy which visited Athens in the twelfth year of the war.[63] Another advantage of secret negotiations was saving face with allies, which was of great concern to the Spartans following the Athenian victory over them at Pylos. They were granted an armistice and allowed to send ambassadors to Athens to sue for a general peace. However, they asked to negotiate its separate points with a committee rather than with the assembly because they were not optimistic of success and did not wish their proposed concessions to get them 'a bad name' with their allies to no purpose. The procedure was refused by the Athenians and the Spartans departed – but, according to Thucydides, Athens was later to regret this decision. Secret negotiations could also spare the public humiliation of a rejected suitor and avoid its possibly dangerous consequences. This was presumably why, following the first peace and alliance between the Athenians and the Spartans, the democratic Argives adopted the discreet suggestion of the Corinthians that, rather than employ their popular assembly for the purpose, they should use 'a few people with special powers' to negotiate the entry of any suitably qualified Hellenic state into a defensive alliance with them. All Thucydides tells us is that the reason for this was to preserve secrecy 'in the cases of those whose applications for alliance were not accepted' – but

---

61   Thucydides, *Peloponnesian War*, pp. 330 [5.36.1], 493 [8.7.1].
62   Thucydides, *Peloponnesian War*, p. 359 [5.8.43].
63   Thucydides, *Peloponnesian War*, p. 336 [5.45.1-4].

the meaning seems clear enough.[64] In the following century, Alcibiades and Demosthenes were both active in this kind of private diplomacy.[65]

Before leaving the topic of private negotiation in ancient Greece it is also interesting to note the numerous occasions on which embassies regularly bumped into each other on missions to the same city – especially Athens, Sparta, Argos and Thebes – thereby providing a further opportunity for secret bilateral diplomacy. This might have been because they had different business in the same city at the same time; because they had been summoned for a particular purpose by one of the leading states;[66] or – admittedly less likely – because a counter-embassy was hurriedly despatched to a third state when it was learned that ambassadors from a rival were heading for it.[67] As to the significance of these circumstances, it seems sufficient to record the observation of Thucydides that there were many discussions between the numerous embassies present in Sparta at the juncture in the eleventh year of the Peloponnesian War when the Lacedaemonians were having second thoughts about the alliance they had made with Athens in 421, the Peace of Nicias.[68] The historian obviously saw nothing remarkable in this sort of private discussion between embassies happening to find themselves in the same city, so if it happened on this occasion it is reasonable inference that it happened on others.

However, intimacy between members of different embassies could go too far. This was the charge levelled against Timagoras, one of the Athenian ambassadors sent to King Artaxerxes in 367, by Leon, one of his colleagues. 'Timagoras had failed to share quarters with him and had taken counsel with Pelopidas [the Theban mission's leader] in all matters,' writes Xenophon.[69] On returning to Athens, where he was also accused of accepting extravagant Persian bribes, Timagoras paid the ultimate price.

---

[64] The Argives empowered 12 men to conduct these negotiations, Thucydides, *Peloponnesian War*, p. 325 [5.27.2-28.1].

[65] Adcock and Mosley, *Diplomacy in Ancient Greece*, p. 168.

[66] For example, the conference at Athens called by the Athenians of all those inclined to ratify the King's Peace of 387.

[67] Such was the Athenian embassy sent in pursuit of one from Thebes to the Persian court in 367, Xenophon, *Hellenika*, 7.1.33.

[68] Thucydides, *Peloponnesian War*, p. 330 [5.36.1].

[69] Xenophon, *Hellenika*, 7.1.38.

Treaties

The treaties of ancient Greece were made for many purposes, among them facilitating the commercial dealings of citizens of one state in another (*symbolai*); and providing for arbitration (see Chapter 3), neutrality, non-aggression, the formation of military alliances (*symmachia*, see Chapter 3), and the making of peace at the end of a war. Although hybrids were by no means rare,[70] peace treaties were generally of two kinds:

• The bilateral peace treaty that was usually time limited and – although it might contain provisions on territorial matters – in practice was little more than a long truce, anything up to 100 years. These were characteristic of the fifth century, when it was still assumed that war was the normal relationship between city-states. The so-called Thirty Years' Peace agreed by Athens and Sparta in 446/5 was a peace treaty of this sort.

• The 'common peace' (*koine eirene*): a multilateral agreement to which, ideally, all Greek city-states were parties, recognised the autonomy and equality of them all irrespective of their military power, and were intended to remain in force for ever. It was less clear on how this should be enforced because 'autonomy' also signified the right to use force, and in practice it relied on a hegemon.[71] This idea of a peace treaty began to take hold imperfectly in the fourth century, beginning with the King's Peace of 387/6, and is perhaps evidence of a significant cooling in attitudes to the normality of war.[72]

If securing a treaty was the task of an embassy and if this were to be achieved, it was sealed not by the 'signature' of a plenipotentiary, in the modern manner, but – as actually spelled out in the Peace of Nicias in 421 – by the public exchange of oaths in the name of gods most respected and feared by each

---

[70] For example, a 'peace treaty' could also set up a new alliance, as in the case of the Peace of Philocrates, which stipulated that Athens should become an ally of Philip of Macedon; and a multilateral alliance could contain elements of a 'common peace'.

[71] Although the concept of 'collective security', fundamental to the League of Nations and the UN in the twentieth century, surfaced in the proposal for an alliance-style duty of mutual assistance in a common peace unsuccessfully advanced by Athens in 371, Perlman, 'Greek diplomatic tradition', pp. 161-2,

[72] On the imperfect application of this idea in and following the King's Peace, see the clear and authoritative *Wikipedia* article, 'Common Peace'; also, Adcock and Mosley, *Diplomacy in Ancient Greece*, pp. 221-2.

party. Treaties themselves, the terms of which were sometimes repeated in oaths, were actually described as oaths (*horkoi*). The oaths were sworn by key figures in each state in the presence of embassies from the other party to the treaty and it may be that each had the right to nominate who should swear these oaths in the other state.[73] Clearly it would have made sense to pin down by this means those with the greatest ability to keep the treaty. In a democracy the administering of oaths by an embassy was usually preceded by confirmation of the treaty's terms by the popular assembly, as is often the case today. This was the procedure followed in Athens in regard to the Peace of Philocrates negotiated by the first embassy to Philip of Macedon. The assembly having voted its approval, oaths were then sworn before Philip's ambassadors in Athens and envoys thereafter despatched to Macedon to receive his own oaths, which were duly given – although it suited him to delay the ceremony.

The terms of a treaty were usually inscribed by each party on a stone or bronze pillar (*stele*); 'the firmest guarantee that such agreements will hold good,' wrote Diodorus the Sicilian, 'is the certainty provided by a written text.'[74] These *stelai* were placed in the temples of the treaty parties, sometimes also at sacred locations elsewhere. Thus the Peace of Nicias of 421 prescribed in one of its clauses that it should be announced in this fashion not only on the Athenian Acropolis (the most common place for inscription of Athenian treaties, where the temple known as the Parthenon was dedicated to the goddess Athena) and in the Spartan temple at Amyclae but also at the religious sites at Olympia, Pythia (Delphi), and the Isthmus.[75] This was clearly another way of warning anyone contemplating breach of a treaty that such an act would invite divine retribution. The oaths confirming the Peace of Nicias, which was to last for 50 years, were also to be renewed annually. Treaty-*stelai* were sometimes destroyed when the treaties they recorded expired or were dishonoured, as in the case of the Athenian *stele* bearing the Peace of Philocrates, urged by Demosthenes

---

[73] This is speculated in Adcock and Mosley, where also the complications attending the administering of oaths for a multilateral agreement are explained, *Diplomacy in Ancient Greece*, pp. 219-21.

[74] Diodorus Siculus, *The Persian Wars*, p. 103.

[75] For the full text, see 'Peace of Nicias'.

to have been breached by Philip of Macedon. But this was rare, a fact which underlined the importance attached to their religious function.

Many alliances and peace settlements, such as the Peace of Nicias, lapsed after only a few years but this was often because of a change of regime in one or other party or because they were negotiated for reasons of the moment rather than as insurance policies against an uncertain future[76] – not because they had been carelessly contrived. Some peace treaties also survived for their full terms; for example, those of Sparta with Argos in 451/0 and with Mantinea in 418/7, both for 30 years.[77] And some very important ones that did not last their full terms at least had a substantial life. For example, the Thirty-Year Peace that ended the First Peloponnesian War lasted for almost half of its time. Breaches in individual treaty provisions were also common but – provided they were not major – did not necessarily lead to the termination of the treaty as a whole. The city-states obviously regarded treaties as valuable otherwise they would not have bothered to negotiate them in the first place, and they did not relish being thought contemptuous of the gods by being seen to be wilfully breaking them. Agreements made with non-Greek ('barbarian') states were also to be honoured.

---

[76] Adcock and Mosley, *Diplomacy in Ancient Greece*, pp. 136-7, 222-6, 231ff.
[77] Adcock and Mosley, *Diplomacy in Ancient Greece*, p. 137.

3   Multilaterals

The multilateral diplomacy of ancient Greece was extensive and extremely important. Some of it took place in ad hoc conferences such as the peace congress at Delphi in 368. Arranged at the behest of Philiscus, vice-regent of the rebellious Persian satrap, Ariobarzanes, the chief parties here were the Thebans and their allies and the Lacedaemonians. But it surely occurred to a greater extent in the states-system's religious leagues and large-member military alliances (or 'leagues'), the last of which were usually temporary arrangements made for joint action with a specific end in view and were not designed to establish states.[78] The religious leagues were the earliest to appear but the alliances were diplomatically by far the most important. International arbitration was also of significance in the ancient Greek system and is considered in this chapter because, by definition, it consisted in the intervention of a third party. The chapter concludes with a lingering glance at the Panhellenic public festivals, events that are normally remembered for reasons remote from diplomacy.

Religious leagues

The religious leagues, or amphictyonies ('dwellers around the temple'), were originally associations of neighbouring communities sharing a deity which, in their religious observance and exchanging of goods, naturally gravitated to the sanctuary of a conveniently situated shrine. The maintenance and defence of the shrine, together with the preservation of harmony between members, were the

---

[78] I exclude from consideration here the numerous federal and confederal states of ancient Greece – although the formation of some was preceded by a military alliance – because it would hardly be right to describe the relations between their members as 'diplomatic'. It is misleading that so many of these *states* are still called 'leagues', since this term is also widely used for military alliances – in the same way that the Greeks applied the term *koinon* (community) to them all. Thus the following have been authoritatively described by Hans Beck as the chief 'federal states' of ancient Greece: the Boeotian *League*, the Thessalian *League*, the Aetolian *League*, the Achaean *League*, and the short-lived Arcadian *League*, Beck, 'Federal states', pp. 294-5.

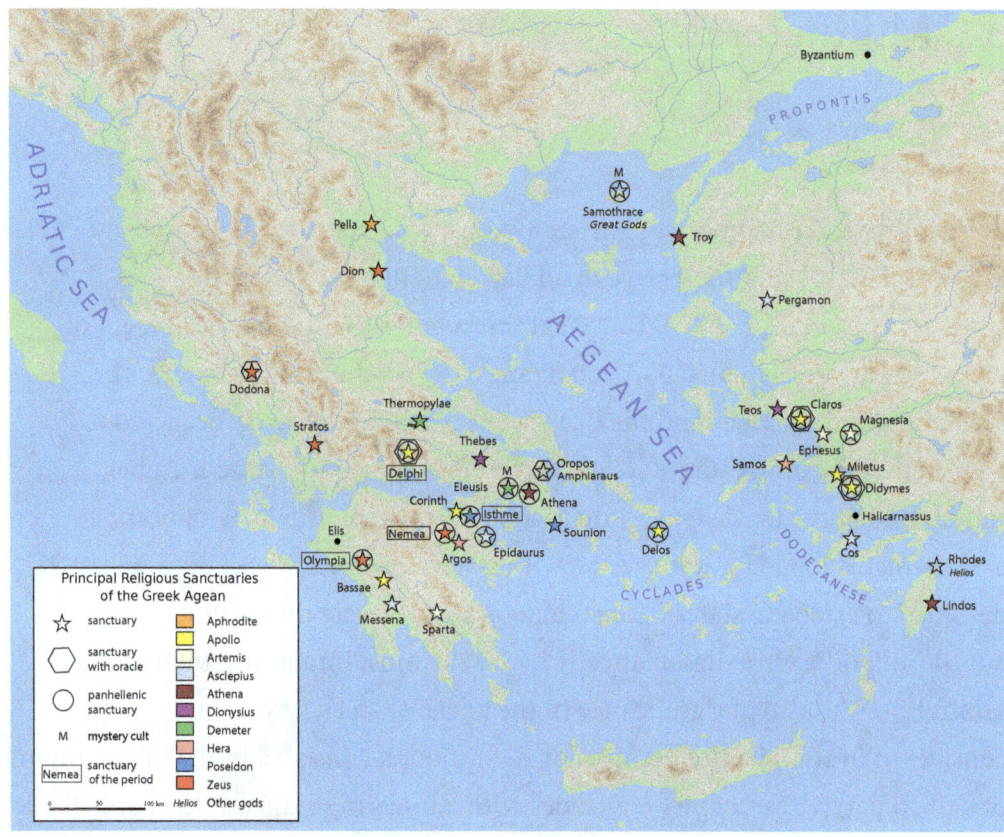

The main sanctuaries of Classical Greece

most important duties of each amphictyony. Those who broke the obligatory oaths underpinning either of these commitments precipitated at the least a fine and at the most a savage reprisal by the other members, a 'sacred war'.[79]

There was certainly an amphictyony based at the sanctuary of the temple of Apollo on the island of Delos that was well established by the early part of the seventh century; another was found at Onchestus, and probably others at Argos and Corinth and many additional places to which there is no record of the technical term being applied. By far the most famous and important, however, was the Delphic Amphictyony, which also honoured

---

[79] The so-called 'First Sacred War', said to have been launched about 590 by an early incarnation of the Delphic Amphictyony and to have resulted in the destruction of the impious city of 'Crisa', has been convincingly demonstrated to be a fiction devised by the supporters of Philip of Macedon to justify his intervention in the 'Third' Sacred War, Robertson, 'The Myth of the First Sacred War'.

Apollo (Box 3.1). The prestige of the 'Great Amphictyony' was reinforced by its legendary oracle, the pronouncements of which were usually treated with great respect by those who consulted it, not least because its role gave its priesthood 'unique opportunities of collecting foreign intelligence.'[80] But not everyone bowed to its judgement. The political influence of the Delphic Oracle was limited chiefly to Western Greece, and it was only occasionally – in the fourth century – consulted by Athens. It played little role in arbitration, no doubt because its methods were suspect: it employed no tribunal, held no inquiry and heard no witnesses. And, describing the conference at Delphi mentioned at the beginning of this chapter, Xenophon tells us drily that the Greeks 'did not consult the god at all about how to make peace but instead discussed it among themselves.'[81]

Box 3.1 The Delphic Amphictyony

Like its Delian counterpart, the Delphic Amphictyony, or 'Great Amphictyony', seems also to have been established in the Archaic period of ancient Greek history. It was at first composed only of twelve tribes of north-eastern Greece in which Thessaly was the most influential member. The others were the Boeotians, Dorians, Ionians, Perrhaebians, Magnetes, Locrians, Oetaeans, Phthiotes, Malians, Phocians, and Dolopians. Its focal point was initially the temple of Demeter at Anthela, near Thermopylae, the sanctuary of Apollo at Delphi being added only later, although this became much the most important.

The association's principal body was a council that met each year in spring and autumn. It consisted of deputies of two kinds. The senior were nominally the *hieromnemones*, two for each tribe holding office for a year. However, being usually appointed by lot, they were often of low ability and little if any experience of public affairs. The consequence was that the second kind of deputy, the *pylagorae* (two for each of the hieromnemones), actually commanded far more influence in the council's deliberations than their 'delegation leader', the reason for this being that they were elected and, in consequence, were orators and statesmen. Matters of special importance had to be approved by an assembly. This consisted of the deputies themselves, the amphictyonic priests, and any other citizens of the association who happened to be present; but this seems to have been little more than a rubber-stamping affair. Sometimes the council took up 'the Hellenic cause' but the association never acquired universal religious authority within the states-system of which it was a part.

Athens, Macedon, Thebes, and the Aetolians subsequently elbowed their way into the Delphic Amphictyony, either via formal membership or control of existing members. As a result, although no member state had a formal veto over important decisions, from time to time it became a vehicle for the policies of the greatest power of the day. For example, in the third century the Aetolians were able effectively to convert the council into an organ of their own league. In such circumstances it would surely have collapsed had it not been for the bond of religion. In the event, it survived until the second century AD.

---

80 'Oracle', *EB*.
81 Xenophon, *Hellenika*, Book 7.1.27.

It is true that the nominal rationale of the religious leagues was wholly religious but it is inherently implausible that, at a time when there was no 'clear division between the secular and the religious',[82] they had no political underbelly. Another reason for this is that oratory was as important at the councils of the amphictyonies as it was in the political relations between city-states. The consequence was that the same statesmen were often active in both. Aeschines, whom we met in Chapter 1, is a well-known example, at one time serving as an elected representative of Athens in the Delphic Amphictyony. In any case, it is firmly established that such bodies tended to become the diplomatic tools of the more powerful military states (Box 3.1). Furthermore, in the event of a decision by the amphictyony to commence a 'sacred war' against a delinquent member, it would have been essential for a council to debate its political implications and negotiate on the division of labour and strategy of the operation. It would also be naïve to assume that private conversations between delegations were any less common in the wings of such meetings than they were between embassies and their hosts, as argued in Chapter 2.

Military alliances

Military alliances (*symmachia*) were established either for defence or – far more often – for both defence and offense. When multilateral they were typically led by the most powerful member, or hegemon. They were confirmed by treaties (see Chapter 2). Most were short-lived but a few lasted for long periods and had an enormous impact on the history of ancient Greece. Notable among these interstate associations were those led by Sparta, Athens, and Macedon.

The Spartan-dominated Peloponnesian League, known at the time as 'the Lacedaemonians and their allies', was more loosely organized than its Athenian rivals although in practice not so different. It lasted from the middle of the sixth century until 366 and, like other such institutions, was held together by bilateral treaties between the leading power and its allies rather than by anything resembling a founding 'constitution'; neither did it have a council or bureaucracy. Conferences of the league, which were rare, were held on an ad hoc

---

[82]   Adcock and Mosley, *Diplomacy in Ancient Greece*, p. 229.

basis as and when occasion demanded; for example, in order to debate and vote on motions to declare war or the proposed terms and procedures for arranging a peace settlement. They usually met in Sparta but only when they were summoned, and there is no evidence – and no convincing reason to suppose – that Sparta was under any obligation either to call for a vote or bow to a majority of which it was not a part. On the other hand, it sometimes found it prudent to consult its allies because the league was 'fractious'; besides, collectively they contributed 'the lion's share of the League's military strength.'[83] But even when the Spartans did support a vote, which was expressed by shouting, this was usually designed to intimidate their allies into endorsing its favoured course of action. Since it did not formally highlight power differentials, this loose form of alliance probably had the advantage of not rubbing the noses of the lesser allies in their individual weaknesses whilst reducing any loss of face on the part of Sparta when it found it expedient to yield to their combined opposition, as on the occasion of its late sixth century proposal to re-impose a tyrant on Athens.

As for the Athens-led military alliances, the first was a naval alliance composed chiefly of the Ionian Greek cities located around the Aegean Sea and on its many islands. It was founded in 478/7 in order to consolidate the repulse of the invasion of Greece by the Persians a few years earlier and go onto the offensive against them in the Aegean and western Asia Minor, later in the eastern Mediterranean. But it was essentially 'a pact of mutual assistance against *all* possible enemies' and from the beginning also had an anti-Sparta edge.[84] Because the sanctuary of Apollo on Delos was venerated by the Ionian Greeks, as well as because the island occupied a central position in the Aegean, it was chosen by the alliance as its base, and in consequence came to be known by modern scholars as the Delian League.[85] The total number of its members has always been difficult to calculate but possibly exceeded 200; from this membership the Athenians did not brook desertions.

---

[83] Lendon, 'Thucydides and the 'Constitution' of the Peloponnesian League', p. 171.

[84] Lendering, 'Delian League'. Sparta, although prominent in the Persian war, held aloof from the new league,

[85] It is also known as the 'First Athenian Confederation'. In ancient sources it is described simply – and more accurately – as 'the alliance' or 'Athens and its allies', Cartwright, 'Delian League'.

The Delian League ('Athenian Empire') in 431

Unlike the Peloponnesian League, the Delian League had a council (*synod*) and a common treasury. As well as discussing contributions of ships and money, the league's council also had before it matters such as the suppression of piracy in the Aegean. Allied members had equal voting rights on the council, although Athens invariably got its way because of its great prestige acquired in fighting the Persians and because the many small states were afraid to vote against it. Furthermore, the council did not sit in permanent session and representatives from its wide membership could not be summoned quickly to debate a policy requiring urgent action.[86] The Athenians also appointed the

---

[86] The alliance with Argos formed hurriedly by Athens in the 460s in fear of Spartan hostility, seems for this reason not to have been brought before the council. This might not have been the only reason, however, because Argos had been neutral in the Persian wars and an Athenian proposal of an alliance with it might, therefore, have been met with a distinctly cool response from the eastern Greeks, Powell, *Athens and Sparta*, pp. 36-8.

board of ten officials charged with looking after the league's funds, which in 454 they removed to their own city. The role of Athens relative to the Delian League was clearly analogous to that of the United States to NATO, and it was not so many years before the body came to be little more than window-dressing for an Athenian 'empire'. The council slowly lost its importance, had probably ceased to exist by 432 and, following defeat at the hands of the Spartans in the Peloponnesian War, the league itself was wound up in 404.

Box 3.2   The Decree of Aristoteles, 377

This famous decree, passed by the Athenian assembly on the proposal of the statesman, Aristoteles, listed the existing members of the recently established Second Athenian League, described its purpose, and invited others to join, including any 'barbarians' (non-Greeks) on the mainland or islands not subjects of Persia. Despite the fact that the decree was evidently conceived as a prospectus, it is sometimes described as the founding 'charter' of the League. A key clause, making clear its purely defensive character, stated that: *'If anybody attacks those who have made the alliance, either by land or by sea, the Athenians and the allies shall support the latter both by land and by sea with all their strength as far as possible.'*

A translation by Stephen Lambert and P. J. Rhodes (from which the above clause is drawn), together with very useful annotations, can be found at *'Attic Inscriptions Online'. The decree was inscribed on a stone *stele*. Images of the reconstructed fragments of this can be seen online in *Christopher A. Baron's 'The Aristoteles decree and the expansion of the Second Athenian League', *Hesperia*, vol. 75 (3), July-September 2006.

The Second Athenian League was a defensive alliance created in 378/7. Its purpose was to guard against a growing fear that Sparta would not honour the 'common peace' provisions of the King's Peace on the autonomy of the Greek cities;[87] later, Thebes became the main threat. It began with a number of bilateral treaties made by Athens, first with Chios, and swelled to a membership that rose to over 70 city-states, a large proportion of which were former members of the Delian League. Each new member affirmed its alliance with the allies of Athens as well as with Athens itself. Its growth was assisted by Athenian propaganda in the shape of the Decree of Aristoteles (see Box 3.2). This time, however, an attempt was made to remove those features of the Delian League that had transformed it into an Athenian empire.

---

[87]   On the King's Peace, see Xenophon, *Hellenika*, 5.1.29-33; 'King's Peace', *Oxford Classical Dictionary*.

Among these was a formal change in the new league's decision-making procedures. Like the Delian League, it had a council (*synedrion*) composed of delegations of the members, which each had one vote. But, although it met in Athens itself, rather than Delos – thereby tacitly acknowledging Athenian leadership – Athens had neither membership of the council nor presiding authority at its frequent meetings. Instead, its own council was nominally just the equal of the allies' council in matters of joint concern. To the extent that the league had a constitution, therefore, it was a 'bi-cameral' one. In practice, however, the allies' council was analogous to what today we would call an advisory council, an official body on which sit the representatives of interest groups with an acknowledged right to convey their views to the executive authority. The council does appear to have had real influence on some matters, particularly the admission of new members and re-admission of old ones. But, in part no doubt because it was seated permanently in Athens and its members were therefore continuously subject to the city's atmosphere and informal pressures, it seems likely that on great issues its impact was not great. While acknowledging that the evidence on procedure is 'partial and confusing', Tuplin judges the likelihood to be that the allies were 'generally manipulated or sidelined.'[88]

The Second Athenian League began to crumble in the mid-350s because the imperial reflexes of Athens could be suppressed no more than could the hostile reaction to them of its proud allies; hence 'the Social War'. But it managed to survive until 338/7, when, following the decisive defeat of Athens and Thebes by Philip II of Macedon at the battle of Chaeronea, its members were absorbed by the king into the awesome League of Corinth. In part to avoid gratuitous humiliation of the Greeks, this was modelled on the hegemonial alliance of Greek diplomatic tradition, with at least one important procedural difference. This is that an element of weighted voting in the council of allies was introduced – each member to have votes reflecting the size of its military contribution to the planned war against Persia. This would flatter the former

---

[88]   Tuplin, 'Second Athenian Confederacy'.

great powers such as Athens and economize on the effort needed to garner votes.[89]

Interstate arbitration[90]

Following the outbreak of a quarrel between states, whether members of the same league or not, a call for 'arbitration' was a common reflex of the Greek cities, and testified particularly well to the cultural solidarity of their world emphasised in the Introduction to this book. Arbitration meant allowing judgment on a dispute to be passed by an impartial third party, which is why it is justified to treat it as an institution of the *multilateral* diplomacy of the Greek system.

By far the most common of the arbitrated disputes involving states were those of a territorial nature: who had rightful possession of a territory or – much the same thing – where precisely did a frontier run. This was partly because fertile land with good irrigation was not abundant and because transport routes, strategic positions, and natural resources all boiled down to the question of territory. Among other arbitrated disputes were unpaid debts and rights over shrines; sometimes arbitrators were even required to pronounce on *all* matters in dispute between two states. But before the middle of the fifth century (it might have been earlier) 'the dispute arose first and then the means of settlement were proposed.'[91] Afterwards, there was a significant change: important treaties sometimes began to provide that any *future* disputes over their clauses – irrespective of their subject – should be referred to arbitration. The first treaty known to be of this sort was the Thirty Years' Peace between Athens and Sparta concluded in the winter of 446–5.

Although supplying arbitrators could be costly and time-consuming and was not without risk, city-states willing to provide the service were not difficult to obtain.[92] This is chiefly because – as in later ages down to the modern

---

[89] Adcock and Mosley, *Diplomacy in Ancient Greece*, pp. 244-5; see also Perlman, 'Greek diplomatic tradition', p. 155. This claim is disputed by others.

[90] Except where otherwise specified, this section draws heavily on Tod, *International Arbitration* and Ager, *Interstate Arbitrations*.

[91] Adcock and Mosley, *Diplomacy in Ancient Greece*, p. 210.

[92] Tribunals of the more 'popular' sort could have memberships running into the hundreds,

day and US President Donald J. Trump – great prestige was to be won by a third party invited to help resolve a dispute, the more so should its efforts be rewarded with success. As a result, even unsolicited offers of arbitration were by no means rare.[93] The important island state of Rhodes acquired a considerable reputation for successful arbitration in the latter part of the Hellenistic period, rather in the manner of Qatar as a mediator in the early twenty-first century AD, and rarely seems to have been shy to offer its services.

Sometimes states asked a foreign citizen with fame for wisdom and fairness to arbitrate in their disputes. Most often, however, they chose a state – usually one of great prestige, not too remote, and to which there were ties of kinship. In the Hellenistic age, the last two desiderata notwithstanding, the great kings were popular. In the interests of producing a verdict that would command maximum respect – as in both modern day international courts and the 'contact groups' that made a strong mark in international mediation in the late twentieth century AD – it was also known for a tribunal to consist of judges from a number of different states (Box 3.3). Whether the tribunal was held in the arbitrator's home state, in one of the disputing states, or on neutral territory, it frequently met at a sanctuary, not least because it was there that the obligatory oaths had most resonance. The character and size of the arbitral tribunal was usually left to the state supplying it.

Box 3.3 The Melitaea-Narthakion arbitration, ca. 143: a multistate tribunal
The small Thessalian cities of Melitaea and Narthakion had a long-running border dispute involving land on which certain temples were also located, the Melitaeans claiming that it was rightfully theirs but had been taken from them by their avaricious neighbour. As a result, two arbitrations were held in the fourth century, one conducted by Medeios of Larisa and the other by the Thessalians; one in the third century, held by the Macedonians; and another in the early part of the second century, once more presided over by the Thessalian League. The first three found in favour of Melitaea and the fourth in favour of Narthakion but on each occasion the unfavoured party evidently refused to accept the judgment. Perhaps it was in despair on the part of the Thessalian League at this situation that, around the middle of the second century, it either encouraged or required the disputants not only to look further afield for arbitrators but also to multiply their number. In any event, the

---

although these normally met in their home state. Those consisting only of 'experts', which were much better suited to site inspections, were far smaller, probably consisting of only three to five members.

93   Mack, *Proxeny and Politics*, pp. 263-4.

agreement of three Greek states from Roman-controlled Asia Minor – Samos, Kolophon, and Magnesia – was duly acquired, each sending two judges. Whether they voted as individuals or as state blocs is not clear but, whatever the procedure, the tribunal smiled once more on the Narthakians. Unfortunately, the multistate tribunal method was no more successful and only a few years later, presumably because of Melitaean obduracy, this 'eternal dispute' was taken to Rome, where, unusually, it was heard – but not pondered in its details – by the Senate itself. No doubt impatient, this told the Greeks to accept the judgment of the Thessalian League; that is to say, to favour Narthakion.
Sources: Ager, *Interstate Arbitration*, p.11 and Cases 32, 79. 154, and 156; Tod, *International Arbitration*, pp. 97, 129-30.

In ancient Greece, arbitration was – as it has been ever since – in principle akin to judicial settlement, and normal court procedure was generally followed: the rival litigants presented their cases (accompanied by documents), witnesses were examined, the judges pronounced their verdict, and the litigants were obliged to accept it, whether they liked it or not. But in the Greek system it is clear that 'arbitration' was very often mediation by another name. There were two reasons for this.

First, mediation by a state anxious to see a settlement to a dispute was often necessary to get the fractious parties to agree to go to arbitration in the first place. This is because – aside from the fact that it was usually only the weaker party that favoured the procedure – acceptance of arbitration was inevitably conditional on securing an arbitrator satisfactory to both sides. Other conditions also had to be agreed; for example, that the precise limits of the subject be clear, that a verdict would not be too long delayed, that the arbitrators should visit in person the territory in dispute, that credible guarantees of fulfilment of the verdict would be provided, that suitable fines would be imposed on any defaulter, and so on. Stipulated in a preliminary agreement, these conditions were best publicised in order to commit both the parties and the arbitrator to them.[94] By the time that agreement to arbitration had been reached, therefore, any mediator required had already done much of the heavy lifting en route to a settlement.

Second, mediation often entered again when the tribunal's formal proceedings had reached a decision. Thus, instead of handing this down as a

---

[94] Publication is attested in some cases but whether this was customary is not clear.

judicial verdict, which would have invited gloating on the part of the victor and openly humiliated the loser, the 'arbitrators' instead encouraged them quietly to accept what they suggested was a fair resolution of the dispute – what our own age would call an 'out of court settlement'. The great advantage of this was that, when possible, it was not only much more likely to gain acceptance of the decision but also restore good relations in general between the disputants and avoid threatening relations between the losing party and the arbitrating state as well.

Interstate arbitration in ancient Greece did not, as might be expected, have a record of untrammelled success, especially in settling conflicts between major alliances such as those led by Athens and Sparta in the Peloponnesian War. While potential arbitrators were always to be found, settling on one acceptable to two powerful parties with many allies was extremely difficult. On those occasions when it was sought by a powerful state, sometimes this seems to have been a ruse to gain the moral ascendancy prior to starting a war. Arbitration was more popular with smaller states, which had fewer options. As for the enforcement of judgments, even powerful arbitrators hesitated over this. Nevertheless, it is evident that a very large number of disputes in ancient Greece – in far from trivial cases – were referred to arbitration and that most verdicts were accepted by both parties. The example in Box 3.3 in a way proves this rule, for it shows that over more than two centuries of one or other disputant not getting the 'right' result, they did not give up on arbitration. Furthermore, employment of arbitration surely became more widespread during the fourth century, as experience with it accumulated and more attention generally was given to safeguards against war; and in the following century it played 'a very prominent part in Greek history.'[95] This is in large part because the arbitration of the ancient Greeks was less legalistic than that of our own day and because it was favoured by the Macedonian conquerors as a useful device for helping to keep the home front quiet while they concentrated on furthering their ambitions in more far-flung places.

---

[95]   Tod, *International Arbitration*, p. 180; see also Bozeman, *Politics and Culture in International History*, pp. 81-5.

Panhellenic public festivals

Panhellenic public festivals held to honour the gods and inspire competition in drama, music, poetry and above all – to the disgust of Isocrates – athletics, were a very important feature of life in ancient Greece.[96] With the stage set by processions and sacrifices, high prestige was to be won by those who excelled on these spectacular occasions, and valuable gifts and privileges were presented to the victors on returning home. But, on the side, they also made a significant contribution to multilateral diplomacy.

Among the greatest of these festivals were the four Panhellenic games, which – so that they did not clash – were held at different junctures in a four-year cycle, the *periodos*.[97] Staged every four years were the Olympic Games and the Pythian Games, the former held in honour of Zeus at the sanctuary of Olympia in Elis in the north-western Peloponnese and the latter for Apollo at Delphi. Held biennially were the Isthmian Games and the Nemean Games, the former taking place every two years on the supremely accessible Isthmus of Corinth, the site of much the most important of the festivals dedicated to the sea god, Poseidon; and the latter at the sanctuary of the same name to Zeus in the north-east of the Peloponnese, later in Argos. There were also more local festivals, among them the 'Great Panathenaia', a set of games added every four years to the annual festival held in Athens in honour of the goddess Athena; the Dionysian festival, held annually also in Athens; Laconia's Hyacinthia, which was marked particularly by the Spartans and the Amyclaeans at Amyclae; and the 'mysteries' of the mythical Persephone and her mother Demeter, celebrated at Eleusis in Attica, the 'lesser' every year and the 'greater' every fourth.

All of these occasions were of some diplomatic significance because they were intervals of political truce in any conflict that happened to coincide with them, and in this regard resembled the funerals of leading political figures in the world diplomatic system over two thousand years later.[98] But this was particularly true of the four major Panhellenic festivals, at which

---

96 Isocrates, *Panegyricus*, 4.41.
97 This is explained fully in Remijsen and Clarysse, 'The periodos'.
98 Some of the ancient Greek festivals themselves originated in funeral games held in honour of a chieftain or others who fell in battle, Gardiner, *Athletics of the Ancient World*, p. 32.

heralds called 'truce-bearers' were commonly sent out ahead of the opening ceremony to announce the 'sacred truce'; this lasted much longer than the games themselves in order to permit visitors to journey to and from them under the direct protection of a god. The truce of the five-day Olympiad, which in most respects was the model for the other games, endured for a full month. Any state breaching the truce and thereby committing an act of sacrilege might be given a hefty fine and, if it refused to pay, banned from the temple of Zeus and thus from taking part in the games. This was the predictable fate of the Spartans on the occasion of the Olympic Games in 420, when – claiming afterwards that news of the truce had not reached them – they made the elementary error of attacking a fort and an important city (Lepreum) belonging to none other than the event's organizers, the Elians, who during the sacred truce of the Olympiad forbad the bearing of arms by anyone in their territory and proclaimed its full length and breadth to be sacrosanct.[99] This was a costly mistake for the Spartans, who were regular winners at athletics. As a rule, the sacred month was widely observed.

At the festivals, sacrifices to deities shared by enemies as well as friends were offered on the first day by special ambassadors sent by the attending states, while envoys were also given the tasks of presenting gifts to the sacred treasury and ensuring the display of 'copies, on tablets of stone or bronze, of treaties and decrees to which they wished to direct the eyes of all Greece.'[100] In his famous *Panegyricus*, Isocrates wrote of the diplomatic value of these festivals:

> Now the founders of our great festivals are justly praised for
> handing down to us a custom by which, having proclaimed a truce
> and resolved our pending quarrels, we come together in one place,
> where, as we make our prayers and sacrifices in common, we are
> reminded of the kinship which exists among us and are made to
> feel more kindly towards each other for the future, reviving our old
> friendships and establishing new ties.[101]

---

[99]   Thucydides, *History*, pp. 340-1 [5.48-51]; Gardiner, *Athletics of the Ancient World*, p. 34.
[100]   Gardner and Jevons, *Manual*, p. 270.
[101]   Isocrates, *Panegyricus*, 4.43.

Isocrates was making the case for the advantages of the Greeks 'assembling together' the better to deal with the barbarian, as well as to assert the claim to leadership of Athens, which, as it happened, excelled in these festivals. So his suggestion that inter-state quarrels were almost automatically settled by diplomacy immediately prior to, during or following one of these occasions must be regarded with scepticism; his wish was in any case too often father to this thought.[102] Nevertheless, he was right to point to their potential for stimulating and facilitating private contacts in the wings of these events (see also Box 2.1), and the fact that he saw it means it was likely that at least some others saw it too.

---

[102]   Romilly, 'Eunoia in Isocrates', p. 99.

4   Conclusion

The view is often heard that failure to keep the peace by diplomacy is evidence of its ineffectiveness. Should this be true, the diplomacy of the ancient Greek city-states can immediately be dismissed as ineffectual, since war between them was a common occurrence even if not the normal characteristic of their relations. But while it is always possible that faulty diplomatic methods or use of suitable methods by incompetent individuals might be a cause of war, it must always be remembered that the instructions on which diplomats act are issued by political leaders. And such individuals might be resolved on war; or set their demands so high that their diplomats have no chance of getting them accepted; or, if more risk-averse, set their demands so low that their diplomats inevitably feed over-confidence on the other side – all with the same result. In fact, war is usually a deliberate or accidental consequence of foreign policy, and for the winning side might well be evidence of the *effectiveness* of diplomacy if its personnel have been successful in solidifying alliances, negotiating base agreements, and securing the supply of strategic materials, all of which are usually vital to victory; and *effective for the losing side as well* if they are able to negotiate the best terms possible in a peace settlement. With such preliminary thoughts in mind, let us turn to the main question: Were the diplomatic methods of the ancient Greeks fit for purpose; that is, for their commercial, cultural, foreign intelligence-gathering, and political/military purposes?

The city-states were clearly anxious for the development of trade not only in the Greek world but also beyond it. Although commerce was despised by the landed aristocrats who tended to hold sway even in the democracies, it was valued for obtaining essential supplies and for the revenues it generated from taxation, including poll taxes on the large number of transient and resident foreigners (*xenoi* and *metics*) amongst the traders. Long-distance trade expanded during the Classical period, for the traders 'took very little notice' of the wars,[103] and it became 'a specialized and important sector of the economy.'[104] This expansion would have been seriously hindered if not rendered impossible in the absence of diplomatic intervention: intervention to conclude treaties facilitating the commercial dealings of citizens of one state in another (especially *symbolai*, whereby foreign nationals were granted legal protection and equal status with citizens in the law courts[105]); to provide assistance (via *proxenoi*) to traders in difficulties; and to cultivate friendly relations with state-suppliers of vital goods and states adjacent to trade routes such as the Hellespont.

The ancient Greeks, as we know, were highly sensitive to their common culture but ethnic and political differences stood in the way of celebrating and enriching this in Panhellenic public festivals. These would have been seriously hindered if not rendered impossible in the absence of the sacred truce announced by heralds.

But were the diplomatic methods of the time also fit for the purpose of collecting foreign intelligence? Allegedly not: 'to the modern eye,' says one respected textbook, 'the diplomatic exchanges of the Greeks were marked by an astonishing ignorance.'[106] Another cites among them the surprise of the Greeks at the Theban defeat of Sparta at Leuctra in 371, and the ignorance of the Athenians about affairs in Sicily prior to the despatch of their ill-fated expedition to that large island in 415, despite their long-standing treaties with two cities on its east coast and naval forays into western waters during the Peloponesian War.[107]

On the other hand, as we now know, even the smallest city-states had the eyes and ears of their *proxenoi* on foreign ground; many states were constantly sending abroad large embassies, which would hardly have had their own eyes shut and ears covered; league councils and Panhellenic festivals were fruitful grounds for obtaining intelligence; and – at least for trading states such as Corinth, Rhodes and Athens – merchants were an additional source of

---

[103]   Michel, *Economics of Ancient Greece*, p. 229.
[104]   Engen, 'Economy of ancient Greece'.
[105]   Michel, *Economics of Ancient Greece*, p. 227; see also Phillipson, *International Law and Custom*, pp. 139-40.
[106]   Hamilton and Langhorne, *Practice of Diplomacy*, p. 15.
[107]   Adcock and Mosley, *Diplomacy in Ancient Greece*, pp. 174-7.

foreign news. So it should not be surprising that there is contrary evidence on the effectiveness of the diplomacy of the ancient Greeks and their 'barbarian' interlocutors in gleaning foreign intelligence. Thus Philip of Macedon is reputed to have been able to discover 'within hours what his arch-opponent Demosthenes had said in his speeches in Athens,' and the Greeks themselves 'were often able to anticipate the moves of others in times of crisis' with 'unerring accuracy.' Among other things, this enabled them quickly to send a counter-embassy when they learned of the despatch of a mission by a rival to a third state.[108]

On balance, then, the collection of information was generally 'a haphazard affair.'[109] The real problem for the ancient Greeks was more the absence of any system of bureaucratic storage and retrieval of information on the capabilities of other states. But when it is also borne in mind that little changed in their wealth production and military technology, this was not usually a fatal weakness. In sum, therefore, the diplomacy of the ancient Greeks was not at all badly set up for the intelligence work required by their times. Spectacular 'intelligence failures' are not exactly unknown in the modern world either.

Last but by no means least, there can be little doubt that the diplomacy of the ancient Greeks was suitable to negotiating agreements of a political and military kind, and then for underpinning them by oaths and publicity on *stelae*. The most important were chiefly peace settlements and military alliances – some of which were the building blocks of major leagues and included arbitration clauses – and these treaties were rarely transient even if it was unusual for them to last for their full terms. By such means the Greeks were able to join forces in resisting the assaults of Persia in the early fifth century and then to sustain a balance of power in the Aegean and the eastern Mediterranean that – notwithstanding a long interlude of Spartan 'hegemony' either side of the end of the century and a shorter one by Thebes later – lasted until the Macedonian conquest confirmed by the battle of Chaeronea in 338.

---

[108] Adcock and Mosley, *Diplomacy in Ancient Greece*, p. 176.
[109] Adcock and Mosley, *Diplomacy in Ancient Greece*, p. 176.

Nevertheless, echoing Demosthenes, Harold Nicolson – the most elegant and well-known writer on diplomacy in the English language in the twentieth century – complains that the democratic procedures of the Greeks placed them at a permanent diplomatic and military disadvantage in dealing with despotic regimes such as that of Philip of Macedon and that this contributed to this king's final victory over them at Chaeronea. Their decisions, he maintained, could 'never be either so secret or so quick,' or even so coherent.[110] This is certainly true.[111] But it is a condemnation of how foreign policy was made and ambassadors were handled, rather than of the diplomatic *methods* of the ancient Greeks – what sort of diplomatic agents they employed and what those agents actually did. In any case, in the 'perfect illustration' of the failings of 'democratic diplomacy' that Nicolson provides – the pre-Chaeronea Athenian bid to fire up Panhellenic resistance – he fails to notice, among half a dozen other things, that the Second Athenian League still provided some allies; that another diplomatic institution, *proxeny*, assisted Athens to enlist the critical assistance of hitherto hostile Thebes; and that the Greeks could well have won the day at Chaeronea against a lesser military leader than Philip II.[112] In so far as Nicolson criticized their diplomatic methods, his main target was the 'mixed embassy', but this had advantages as well as disadvantages. He also makes no allowance for the extensive but little-remarked resort to private diplomacy that was also a feature of the Greek system, as we have seen.

Conditions in ancient Greece favoured an energetic diplomacy, as emphasised in the Introduction, but others imposed heavy handicaps on its mechanisms and gave them an excessive workload. An exceptional burden on both was the enormous number of city-states, which made agreement on matters of common concern more difficult to achieve, while their long

---

[110] Nicolson, *Evolution of Diplomatic Method*, p. 11: 'delays and *confusions* [were] inherent in democratic diplomacy' (emphasis added).

[111] See also Green, *Alexander the Great*, p. xix: 'The cumbersome democratic process met efficient autocracy and failed.'

[112] Demosthenes was *proxenos* of Thebes in Athens, and it was chiefly his personal diplomacy that persuaded the Thebans to stand with the Athenians at Chaeronea, Adcock and Mosley, *Diplomacy in Ancient Greece*, p. 96; see also, Demosthenes, 18.169-79. It is instructive to compare Nicolson's account of the pre-Chaeronea diplomacy with that of Ryder, 'Demosthenes and Philip II'.

peripheries relative to their area led to countless boundary disputes. In all of the circumstances, particularly these, the diplomacy of the ancient Greeks was remarkably effective, and certainly more so than might be concluded from a hasty reading of their recurring wars and occasional disposition to 'lay waste' to the countryside and level the city of a defeated rival. I am inclined to agree with Adam Watson that the ancient Greeks produced 'one of the most developed periods of diplomacy before our time.'[113]

---

[113] Watson, *Diplomacy*, p. 86.

Some important dates

480	Conventional start of 'Classical' Period, marked by end of Persian threat
478/7	Formation of Delian League
458	Outbreak of First Peloponnesian War
454	Delian League treasury moved to Athens
449	Peace of Callias between Athens and Persia
446/5	Thirty Years' Peace treaty (with arbitration clause) ends First Peloponnesian War
431	Outbreak of (Second) Peloponnesian War
429	Death of Pericles
423	Year's Truce between Athens and Sparta
421	Peace of Nicias in Peloponnesian War, and Athens-Sparta defensive alliance
418	Battle of Mantinea, at which Peloponnesian League defeats Athens and its new democratic allies in Peloponnese and Peace of Nicias in tatters
415	Athenian military expedition to Sicily
413	Catastrophic Athenian defeat in Sicily and Nicias executed Renewal of Peloponnesian War
411	Persians intervene in war
405	Artaxerxes succeeds to throne of Persia Spartan admiral, Lysander, destroys Athenian fleet at Aegospotami
404	Surrender of Athens to Sparta and winding up of Delian League

395	Death of Thucydides
394	Thebes and Athens form coalition against Sparta Outbreak of Corinthian War
387/6	The King's Peace/ Peace of Antalcidas between Sparta and Persia
382	Spartans seize Thebes
378/7	Second Athenian Confederacy established
377	Decree of Aristoteles
371	Thebes defeats Sparta at Leuctra, and subsequently sets up Arcadian League
370	Athens switches to Sparta's side
362	Battle of Mantinea, a re-match of Leuctra again won by the Thebans, but their leaders killed
356	Outbreak of war between Athens and Macedon
355	Outbreak of 'Third Sacred War', between Delphic League and Phocians
346	Peace of Philocrates: Philip II of Macedon imposes peace and alliance on Athens
338	Battle of Chaeronea, decisive victory of Philip II of Macedonia over Greek forces led by Athens and Thebes
338/7	Formation of League of Corinth
323	Death of Alexander the Great and conventional start of the 'Hellenistic' period

References and select bibliography

An *asterisk preceding a reference indicates online availability at the time of writing, usually without a paywall.

Adcock, Sir Frank and D. J. Mosley, *Diplomacy in Ancient Greece* (London, 1975)

*Aeschines, 'Against Ctesiphon', Perseus Digital Library

*Aeschines (Greek statesman), *Encyclopedia Britannica, 1911 edition, vol. 1*

*Aeschines, 'On the Embassy', Perseus Digital Library

Ager, Sheila L., *Interstate Arbitrations in the Greek World, 337-90 B.C.* (Berkeley, 1996)

*'Amphictyony', *Encyclopedia Britannica, 1911 edition* [G. W. Botsford]

Anderson, J. K., *Xenophon* (London, 2001)

Badian, E., 'The Peace of Callias', *The Journal of Hellenic Studies*, vol.107, 1987

*Baron, Christopher A., 'The Aristoteles decree and the expansion of the Second Athenian League', *Hesperia*, vol. 75 (3), July-September 2006

Beck, Hans, 'Federal states', *Encyclopedia of Ancient Greece*, ed. Nigel Wilson (London, 2006)

Berridge, G. R., *Diplomacy: Theory and Practice*, 6th ed (Cham, Switzerland, 2022)

Boak, A. E. R., 'Greek interstate associations and the League of Nations', *The American Journal of International Law*, vol. 15 (3), July 1921

Bolmarcich, Sarah, 'The afterlife of a treaty', *Classical Quarterly*, vol. 57 (2) (December 2007)

Bonner, Robert J. and Gertrude Smith, 'Administration of justice in the Delphic Amphictyony', *Classical Philology*, 38 (1), January 1943

Bozeman, Adda B., *Politics and Culture in International History: From the Ancient Near East to the Opening of the Modern Age*, 2nd ed (Transaction: London, 1994)

Bruce, I. A. F., 'Athenian embassies in the early fourth century B.C.', *Historia*, 15 (3), August 1966

Buckler, John, 'Demosthenes and Aeschines', in Worthington, I. (ed), *Demosthenes: Statesman and orator* (London, 2000)

*'Caduceus', *Encyclopedia Britannica, 1911 edition*

*Cartwright, Mark, 'Delian League', *Ancient History Encyclopedia*, 4 March 2016

*Cartwright, Mark, 'Trade in ancient Greece', *Ancient History Encyclopedia*, 22 May 2018

Casson, Lionel, *Travel in the Ancient World* (London, 1974)

'Common Peace', *Wikipedia*. This is a clear and authoritative exercise in history of ideas and diplomatic history, based largely on German sources.

*'Decree inviting states to join the Second Athenian League', 378/7BCE [Decree of Aristoteles], trsl. S. Lambert and P. J. Rhodes, *Attic Inscriptions Online*, RO22

*'Delian League', *Encyclopedia Britannica, 1911 edition* [J. M. Mitchell]

*'Demosthenes', *Encyclopedia Britannica, 1911 edition* [R. C. Jebb]

*Demosthenes, 'On the Crown', 18.169-79, Perseus Digital Library

*Demosthenes, 'On the False Embassy', 19, Perseus Digital Library

Diodorus Siculus: *The Persian Wars to the Fall of Athens: Books 11-14.34 (480-401 BCE)*, translated, with introduction and notes by Peter Green (Austin, 2010)

Diodorus Siculus, vols. 4-8, translated by C. H. Oldfather (London, 1989). Perseus Digital Library

*Duke, George, 'The Sophists (Ancient Greek)', *Internet Encyclopedia of Philosophy*

*Engen, Darel, 'The Economy of Ancient Greece', EH.net Encyclopedia [Economic History Association], ed. Robert Whaples 31 July, 2004

*'Ephor', *Encyclopedia Britannica, 1911 edition* [M. N. Tod]

Frey, Linda S. and Marsha L. Frey, *The History of Diplomatic Immunity* (Columbus, Ohio, 1999)

Gagarin, M. and Fantham, E. (eds), *The Oxford Encyclopedia of Ancient Greece and Rome*, vol. 4 (Oxford, 2010)

Gardiner, E. Norman, *Athletics of the Ancient World* (Oxford, 1930)

*Gardner, P. and F. B. Jevons, *A Manual of Greek Antiquities* (New York, 1895)

Grant, J. R., 'A note on the tone of Greek diplomacy', *The Classical Quarterly*, New Series, 15 (2), November 1965

Green, Peter, *Alexander the Great and the Hellenistic Age: A short history* (London, 2007)

Hamilton, K. and R. Langhorne, *The Practice of Diplomacy: Its evolution, theory and administration*, 2nd ed (London, 2011)

Hansen, M. H., *Polis: An introduction to the ancient Greek city-state* (New York, 2006)

Herodotus, *The Histories*, translated by Robin Waterfield with an Introduction and Notes by Carolyn Dewald (Oxford, 1998). An earlier English translation, *Herodotus, The Histories A. D. Godley, Ed. is readily available online.

*Isocrates, 'On the Peace', in *Isocrates*, with an English translation by George Norlin, vol. 2 (New York, 1929)

*Isocrates, 'Panegyricus', in *Isocrates*, with an English translation by George Norlin, vol. 1 (New York, 1929)

Kagan, Donald, *Pericles of Athens and the Birth of Democracy* (London,1990)

Kent, Peter (ed), *The Oxford Companion to Ships and the Sea* (Oxford, 1988)

*'King's Peace', *Oxford Classical Dictionary*,

Kralli, Ionna, 'Athenian proxeny decrees'. Review of E. Culasso Gastaldi, *Le prossenie ateniesi del IV secolo a.C. Gli onorati asiatici* (2004), *The Classical Review*, 56 (2), October, 2006

*Lendering, Jona, 'Delian League', *Livius.org* 19 August 2017

*Lendering, Jona, 'Peloponnesian League', *Livius.org* 19 June 2017

Lendon, J. E., 'Thucydides and the 'Constitution' of the Peloponnesian League', *Greek, Roman and Byzantine Studies*, vol. 35 (2), Summer 1994

Mack, William, *Proxeny and Polis: Institutional Networks in the Ancient Greek World* (Oxford, 2015)

Michell, H., *The Economics of Ancient Greece* (Cambridge, 1940)

Nicolson, Harold, *The Evolution of Diplomatic Method* (London, 1954)

*'Oracle', *Encyclopedia Britannica, 1911 edition* [L. R. Farnell]

Ormerod, H. A., *Piracy in the Ancient World* (Liverpool, 1924)

*'Peace of Nicias', Livius.org [This includes the text of the peace treaty and of the defensive alliance signed by Athens and Sparta in the same year.]

*'Peloponnesian War', *Encyclopedia Britannica, 1911 edition* [J. M. Mitchell]

Perlman, S., 'Greek diplomatic tradition and the Corinthian League of Philip of Macedon', *Historia: Zeitschrift für Alte Geschichte*, Bd. 34, H. 2, 1985

*Phillipson, Coleman, *The International Law and Custom of Ancient Greece and Rome*, vol. I (London, 1911)

*Planeaux, Christopher, 'The Delian League, Part 1: Origins down to the Battle of Eurymedon (480/79-465/4)', *Ancient History Encyclopedia*, 13 September 2016

Plato, *The Republic*, trsl. H. D. P. Lee (Harmondsworth, 1955)

Plutarch's Lives: The translation called Dryden's, rev. A. H. Clough (London, 1905), vol. 3 ('Cimon')

Plutarch's Lives: The translation called Dryden's, rev. A. H. Clough (London,1905), vol. 3 ('Nicias')

Powell, Anton, *Athens and Sparta: Constructing Greek political and social history from 478 BC*, 2nd ed (London, 2001)

Pretzler, Maria, *Pausanias: Travel writing in Ancient Greece* (London, 2007)

*Proxeny Networks of the Ancient World (a database of proxeny networks of the Greek city-states)

*Rapp, Christof, 'Aristotle's Rhetoric', *The Stanford Encyclopedia of Philosophy*, Spring 2010, Edward N. Zalta (ed.)

*Remijsen, Sofie and Willy Clarysse, 'Heralds and trumpeters', *Ancient Olympics*

*Remijsen, Sofie and Willy Clarysse, 'The periodos', *Ancient Olympics*

Rhodes, P. J., 'Political leagues (other than Sparta's)' in Xenophon's *Hellenika*, App. H in Strassler, R. B. (ed.), *The Landmark Xenophon's Hellenika*, trsl. by J. Marincola (London, 2011)

Rhodes, P. J., 'Making and breaking treaties in the Greek world', in Philp de Souza and John France (eds), *War and Peace in the Ancient World* (Cambridge, 2008)

Roberts, Jennifer T., *The Plague of War: Athens, Sparta, and the struggle for ancient Greece* (New York, 2017)

Robertson, Noel, 'The myth of the First Sacred War', *The Classical Quarterly*, 28 (1), 1978

Roebuck, Carl, 'The settlements of Philip II with the Greek states in 338 B.C.', *Classical Philology*, vol. 43 (2), April 1948

Romilly, Jacqueline de, 'Eunoia in Isocrates or the political importance of creating good will', *Journal of Hellenic Studies*, vol. 78 (1958)

Rung, Edward, 'War, peace and diplomacy in Graeco-Persian relations from the sixth to the fourth century BC', in Philp de Souza and John France (eds), *War and Peace in the Ancient World* (Cambridge, 2008)

*Rung, Edward, 'The Mission of Philiscus to Greece in 369/8 B.C.', *Anabasis. Studia classica et orientalia*. vol. 4, 2014

Ryder, T. T. B., 'Demosthenes and Philip II', in Worthington, I. (ed), *Demosthenes: Statesman and orator* (London, 2000)

Sealey, R., *Demosthenes: A study in defeat* (New York, 1993)

Sommerstein, A. H. and A. J. Bayliss, *Oath and State in Ancient Greece* (Berlin, 2013), Part 2 ('Oaths and Interstate Relations', by Bayliss)

Starr, Chester G., *The Influence of Sea Power on Ancient History* (Oxford, 1989)

Thucydides, *History of the Peloponnesian War*, translated with an Introduction by Rex Warner (Harmondsworth, 1954)

Thucydides, *The Landmark Thucydides: A Comprehensive Guide to the Peloponnesian War*, ed. Robert B. Strassler (New York, 1998)

*'Thucydides on the Peace of Nicias', Livius.org

*Thucydides, *The Peloponnesian War*, trsl. Richard Crawley (London, 1910). Perseus Digital Library

Tod, M. N., *International Arbitration amongst the Greeks* (Oxford, 1913)

Toynbee, Arnold, *The Greeks and their Heritages* (Oxford, 1981)

Tozer, Rev. Henry Fanshawe, *Lectures on the Geography of Greece* (London, 1873)

Tuplin, C. J., 'Second Athenian Confederacy', *Oxford Classical Dictionary*, March 2016

Wallace, M. B., 'Early Greek *proxenoi*', *Phoenix*, vol. 24 (1970)

Wardman. A., *Rome's Debt to Greece* (London, 2002)

Watson, A., *Diplomacy: The dialogue between states* (London, 1982)

*Westermann, W. L., 'Interstate arbitration in antiquity', *The Classical Journal*, vol. 2 (5), March 1907

Westlake, H. D., 'Diplomacy in Thucydides', *Bulletin of the John Rylands Library*, vol. 53 1970–1

Wilamowitz-Moellendorff, Ulrich von, *Reden und Vorträge*, 3rd ed (Berlin, 1913)

Xenophon: Strassler, R. B. (ed.), *The Landmark Xenophon's Hellenika*, trsl. by J. Marincola (London, 2011). An earlier translation is available in *Wikisource

Zimmern, Alfred, *The Greek Commonwealth: Politics and Economics in Fifth Century Athens*, 5th ed revised (Oxford, 1931)

Diplomacy, Satire and the Victorians
The Life and Writings of E. C. Grenville-Murray

Abridged Edition

G. R. Berridge

Emeritus Professor of International Politics,
University of Leicester, UK
and

Senior Fellow, DiploFoundation

Contents

Preface

I came to Eustace Clare Grenville-Murray via a book called *Embassies and Foreign Courts* published in 1855 and written by 'The Roving Englishman'. Although for a long time vaguely aware of it, I had ignored it because put off by its pseudonymous authorship and neglect by other scholars: I thought it could not be serious. When, however, curiosity finally got the better of me, I found it to be certainly an eccentric kind of diplomatic manual but acute in many of its observations and written with an irreverence, verve, and elegance that placed it in a galaxy light years remote from that occupied by the more well-known examples of this genre. This discovery led me to ask the same question which for a while plagued the author's employers more than a century and a half earlier: Who on earth was 'The Roving Englishman'? It did not take long to establish his real name and that he was a British diplomat who had turned to 'scribbling' in part to blow the whistle on abuses in the Diplomatic Service and the then separate Foreign Office, and I became intrigued by his career. To my initial surprise, I found that there was no full-length biography of him and that the few biographical essays of which he was the subject were not only riddled with errors but also displayed enormous gaps. Hence this book.

The failings of the extant treatments of Grenville-Murray, I now realise, are not so surprising after all, for establishing the facts of his life and the workings of his mind were both extremely difficult to accomplish. The reasons for this are as follows. First, his birth was illegitimate, so the records of his early life are either non-existent or largely fictitious. Second, because he was a whistleblower but relatively impecunious, he went to great lengths to cover his literary tracks in order to safeguard his salaried income, so it is by no means easy to identify much of his writing, especially his newspaper articles. Third, because aristocrats both inside and outside the Foreign Office were desperate to contrive his downfall, a whole raft of damaging myths was created about his official conduct and particular events in his life, and these have been constantly re-cycled – and inevitably embellished. For example, not so long ago in *The Telegraph* Andrew Marr repeated the myth that he was 'horse-whipped' by Lord Carrington; while even more astonishingly the historian John Vincent, in his *Disraeli, Derby and the Conservative Party* (p. 42), describes him, among other things, as a 'pornographer'. Finally, he left no accessible personal collection of private papers – no private correspondence, no diaries, no unpublished memoirs – and the only readily traceable private letters of his own held in other collections are those to be found in the Stowe Papers at the Huntington Library in California and the papers of Sir Henry Bulwer at the Norfolk Record Office. On the other hand, Grenville-Murray's literary output was prodigious and, precisely because key Foreign Office officials loathed him, there are also entire volumes of documents in The National Archives in London dealing with 'The Case of Mr. G. Murray.' It was chiefly because I concluded that there was sufficient material in these sources to make a go of the project that I took the decision – probably still a rash one – to launch it.

I am grateful for assistance with various aspects of this work to Troy Bassett, the late Philip Cottrell, Penny Hatfield, Clare Mence, Thomas Otte, Mary L. Robertson, Jackie Smith, Jelena Jakovljevic and David Tothill. I must also record my gratitude to the University of Leicester, particularly the Department of Politics and International Relations, for enabling me to preserve my access since retirement to invaluable Library databases. Finally, I would like to thank the executive committee of the British International History Group, especially John W. Young, for permitting me to give a lecture on Grenville-Murray at the group's annual conference in September 2012, for this helped to preserve the momentum of my project. John Young also did me the honour of casting a critical eye over the whole manuscript of the book in first draft and, because of this as well as in testimony to our long friendship, it is to him that I have dedicated it.

In abridging the book for inclusion in this three-work omnibus I have pruned sections dealing chiefly with Grenville-Murray's personal circumstances and literary output and also most footnotes. A full Note on Sources by chapter is found at the end of the book. Those wishing to plunge deeper and track details to precise documents should consult the first edition, which was published under the title *A Diplomatic Whistleblower in the Victorian Era* (Isis Press: Istanbul, 2017).

G.R.B., Leicester, September 2025.

List of Acronyms and Abbreviations

2DBC   Second Duke of Buckingham and Chandos

3DBC   Third Duke of Buckingham and Chandos

AYR   All the Year Round [successor to Household Words]

BB   ['Blue Book'] HCPP (4163), 14 June 1869: Papers Relative to the
            Complaints made against Mr. Grenville-Murray as Her Majesty's
            Consul-General at Odessa; and to his Dismissal from Her Majesty's
            Service

BL   The British Library

CM   The Cornhill Magazine

DNB   Dictionary of National Biography

FO   Foreign Office

FO   List The Foreign Office List and Diplomatic and Consular Hand Book

G-M   Grenville-Murray, Eustace Clare

HCDeb.   House of Commons Debates (Hansard)

HCPP   House of Commons Parliamentary Papers

HL   Huntington Library, California

HW   Household Words

LCD   The Letters of Charles Dickens (The Pilgrim Edition)

LMA   London Metropolitan Archives

NRO   Norfolk Record Office (Norwich)

ODNB   Oxford Dictionary of National Biography (Oxford University Press,
            2004)

QM   The Queen's Messenger: A Weekly Gazette of Politics and Literature
            [1869]

TNA   The National Archives [British]

List of Illustrations

Prologue

In the Victorian era, British diplomatic couriers, who were usually retired
military officers carrying documents between London and posts abroad so
secret they were required to guard them with their lives, were styled 'Queen's
Messengers'. It was therefore with mischief in mind that in January 1869
Grenville-Murray launched a satirical weekly entitled *The Queen's Messenger*.
It was designed chiefly to exact his revenge on the Foreign Office, which had
dismissed him from government service ostensibly for failures of duty while
consul-general at Odessa but in reality for acting as a whistleblower while
moonlighting as a journalist. *The Queen's Messenger* swiftly multiplied the
ranks of his enemies and in late July of the same year he had to flee to France.
In its last issue before the start of parliament's summer recess, two small
notices tucked away at the bottom of a column demonstrated at once its editor's
cleverness, wicked sense of humour, and unashamed belief in his own genius:

> A very brilliant meteor (writes Sir A. S. Herschel) was seen last
> Friday evening, at 11.35 P.M., crossing the Channel. A morning
> paper declares this must have referred to Mr. Grenville Murray.
>
> ASTRONOMICAL NOTICE FOR 1870. – *The Queen's Messenger*
> will reappear in February; several eclipses are expected to follow.[114]

In fact *The Queen's Messenger* was never to come back but no-one could
have doubted that the world would hear again from its editor, who by this time
had firmly established himself in the eyes of the governing circles of Britain as
the irrepressible evil genius of 'scurrilous' journalism.

Until diplomacy began to be properly professionalized and better
paid during the latter half of the nineteenth century, British diplomatists had

---

[114]   *QM*, 12 August, 1869, p. 338. Herschel was a leading British astronomer, then at the University of Glasgow, and produced annual reports on bright meteors observed for a committee of the British Association.

rarely been above moon-lighting. This was particularly the case when they found themselves at posts where the cost of living was exceptionally high or the opportunities too tempting to resist. In the Orient, some traded on their own account in jewels, currencies, and letters of protection; others bought or stole statuary and other ancient artefacts, whether for themselves or for rich and influential patrons at home. Perhaps more common, although less profitable, was the activity of the scholar-diplomat, who sought to supplement his income and burnish his reputation by writing books and occasional articles on the languages, history, and contemporary features of interest of the countries with which he had become professionally acquainted; Sir Ernest Satow, who served first in Japan and then China, is the classic example. And then there was the diplomat-journalist.

Diplomats and journalists – as still today – had in common the gathering and reporting of information, while some journalists specialised in foreign affairs and were often well connected with politicians. It is hardly surprising, therefore, that from time to time members of one of these profession should have been tempted to swop one role for the other, and sometimes back again. Well known examples in Britain in the nineteenth and early twentieth centuries were Henry Southern, Valentine Chirol, Harold Nicolson, and Robert Bruce Lockhart; in France Henri Beyl, better known as the great novelist Stendhal; in Russia Petr Botkin, the late nineteenth/early twentieth century Russian diplomat who scribbled for *Novoye Vremya*; and in the United States John Moncure Daniel, the incendiary pro-slavery editor of the *Richmond Examiner*. In the twentieth century it was not unusual, especially in wartime, to find journalists recruited to the more specialized diplomatic work of the press attaché.

What was much rarer was the person who worked both as a diplomat and a regular journalist *simultaneously*. Sir Henry Bulwer, who ended his career as British ambassador at Constantinople, was certainly one example; and Lockhart was another.[115] But insofar as Grenville-Murray appears to have

[115] Following his low-paid appointment as British vice-consul in Moscow at the beginning of 1912, Lockhart – who also wrote under a pseudonym – became a regular contributor to the *Morning Post* and the *Manchester Guardian* until the outbreak of war. In September 1917,

divided his time more evenly between the two professions over an exceptionally long period, he remained extremely unusual and was without doubt the diplomat-journalist par excellence.

For reasons that will become evident, we have no photograph or portrait of Grenville-Murray. However, he was described by those who knew him as slim and rather short in build, with curly hair, well-cut features, a dark complexion, and very bright eyes. He was brilliant and knew it, restless, vivacious, and furiously hard-working. Henry Labouchere, the radical politician who was equally familiar with the world of the press and nobody's fool, judged him after his death to have been 'the ablest journalist of the century.'[116] This was not an unusual opinion but no-one has ever had a good word to say about his conduct as a diplomat or even given a moment's thought to his broad-ranging reflections on diplomacy, his first-chosen profession.

What was Grenville-Murray's background? What were his connections to the novelist Charles Dickens and to the foreign secretary and later prime minister Lord Palmerston? What were the themes of his writing? Was he really a useless diplomat? How did he manage to juggle journalism and diplomacy for over 17 years, especially since he specialised in satire and ridicule directed chiefly at his own employers? How did the Foreign Office finally manage to get rid of him? What did he do afterwards and what is his lasting importance? These are the questions which shape this biography as it follows Grenville-Murray's adventures: first as the 'Roving Englishman' in Vienna, Constantinople, and the Crimean War; then to Tehran following the comic opera war between Britain and Persia which succeeded it; and afterwards during his diplomatic nemesis in Odessa. The tale ends with his literary rebirth during an exile to France which began in 1869. This coincided with the collapse of Louis Napoleon's Second Empire, the Prussian siege of Paris, the short-lived Paris commune, the second siege of Paris, and the birth of the Third Republic. This, on the face of it, was great timing for a determined journalist who by this time had nothing else to do.

---

once more writing anonymously because still 'a Government servant', he made his first foray into 'frenzied journalism', Lockhart, *Memoirs of a British Agent*, pp. 77, 102, 196.
[116]   Quoted in Hatton, *Journalistic London*, p. 109.

1   Powerful Patrons

Eustace Clare Grenville-Murray, as he eventually called himself and as he duly came to be known by others, was a bastard. He was also born into and acquired the expensive tastes of the English aristocracy. Together these facts made it doubly important that he should obtain powerful patrons.

Eustace was the illegitimate son of the 1st Duke of Buckingham and Chandos, the immensely wealthy Richard Grenville, and Emma Murray, an actress and courtesan of the aristocracy and London political class, said in the 1830s by the *Satirist* to have been the daughter of an innkeeper in Hereford. In order to gloss over the social embarrassment of this birth, on his baptism on 29 December 1823, Eustace was provided with the invented but comparatively common surname of Clare: 'Eustace, son of Richard and Emma Clare.' But this was just an expedient of the moment, and he must very soon have been given Emma's purported surname as his own, 'Clare' then becoming a second forename.

'A thousand scrapes'
What became of Eustace Clare Murray in the first 20 years of his life is difficult to penetrate. It is evident that he did not lack some financial support, whether this came from his parents or – for reasons we shall see later – Lord Palmerston. On the evidence of his first writings, it is also clear that he was a respectable classical scholar; so, on the basis of this and other hints, it is likely that he had the typical education of a young gentleman of the upper class, probably at Eton College.

In 1839, on the death of his father – whose odious character and spectacular extravagance had laid the ground for the mid-century financial collapse of the Grenville family – it is likely that a promising school career was prematurely ended; and that, in this respect like the hero of his little remarked first novel, *Walter Evelyn*, at the age of 14 or 15 Eustace was required to accompany his mother on long visits to Paris. There he became fluent in French but also seems to have got himself into 'a thousand scrapes'.

One of these scrapes, as we shall see, was the consequence of acquiring debts, which was regarded as 'a fine dashing manly habit' by the spendthrift element of the aristocracy.[117] The thorough nobleman, he had evidently been led to believe, never paid his debts on principle, for he did his tradesmen great honour by dealing with them at all, so actually to give them money as well would be 'to pay them twice over.'[118] Another of his youthful follies was siring bastards. Generally credible letters preserved among Foreign Office papers claim that he was the father of a baby girl born in about 1842 that two years afterwards he left – with financial provision for her board and education – in the care of a woman in France.

As Eustace later admitted, at this stage in his life he still had little idea of what he wanted to do but achieved at least some stability when in 1844 he married a widow, Sarah Lake of Brompton (later 'Clara), who was of roughly the same age. In due course, the couple settled at a house in the bohemian district of central London later known as Fitzrovia.

Clara had brought £1200 to their union but this was not going to be enough. Unfortunately, Eustace could expect no further support from his mother, for her own income was drying up and by 1850 she had been forced to abandon her fine London life-style and live – among other compatriots in adversity – in Calais. Adding to the couple's worries was the arrival of children: Reginald, on 29 August 1846, and Wyndham, on 1 January 1848. To make matters worse, just two months after Wyndham's birth Eustace chose to become a student at Oxford, where he acquired debts but no degree. In desperation, he rashly lent the 2nd Duke his wife's money in hope of a generous annuity but probably with the added calculation that the loan would encourage the duke to recognize him as natural heir to his title instead of the son, Richard, Marquess of Chandos, with whom the duke was warring. Still floundering, in early 1850 he briefly flirted with legal studies at the Inner Temple, before concluding that

---

[117] *Walter Evelyn*, vol. 3, p. 39.
[118] *Under the Lens*, vol. 2, p. 46.

the 'great expectations' to which he had been born had been a pantomime trick played on him by 'Miss Fortune', and deciding to sell his horses and go abroad.[119]

Palmerston and Dickens

'Miss Fortune' was, however, to change her tune, for Grenville-Murray was soon to have not one but two patrons who were far more serviceable to him than the 2nd Duke of Buckingham. These were the Irish peer, Lord Palmerston, and the novelist, Charles Dickens.

Before Grenville-Murray was even born, Henry John Temple, 3rd Viscount Palmerston, was already a prominent figure in politics. Generally regarded as a conservative-leaning liberal, he had been a member of parliament since the first decade of the century and served as secretary of war under five prime ministers before 1828. Thereafter, in Eustace's formative years, he came to dominate the Foreign Office: he was foreign secretary for almost all of the time from November 1830 until August 1841, and again from July 1846 until December 1851. He was a major figure on the European stage and had admirers across the political spectrum, although within the Foreign Office itself he was such a hard task-master that, with only few exceptions, he was hated by the clerks. In the early stage of his ministerial career, Palmerston – who was a famous womanizer and did not marry until 1839 – also happened to have been another of the lovers of Eustace's mother, Emma Murray.

As Emma was one of his favourites and in January 1816 had borne him a son, at about this time Palmerston had installed her first at a Pall Mall address and later in Piccadilly. Here he bought her the lease on a house and gave her financial support for many years afterwards. This included assisting with the education of their son and several of her other children. Since it has also been reliably reported that Grenville-Murray 'attracted the attention of Lord Palmerston when a mere lad,'[120] it is a reasonable supposition that Eustace was among those whose education he assisted. The rising politician must have noted

---

[119]   *The Roving Englishman*, pp. v, vi, vii.
[120]   Henry Labouchere in *Truth*, 29 December 1881.

the boy's striking potential, and gave him occasional diplomatic errands to run in the 1840s after he had reached the age of 18; this was the kind of informal training in diplomacy that had been going on since Elizabethan times.

A diplomatic career might for long have been a possibility considered by Eustace, but it seems that this was by no means uppermost in his mind in the spring of 1850. Instead, this was combining entry into the Austrian army with journalism. In the latter field, at least, Palmerston, who was adept and energetic at manipulating public opinion through the press and had a weakness for journalists, could assist him as well. And, when openings were offered to Eustace at this juncture, he seized them greedily.

The first of these offers was an appointment as the Vienna correspondent of the Palmerston-supporting London *Morning Post*, then edited by the former Tory MP and friend of Palmerston, Peter Borthwick. Palmerston probably wished to use Eustace as an alternative to the British Embassy in Vienna as a source of news on Austrian affairs, for he had been doing the same sort of thing in Paris. Having accepted the offer, Eustace promptly departed for Vienna.

At the same time, Eustace had taken up another offer of journalistic employment. This was an invitation from William Henry Wills to write for *Household Words*, a weekly periodical launched at the end of March of which he was part proprietor, business-manager, and sub-editor. The editor and chief proprietor was the novelist, Charles Dickens, who himself had started writing as a journalist, but by this time was a long-established literary celebrity.

Dickens especially wished his new periodical to expose social evils and abuses of power and privilege, but ruled out no subject for inclusion. He also wanted it to appeal to all social classes, to young and old, and to women as well as men. In style, he wished it to be entertaining as well as instructive; in other words, while being scrupulously true to the facts, non-fiction articles were to be as lively as possible. Since he saw *Household Words* as a vehicle for his own voice, he wrote many articles himself, edited it brutally, and laid it down as general policy that all articles were to be anonymous. Although it received a

1. Lord Palmerston ('Cupid')

mixed reception from literary critics, it was extremely popular with the public and turned a handsome profit for its owners.

In August 1850, having been asked to concentrate on providing practical tips on foreign travel and sketches of foreign manners, Eustace published his first article in *Household Words*, and thereafter became a regular contributor. As this testifies, he had found in Charles Dickens another admirer.

Caught out by 'Lord Fiddlededee'

In the spring of 1850, Eustace arrived in Vienna and, to give himself an edge, had decided to advertise his connection to his father's ducal family by changing his surname from 'Murray' to 'Grenville-Murray'; such a moniker would have been particularly valuable in the notoriously status-conscious Austrian capital. One of his letters of introduction was from his half-brother, Buckingham, and commended his suitability for the Austrian army to Field Marshall Laval Graf Nugent von Westmeath, though this proved redundant because he soon dismissed the idea.[121] The other was from Palmerston, which asked the British ambassador to assist Eustace in discharging his duties as correspondent of the *Morning Post*, and he remained in Vienna in this capacity until the following spring.

The earnings of his pen alone would not support his life-style and his family, however, and in Vienna he had run up large debts to Leo Wolf, an American resident of the city at whose house and table he had been a constant guest. With the active encouragement and support of Palmerston, therefore, in July 1851 he accepted appointment as an attaché at the British Embassy in the Austrian capital.

The Vienna position was unpaid, as was the custom with initial appointments in the diplomatic service, but could be expected eventually to carry a small salary. Meanwhile, it would provide Eustace with some expenses for travel and subsistence – and, most importattly, mail facilities for the

---

[121]   The Austrian army was a multi-national service that was the preferred destination for minor British aristocrats and gentry, especially if they were Catholics or if there was – as in Eustace's case – a question mark over their social standing. I am indebted to T. G. Otte for this information.

despatch of his articles to London. For, with the blessing of Palmerston, who is said to have wished him to write in unfriendly tones about the Austrian prime minister, he was determined surreptitiously to keep up his position as correspondent of the *Morning Post* in the Austrian capital.

After several months in London familiarizing himself with the work of the Foreign Office, in the autumn of 1851 Grenville-Murray was back in Vienna but made the mistake of failing to make a prompt appearance at the embassy. Instead, what did turn up, on the day in each week when the messenger left for London, was a packet from him addressed to 'Peter Borthwick, Esq.', whose position as editor of the *Morning Post* was well known in the mission. To the minds of his chancery colleagues, Grenville-Murray was an arrogant free-loader who was trading on the influence of his eminent connections and had no intention of taking his diplomatic duties seriously. As a result, they reported his behaviour to the new ambassador who arrived in October.

The new head of the British Embassy at Vienna was the ageing 11th Earl of Westmorland, whose ambitions as a musical composer caused him later to be immortalized by Grenville-Murray as 'Lord Fiddlededee'.[122] Duly summoning the miscreant to his presence, Westmorland informed him that it was contrary to royal instructions to permit a member of a mission to correspond with a newspaper. It was certainly true – as Sir Ernest Satow later confirmed approvingly in his famous manual – that the British diplomatic service was 'very strict' on this sort of thing,[123] although it is highly unlikely that Grenville-Murray was the first to treat it lightly – and he was certainly not the last.[124] Westmorland duly ordered him to desist, and he gave his word of honour that he would not write newspaper copy while remaining at the embassy. From that day onwards he took his place in the chancery.

---

[122] A 'fiddle' was a violin, while 'fiddlededee' meant nonsense; hence the perfection of this nickname.

[123] Satow, *A Guide to Diplomatic Practice*, vol. 1, p. 136, para. 152.

[124] As a young man at the British Legation in Yedo in 1866, Satow himself published anonymously three articles on British policy to Japan in the English-language *Japan Times* (owned and edited in Yokohama by his friend Charles Rickerby), without the knowledge of his head of mission. 'It was doubtless very irregular, very wrong, and altogether contrary to the rules of the service, but I thought little of that,' he admitted in *A Diplomat in Japan*, p. 159.

Despite this undertaking, Grenville-Murray continued to write newspaper articles, but chiefly for the *Daily News*, the radical paper established by Charles Dickens in 1846, rather than the *Morning Post*. Since his copy was anonymous, he must have thought that he was safe. Alas, due to a mishap, in January 1852 two of his drafts, addressed to Frederick Knight Hunt, chief editor of the *Daily News* and a fellow contributor to *Household Words*, ended up in the hands of the ambassador, who eventually reported him officially to the Foreign Office.

Grenville-Murray had good reason to be alarmed at this turn of events. The affair had come to the unfavourable notice of Queen Victoria, who had been reportedly 'furious' at the young Prince of Wales for siding with the attaché. And only shortly before, Palmerston's protection had been jeopardised by his departure from the Foreign Office. Fortunately for Grenville-Murray, however, his diplomatic patron was not alone in regarding Westmorland as professionally useless, and his inexperienced successors at the Foreign Office – first Lord Granville and then Lord Malmesbury – were heavily reliant on his detailed briefings. It is probably for this reason that Thomas Seccombe, the young but respected assistant editor of the *Dictionary of National Biography*, was able to state with confidence that it was the continuing influence of the great man that decided Grenville-Murray's fate in favour of leniency: removal to another post rather than dismissal from the service. It seems likely that Palmerston favoured this course not only because Grenville-Murray was his own protégé, but also because it was his general rule that people should be taken as they are and the best made of their good qualities, 'without dwelling too much on their bad.'[125]

---

[125] Palmerston to Bulwer, 13 Sept. 1838, in Bulwer, *The Life of Henry John Temple*, p. 285. Bulwer adds that Palmerston 'frequently' made this observation.

2 'The Roving Englishman'

In politics, Grenville-Murray was a conservative in the tradition of Edmund Burke. In other words, he rejected the blinkered, reactionary conservatism of the landed aristocracy and favoured, instead, moderate administrative and constitutional reform. In 1855 he joined the Conservative Club. This was nominally established for those unable to gain immediate entry to the hub of the Tory social network in the Carlton Club, but it did not mark him as a party man because it was in reality a dissident group. In short, he was a Burkean conservative without political ambitions.

Since his own experience of government service was with the Foreign Office and the diplomatic service, it was naturally these institutions on which Grenville-Murray was to cast his merciless eye. In the process of what became a sustained reformist campaign, he emerged as their most damaging whistleblower; as, indeed, the only one of any significance at the time. Consequently, the official loathing for him that had begun in Vienna increased further. All of this came to a head against the background of the Crimean War, the horrifying mid-century clash of arms on the front line between Russia and Turkey in the Danubian Principalities and the Black Sea, a conflict in which Britain and France came to the assistance of the Turks for fear of the impact on their own interests should the Ottoman Empire, as had long been predicted, finally collapse. As it happened, this great episode in the history of the European balance of power was not just incidental background noise to Grenville-Murray's early career; he was closely involved in it, and it marked his thinking in a decisive manner.

In April 1852, Grenville-Murray was transferred to the legation at Hanover. This was a mission of startling obscurity where the minister, the Hon. John Duncan Bligh, second son of the 4th Earl of Darnley, had been nominally in charge since as far back as 1838. However, he usually left his post in August, and did not return until late in the following spring. He was, Grenville-Murray later told the readers of the *Daily News*, paid £3,400 a year for doing nothing. Meanwhile, his office over an eating-house was kept by a 'cobwebbed attaché' who spent most of his time fishing in an adjoining street.[126]

If not enthralled by the prospect of Hanover, it was no doubt with some relief that the disgraced attaché had departed the embassy in Vienna, where he had been socially ostracized by its staff. Nevertheless, Grenville-Murray must soon have realised that he had become the object of a game of diplomatic pass-the-parcel, for Bligh seems to have been keen that he be hurried on. When the music stopped, in October, Grenville-Murray discovered that he had been appointed to the embassy at Constantinople. This at least was a vastly more important post, and had marvellous potential for a budding travel writer. It also marked a promotion, for he was to be 5th *paid* attaché, even if his annual salary of £250 was not eye-watering.

Although told to proceed to the Ottoman capital without delay, he did not arrive until five months later. During this interval he completed his first novel: the 900-page long triple-decker, *Walter Evelyn; or, The Long Minority*, published anonymously on 1 November 1853 by Richard Bentley, the once leading but by then struggling London publisher. He was also scribbling feverishly for *Household Words*. Dickens had initial reservations about Grenville-Murray's articles, which were occasionally described as empty, conceited, slovenly, or containing statements difficult to believe. He was an unsparing editor, and a few of these qualms endured. Nevertheless, it was a common view at the time that Grenville-Murray remained one of his happiest finds.

His first pieces in *Household Words* had appeared with strict anonymity, but by November 1851 he was writing as the 'Roving Englishman'. This was a good *nom de plume* for a travel writer, and was soon to be well known. Before long, however, his pen was straying into more controversial areas, and for this Charles Dickens must take some responsibility. For apart from the Roving Englishman's obvious, raw potential as a perceptive, witty, and elegant travel writer, what the 'conductor' of *Household Words* also spotted

---

[126] *Pictures from the Battle Fields*, pp. 305-13; *Daily News*, 3 April 1855.

was the likelihood that he would be able and willing to write critically about the diplomatic profession. This appealed to Dickens because the aristocratic stranglehold on the upper reaches of this profession was among the social evils the great novelist himself wished to see attacked. Wills, the weekly's business-manager and sub-editor, must have expressed the same view, for as early as September 1850, in replying to one of his letters, Dickens wrote: 'The diplomacy, splendid. I should like to begin that, with a Sketch of an aristocratic attaché and so forth. I know the reality very well, having seen a good deal of it abroad.' Nothing remotely of this sort appeared in *Household Words* for nearly three more years but, when it did, it came from the pen of Grenville-Murray – and it got him into serious trouble with his new chief.

Arise, 'Sir Hector Stubble'!

Like many men who passed through the British Embassy in Constantinople, Grenville-Murray did not hit it off with the ambassador, Stratford Canning, who had been at the embassy on and off since 1808 and had a reputation for unrivalled influence with the Ottoman authorities. However, he was by then 66 years of age, perpetually harassed and inclined to bad fits of gout. He was also notoriously short-tempered, especially when he thought himself slighted, and his temper had not been improved by his orders to return once more to Constantinople instead of being rewarded with either the coveted Paris embassy or the post of foreign secretary; it was only as a consolation that he had just been raised to the peerage as Viscount Stratford de Redcliffe.

The man who was actually preferred for the Foreign Office, Lord Malmesbury, had no illusions about Stratford's volcanic personality, so it is surprising that he should have sent him someone like Grenville-Murray, though he had a reputation for putting round men in square holes. The great ambassador evidently regarded Grenville-Murray as too clever by half, and inclined to show insufficient respect for his rank and achievements. Besides, the new attaché's reputation had preceded him to Constantinople. Inevitably, their relations were 'from the first the reverse of cordial.'[127]

---

[127] Seccombe, 'Murray'.

For his own part, Grenville-Murray was bored with the routine embassy work given him and increasingly contemptuous of the perfumed non-entities who, through patronage and favouritism, peopled just about every reach of the British diplomatic service; so he continued to concentrate on his writing. Two more books were produced. The first was *From Mayfair to Marathon*, a collection of essays new and old that appeared anonymously at the end of 1853, one of which ('A Lost Chapter') was eloquent of the bitterness he nourished over his experiences at Vienna, Hanover, and then Constantinople. The other was *Doĭne: Or, the National Songs and Legends of Roumania*. He had also continued to bombard Dickens with articles.

One of these pieces was a heavily disguised first shot across Stratford's bows, fired while the ambassador was still in England. On 20 November 1852, the Roving Englishman published a piece in *Household Words* called 'His Philosophy of Dining', which surely had more to do with diplomacy – and the irascible Stratford Canning – than Dickens perhaps realised, for dining was regarded as an important tool of the craft, not least by Lord Palmerston. The piece began: 'Let us by all means try to sit down to dinner in a good temper. Nothing,' it continued, 'spoils the digestion like anger.'

Had it been brought to Stratford's attention on his return to Constantinople in April, and its authorship revealed, this piece was well designed to produce more than a growl from the ambassador. The real identity of the Roving Englishman was probably already strongly suspected because – astonishing to report – the office of *Household Words* made no attempt to keep secret the authorship of its articles; readers just had to enquire in order to be enlightened.

In June 1853, the Roving Englishman launched in *Household Words* a less veiled attack on Lord Stratford. Appearing in the guise of 'Lord Loggerhead', he is employed to illustrate the 'laughable incapacity' of certain English diplomats at difficult courts: stupid, excitable, bad-tempered, and linguistically challenged.[128] Whether because this piece had been drawn to his attention, or

---

[128] 'Diplomacy', *HW*, 18 June 1853. 'Loggerhead' meant thick-headed or stupid, but also carried the connotation of being locked in dispute.

2. Lord Stratford de Redcliffe ('Sir Hector Stubble')

because by this time he could no longer stand the sight of Grenville-Murray, four months later Stratford banished his insufferable attaché. His post of exile: acting vice-consul at Mytilene, the chief town of the predominantly Greek island of Lesbos, then still part of the Ottoman Empire.

For the Roving Englishman, this was nevertheless an exile with compensations. 'I am in Mytilene,' he announced to the readers of *Household Words* two months after his arrival, 'on storied grounds, for Mytilene is the ancient Lesbos, and one of the largest and most beautiful islands of the Aegean Sea.'[129] It also enjoyed frequent sailings to Smyrna and Constantinople, of which he evidently availed himself. Above all, he had no-one breathing down his neck, and – with little shipping to worry about – ample leisure both to reflect on his profession and to write up the acute observations of people and places that by then were the hallmarks of his journalism. Dickens 'liked them greatly,' said their mutual friend, Edmund Yates, of the sketches of Greek and Turkish life he wrote at that time; they were 'immediately published and eagerly read.' But 'On Her Majesty's Service', which was the front-cover lead item of *Household Words* on 7 January 1854, attracted far more attention than the rest.[130] And here – even though Dickens only discovered this later – Lord Stratford held centre stage.

This article turned on a description of the political staff of the British Embassy to the Ottoman Empire, thinly disguised as the mission to the notorious, slave-trading principality of Dahomey on the coast of West Africa. This was a perfect choice: not only was its warlike king one of the great pantomime villains of the mid-Victorian era, but it was also likely to catch the eye of Palmerston, who was a passionate opponent of the slave trade and favoured armed intervention to crush it in that kingdom.

Revealing that he had been the sub vice-consul in Dahomey and the only salaried functionary of the kind extant, the author explained that he had been given the appointment because Her Majesty's ambassador at Dahomey – formerly Lord Loggerhead but now renamed 'Sir Hector Stubble' – had quarrelled with him. There followed what Edmund Yates rightly described as

---

[129] The Roving Englishman, 'A Greek Feast', *HW*, 24 December 1853.
[130] The article was nine columns long, and for it G-M was paid the then princely sum of five pounds.

" *Familiar in their Mouths as* HOUSEHOLD WORDS."—Shakespeare.

HOUSEHOLD WORDS.

A WEEKLY JOURNAL

CONDUCTED BY CHARLES DICKENS.

Nº· 198.]   SATURDAY, JANUARY 7, 1854.   [Price 2*d.*

ON HER MAJESTY'S SERVICE.

I do not know that I had anything to do at Dahomey, when I used to put this magnificent heading outside my letters to my brother Tom ; but I do know the name of my appointment, which is more than most of us did. I was called Sub Vice-Consul, and I think I was the only salaried functionary of the kind extant. I was appointed because Sir Hector Stubble, Her Majesty's Ambassador at Dahomey, had quarrelled with everbody about him, so violently and so often that the service could no longer go on. I need scarcely add that he also quarrelled with me. He would not have anything to say to the Honourable Mr. Faddleton, our secretary, because he lisped ; nor to his first *attaché*, because he squinted ; nor to the six other *attachés*, for equally cogent reasons.

Between the Consulate and the Embassy there was open war ; one pretending to all authority, and the other granting none. A person arriving as I did in Dahomey, from any other quarter of the world, and finding himself in an official situation, might have thought easily enough that he had lost his way and got into the Inquisition.

Sir Hector Stubble had set every living being within his influence by the ears. He had a talent for it. You could not walk across the street with a British subject, whom you met by accident, without that British subject immediately falling foul of every other British subject in the place—and there were a good many of them—all at loggerheads. Slander and backbiting, complaints and annoyances, quarrels and jars of all kinds were going on from morning till night. The very cats and dogs about the premises learned to look shyly at each other.

I never could account for, or explain to myself how a man so thoroughly respectable as Sir Hector could have contrived to make himself so disagreeable. He was a man of fair average capacity, upright, and hardworking. But a more hard, stern, unjust, unkind, unloveable man never stood within the icy circle of his own pride and ill temper. He was haughty and stiff-necked beyond any man I have ever seen. He trampled on other men's feelings as deliberately and unflinchingly as if they were wooden puppets made to work his will. He was not a greatminded man, for he had favourites and jealousies and petty enmities ; he had small passions, and by no means an intellect mighty enough to make you forget them. He was a fine specimen of the British Bigwig, and would have figured well as the head of a public school, or the principal of a college.

He had been at Dahomey nearly all his life. Dahomey was a very bad school for the rearing of an English gentleman. He had exercised too much power over others so long, that at last he could speak to none save in the grating language of harsh command. He seemed to look upon mankind as a mere set of tools : when he wanted an instrument he took it ; and when he had done with it, he put it aside. Perhaps it was the long habit of dealing with persons placed in an improper position of subordination to him which made him treat every one under him as a slave. Nature never could have made a man so thoroughly unamiable.

Sir Hector Stubble had no heart, no feeling, no eyes, ears, thoughts for any one but Sir Hector Stubble. For him the world was made, and all that in it is ; other people had no business there except in so far as they were useful to him. His private secretary or his valet—any one upon whom his completeness in any way depended —would have appeared to him an individual of much more importance than the greatest practical thinker who ever served mankind.

No one had ever owed him a service or a kind word. In seventy long years of a life passed in honour and fair public repute, he had never gained a private friend. He had been appointed at twenty-one to a position for which he was unripe—that of Secretary of Embassy at Dahomey. He had passed nearly the whole of his subsequent life among slaves and orientals, until he had become incapable of holding equal commerce with free men.

Now, this kind of thing will not do among Englishmen ; few Englishmen are so much superior to the rest of their countrymen, as

3. 'On Her Majesty's Service', Household Words, 7 January 1854

'a merciless but unmistakable caricature' of the head of Grenville-Murray's embassy.[131] It began by admitting that he was 'a man of fair average capacity, upright, and hard-working' but then charged that 'a more hard, stern, unjust, unkind, unloveable man never stood within the icy circle of his own pride and ill temper,' and continued in like vein until concluding that 'he had passed nearly the whole of his subsequent life among slaves and orientals, until he had become incapable of holding equal commerce with free men.'

A year later, in January 1855, a further outing was given to Grenville-Murray's ruthless character assassination of Lord Stratford in *The Roving Englishman in Turkey. Sketches from Life*. And just a few months after this, his onslaught was broadened with the appearance of his *Pictures from the Battle Fields*, a book inspired by a short visit to the theatre of war in the Crimea. This contained blasts at a number of lesser diplomats, among them Westmorland again, chiefly for failing to manoeuvre the Austrians into a more anti-Russian posture. But the main target – now named openly – was once more Lord Stratford. In 40 years in the East, charged the Roving Englishman, he had done hardly any good at all. As a result, 'the great British embarrasser' at Constantinople had made Turkey an attractive prey to Russia and then, as if this were not bad enough, so mishandled Russian demands as to precipitate the war.

These were strong views, so much so that the reviewer in *The Times* thought their author must have left the diplomatic service. But they struck a chord with the public, already well prepared to believe any charges of official bungling in connection with the Crimean War as a result of the famous despatches of W. H. Russell, the same newspaper's correspondent on the front line. Furthermore, they could not be construed as critical of Lord Palmerston, who was out of the Foreign Office at the crucial moment and therefore escaped the popular censure of the government's Eastern policy. Just to be on the safe side, however, Grenville-Murray remarked on Palmerston's 'wonderful aptitude for every department of public business, and his paramount influence, his active reforms in all; his vast English mind and genial nature; his wise and winning

---

[131]   *His Recollections and Experiences*, p. 448.

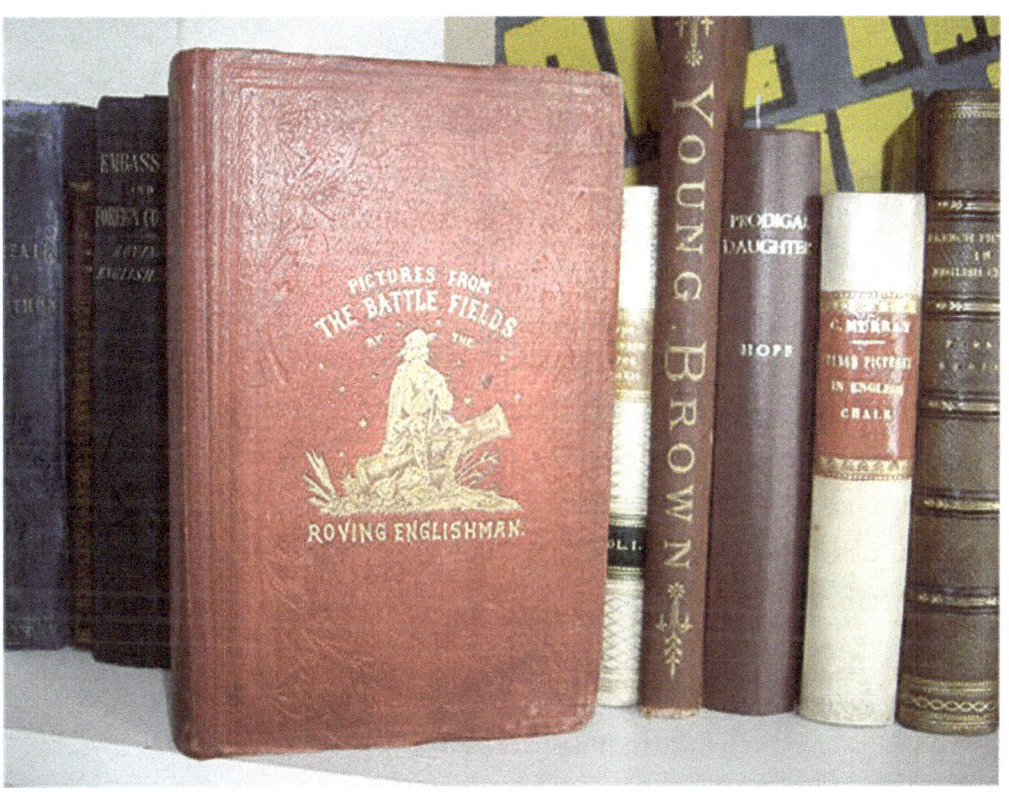

4. *Pictures from the Battle Fields,* on the Author's bookshelf

courtesies.'[132] *Pictures from the Battle Fields* and *The Roving Englishman in Turkey* were both warmly received by the public; the former sold 2,000 copies in the first three days and was already re-printing, boasted its publisher, at the beginning of June.

British diplomacy – 'a lugubrious farce'

During the mid-1850s, when Grenville-Murray launched his personal campaign for diplomatic reform in earnest, the Foreign Office was a small ministry firmly believing that the character of its work – highly confidential and requiring irregular hours – set it apart from all other departments of state. There was no open competition for appointments; nor did key position holders change often. Thus for most of the time between 1853 and 1870 the foreign secretary, who was nearly always second only in standing to the prime minister, was either the 4th Earl of Clarendon or Lord John Russell; and as for the permanent officials, Edmund Hammond, was permanent under-secretary from 1854 until 1873, and G. Lennox-Conyngham chief clerk from 1841 until 1866. Family dynasties among the clerks were also pillars of the status quo, the most remarkable of which was that of the Bidwell family, four generations of which had served at the Foreign Office.

As to the mid-Victorian diplomatic service, here the need for reform was possibly more urgent than in the Foreign Office itself, from which it was at that time administratively separate. It is true that professionalization was slowly on the way: the number of paid junior diplomatists was increasing and a qualifying examination for candidates proposed in 1851 was introduced five years later. The custom that heads of mission owed their positions to their political allegiance to the government of the day rather than to seniority and professional competence was beginning to erode. The diplomatic service as a whole was also no more socially exclusive than the rest of the mid-Victorian governing elite, and if those in its top tier – the 'ambassadors' in their embassies – were very expensive, at least there were very few of them, as opposed to the 'ministers' in their more lowly legations.

---

[132] *Pictures from the Battle Fields*, p. 3; see also p. 203.

5. Edmund Hammond, Permanent Under-Secretary at the Foreign Office

Nevertheless, in the 1850s the members of the diplomatic service were still drawn chiefly from the aristocracy, and those attaining the rank of ambassador overwhelmingly so. Only those nominated by the foreign secretary could sit the new exam, which was in any case not a stiff one. A wealthy background was even more important for young attachés than young Foreign Office clerks because they were still initially 'unpaid', could remain so for up to five years, and – with the passing of the family embassy – could no longer rely on their head of mission for board and lodging.

The degree of foreign language expertise among diplomatists was also lamentable, as admitted by those interrogated by the Select Committee on Official Salaries in 1850, which turned out to be the starting point of the 'age of inquiry'.

Despite the recommendation of an 1850 committee for their merger, numerous missions of little value remained a fixture in central Germany and, to a lesser extent, in Italy. A serious block on promotion within the service had also developed with the increase in the number of paid attachés with career ambitions. As to the duties of the diplomatic service, here an emerging point of concern was its restricted conception of its responsibilities to Britain's foreign commerce. Like the Foreign Office, the diplomats were wedded to the view that – if they had any responsibility for this at all – it lay only in negotiating commercial treaties providing the best terms possible for British trade *as a whole*. It did not extend to canvassing for trade or contracts on behalf of individuals or companies, and certainly not small ones; that is, the ones that needed it most.

Grenville-Murray was appalled by the state of affairs both in the Foreign Office and the diplomatic service, and his ideas for reform were many and detailed. They were shaped by his diplomatic experience, active interest in current events, and extensive reading on the law and history of diplomacy. His criticisms, which were always constructive and quickly increased in ferocity, surfaced not only in *Household Words* and *Pictures from the Battle Fields* but also in anonymous leading articles in the *Daily News* in March 1855 and above all, in the following August, in a lengthy book called *Embassies and Foreign Courts: A History of Diplomacy*.

Much of the ground work for *Embassies and Foreign Courts* had been laid by his *Droits et Devoirs des Envoyés Diplomatique* [Rights and Duties of Diplomatic Envoys], which had appeared rather obscurely two years earlier, and was evidently conceived as a manual for the profession. However, it was also an exercise in professional self-improvement, for he still very much wanted to be a successful diplomatist. In an otherwise favourable review, *Droits et Devoirs* had been criticised for not having been written in English and for having insufficient modern examples. It is also possible that Palmerston, who in May 1855 was confronted with a complaint in parliament that British diplomatists had not written books on diplomacy, shared this view and encouraged him to revise it accordingly. In any event, the new book corrected the perceived errors of *Droits et Devoirs*. It also had a broader range and a more polemical edge and, to cash in on the popularity of the 'Roving Englishman', was published under this pseudonym.

Embassies and Foreign Courts made no reference to *Droits et Devoirs* for the obvious reason that the earlier work had appeared under the author's real name. Trying to be a campaigning book as well as a manual for the profession, inevitably it ended up serving neither purpose particularly well. Its extensive technical detail made it unattractive as a polemic, while being a polemic it engendered – and still engenders – suspicion of its trustworthiness as a manual. Nevertheless, among those who have taken the trouble to read it, Kenneth Bourne – Professor of International History at the LSE and otherwise no great admirer – admitted that there was a good deal in this book, as well as in Grenville-Murray's other work on diplomacy, that was 'shrewd and well-informed.'[133]

Taking sardonic delight in the ammunition provided by the recently inaugurated *Foreign Office List*, which contained much information on the previous appointments of British diplomatists and consuls,[134] Grenville-Murray

---

[133] *Palmerston*, pp. 205-6.
[134] The *FO List* was launched in 1852 as a private venture by Francis Cavendish, then an assistant junior clerk in the Foreign Office.

slammed into the patronage system. It was by means of this, he maintained, that the men favoured for the profession were too often 'fashionable idlers', with neither brains, historical learning, foreign languages, nor appropriate experience; and that men of humble origin like the naturally gifted Oriental Secretary at Constantinople, Charles Alison, were repeatedly passed over for important posts. 'I am very much afraid,' he wrote when launching his reformist campaign in 1853, 'that a more completely incapable body of men (taken *en masse*) do not exist than our diplomatic servants.'[135] The only value of 'your Great Nobody', he maintained, was in countries blighted by 'cringing and lord-reverence'.[136] By early 1855, he was describing the families from which such diplomats came as the 'cousinocracy', later the 'white-gloved cousinocracy'. British diplomacy, he concluded, was at once an 'occult science' and a 'lugubrious farce.'[137] What were the consequences, and what should be done?

The most serious result of this state of affairs, believed Grenville-Murray, was that policy was made in ignorance of local conditions; and it was for this reason that so many disasters had occurred in the Crimean War. Not even a Palmerston, he maintained, could 'attend to the details of all the business of all the countries in the world.'[138] Another drawback, however, was that British diplomacy took no interest in commerce – despite the fact that the British were essentially a commercial people – because the aristocracy had always considered trade beneath it. The last evil was that whereas the lowly consul could be told what to do, the lordly diplomatist could not; in consequence, the diplomatic service had been 'allowed to run riot.'[139]

To rectify this situation, Grenville-Murray urged adoption of the rule that ministerial recommendations for appointments to the diplomatic service should be ratified at least by the tacit consent of parliament. 'Most ministers,' he said, 'would be ashamed to recommend a Fiddlededee or a Tweedledum if the thing were not done snugly, in the dark.'[140] Later he went further, saying

---

[135] 'Diplomacy', *HW*, 18 June 1853.
[136] 'Diplomacy', *HW*, 18 June 1853.
[137] *Daily News*, 10 March, 1855.
[138] 'On Her Majesty's Service', *HW*, 7 January 1854.
[139] 'On Her Majesty's Service', *HW*, 7 January 1854.
[140] 'On Her Majesty's Service', *HW*, 7 January 1854.

that ministers should also be required to state the grounds on which they gave places and promotions when announcing them in the *London Gazette*. As for diplomatists unfamiliar with the language of the country to which they were to go, they should be allowed six months to acquire its rudiments before starting out.

Less well judged among the Roving Englishman's other targets was the 'secrecy and hocus-pocus of diplomacy.' Only by getting rid of this, he claimed, could statesmen be held to account for any mischief they might do and private experts be encouraged to offer advice. Anticipating the great cry for 'open diplomacy' well over half a century before it became fashionable, he also stressed that 'suspicion always attaches to mystery,' and that if official mysteries were exposed sooner, 'wars and other great evils would often be prevented.'[141] Only two exceptions were to be admitted to his general rule of openness: first, when secrecy was dictated by 'the immediate concerns of actual warfare'; and second, when it was needed 'to spare humiliation to the feelings of private persons, who sometimes become unavoidably mixed up with some scandalous affair.'[142]

Grenville-Murray also thought that diplomatists should not be allowed to remain in any one post beyond three years; by this means they might avoid growing 'brimful of rules, orders, regulations, etiquette, and local prejudices' and understand one country the better for knowing more of others.[143] With his bitter experience at Constantinople in mind, he also insisted that an ambassador should be obliged to listen to the advice of his diplomatic staff rather than entertain their opinions only as grudgingly as an absolute monarch granted a parliament.

He was even further ahead of his time by stressing that British embassies should, like those of France, include attachés from different professions. 'Let us,' he begged, 'be represented abroad as we really are; in our best colours; by our best men who have really shown ability, and earned (not inherited) distinction.' They should include 'draughtsmen, surveyors, engineers,

---

[141] *The Press and the Public Service*, pp. 160-1, 168-9.
[142] *Embassies and Foreign Courts*, pp. 135, 235 (see also pp. 33-4); and *The Press and the Public Service*, p. 164.
[143] 'Diplomacy', *HW*, 18 June 1853.

physicians, soldiers, lawyers, sound men thoroughly accustomed to observe, and scholars!' By this means, he said, Britain's embassies might 'help to advance the progress of science and civilization all over the world … and bring us back numberless practical benefits in return.'[144] He gave to such ideal missions the name 'practical embassies'.[145]

If embassies were to be staffed by men of genuine distinction, there should also, he continued, be no flinching from treating them well. They should have high salaries, and houses should be bought rather than – as had hitherto been customary – rented for their residences.[146] Some diplomatic missions should also have larger staffs. 'At Paris, Vienna, Constantinople, Berlin, Naples, Madrid, we could hardly have too many clear-headed, hardworking men,' he maintained. Meanwhile, agreeing on the basis of personal experience with the select committee on official salaries of 1850, he believed economies might be made by closing missions that were a farce, such as those at Hanover, Stuttgart and Dresden. But, except on special occasions, grand missions headed by an ambassador – characteristically dressed like a harlequin, surrounded by a vast retinue, and demanding sovereign honours by virtue of holding the full representative character (a 'singular hallucination') – were obsolete, he believed. Why? Because the intercourse between nations being no longer rare and difficult, nations knew each other better, and so no longer needed absurdly expensive embassies as reminders that they were not to be treated with contempt. This was an acute point.

In regard to the dark arts of diplomacy, Grenville-Murray's hostility was unremitting. No doubt with the fate of his own letters at Vienna much in mind, he regarded the secret opening and re-sealing of the despatches of foreign envoys as simply an infamous species of theft. As for cyphers, he thought these at best useless, because they could be so easily broken; and at worst dangerous, because of the ease of making mistakes in both encrypting and decrypting

---

144 'On Her Majesty's Service', *HW*, 7 January 1854. He later claimed credit for the appointment of military attachés to some British embassies as a result of his inclusion of 'soldiers' in this list, *Turkey, being Sketches from Life*, p. 29.

145 *Embassies and Foreign Courts*, p. 238; see also pp. 175-6.

146 *Embassies and Foreign Courts*, p. 149. On this subject generally, see my *Outposts of Diplomacy*, pp. 112-16.

messages. Anyway, he observed with heavy sarcasm, 'few ambassadors appear to need a cypher to render their despatches completely incomprehensible to anybody.' For important messages, he believed there to be no substitute for a trustworthy messenger, who had the incidental advantage of being a valuable source of intelligence on the countries through which he passed.[147] The use of bribery and secret agents as means of obtaining information also suffered condemnation at his hands: they were ungentlemanly, expensive, and, above all, unnecessary. When secrets became serious, he insisted, they always became known, especially to an observant man who was liked and respected, gave good dinners, and kept his lines open to the opposition – for 'disappointment,' he observed, 'is open-mouthed.'[148]

Grenville-Murray also had firm and detailed views on the reforms needed by the consular service. Notable among these were his belief that consuls should be paid decent salaries so that they would not need to pocket the fees for their services, a system not only open to notorious abuse, he maintained, but also one that inevitably led to 'serious altercations with sea-captains'; fees collected should instead be for government account. Second, their annual commercial reports should be improved in quality, timeliness, and public availability but this would never happen while the Foreign Office failed to show interest in them, merely shunting them to the Board of Trade. And third, the 'astounding' system of patronage should be drastically limited in favour of the appointment of men either properly trained or suitably experienced for consular work.

Turning to the Foreign Office itself, Grenville-Murray's remaining target was the one for which he was to be best known, and which made him his most bitter enemies: the so-called agency system. This consisted of the informal arrangement whereby a clerk keen for the work took under his wing any diplomatist and consul who thought he would serve him well. The 'agent' ensured that his quarterly salary payments were safely banked, and, among other chores, forwarded his private correspondence, alerted him to vacancies

---

[147] *Embassies and Foreign Courts*, pp. 138-45, 178-99.
[148] *Embassies and Foreign Courts*, pp. 260-2.

at attractive posts, and helped to arrange exchanges with other colleagues. In return, the agent was paid annually 1 per cent of the salary and outfit allowances of his diplomatic client (excepting unpaid attachés, who were not charged), and a flat rate of usually about ten guineas by his customers among their poor relations in the consular service. Any clerk could become an agent, although in practice there were only six in the Foreign Office in the mid-nineteenth century. The arrangement was nominally voluntary: diplomats and consuls were not *obliged* to hire a Foreign Office agent, although in practice almost all did.

The agency system was defended on the grounds that it was convenient to all concerned, increased understanding between officers at home and officers abroad, assisted security in the Foreign Office building by keeping 'out-of-door' agents to a minimum, and provided a valuable supplement to the salaries of those clerks who took on the work. It was probably for the last of these reasons that while Palmerston himself was at the Foreign Office – and often under pressure from the Treasury to economise – he left the system alone.

The agency system, however, was controversial. It had been said, for example, that the services provided by the clerks as 'agents' should have been free to their fellow officers, and that the private profits it generated encouraged them to devote disproportionate time to this work at the expense of their official duties. As a result, the system had been challenged periodically since the late eighteenth century, and had been abolished by the Colonial Office in 1837. Enter the Roving Englishman, injecting unprecedented invective into the campaign against the Foreign Office agents.

Notwithstanding their 'true British official contempt for the ordinary pursuits of trade,' wrote Grenville-Murray, the time of the Foreign Office agents was *chiefly* spent on 'the lucrative and important duties of bankers and monopolists.' In consequence, the real earnings of these magnificent hypocrites were far higher than officially recorded. Holding 'the keys of promotion,' they were in a position to sabotage the careers not only of those who refused to employ them but also of those among their poorer clients who had the effrontery to require their salaries to be paid with 'inconvenient regularity.' A person such as this, inevitably suspect in the eyes of the men of substance in the Foreign

Office, would receive no early notice of 'snug vacancies,' while every opportunity would be taken of 'giving currency to ingenious slanders about him.' By contrast, he continued, there is 'overflowing sympathy and generous kindness for the excellent officer who allows his salary to accumulate in the hands of his mollified agent.' In sum, wrote Grenville-Murray, the Foreign Office was 'one of the oldest established shops in London ... the job-shop of several of the most prudent, accomplished and thriving traders in this kingdom.' The greatest of all of these traders might recently have retired, 'with all the respect which is due to a large realized fortune,' and then died – but the system still flourished.[149]

This last jab was to cost the Roving Englishman dear, for it was clearly directed at John Bidwell, and so made a serious enemy of his son, also called John Bidwell and also a Foreign Office clerk. He also happened to be Grenville-Murray's own private agent. John Bidwell junior, who was also a candidate member of the cousinocracy (he later married the daughter of the 3rd Earl of Clanwilliam), was so deeply hurt by the attack on his father that he refused any longer to serve Grenville-Murray in this capacity, and returned his power of attorney.[150] In the long run, Bidwell's enmity was to be more serious for him than this loss.

In advancing his recommendations for the reform of the diplomatic and consular services, the Roving Englishman was on most points stiffening a strong wind already starting to blow. On the agency system, however, he was stirring up his own gale. He was out of the country when a parliamentary select committee on the consular service began to take evidence in the early summer of 1858 (the first since 1835), and similarly absent abroad when the select committee on diplomatic service was in session in the first half of 1861 – and so never appeared as a witness before either; nor did he send them any memoranda, or at least any that were among the selections published in their reports. Nevertheless, his books, the weekly in which he had a regular column and his articles in the daily press were widely read. This was sufficient for his

---

[149] *Pictures from the Battle Fields*, pp. 279-85.
[150] Thereafter, he appears instead to have employed his wife and a firm of solicitors, Clayton and Cookson, of Lincoln's Inn, to look after his interests at the FO.

influence on reform to be felt and, as we shall see, it was reinforced by a press campaign at the end of the 1860s.

Satire and anonymity

Satire was Grenville-Murray's chief mode of attack, and anonymity his principal method of defence. Both were employed in his novels – a genre which, like Dickens, he believed should have a strong moral purpose – as well as his journalism and, with exceptions, in his non-fiction works as well. However, satire had a low reputation in the Victorian era, while anonymity, although still the norm, was itself beginning to come under pressure. As a result, he was at pains to justify both.

In *The Press and the Public Service*, published in March 1857 and the nearest thing to a political testament he ever wrote, Grenville-Murray was keen to stress that satire should not be employed for attacks on 'private character, upon private grounds.' This, he believed, following the divine master, would be neither pious nor politic. However, he proceeded, it was necessary that all private considerations should yield to public duty. Public men could not be separated from their public misdeeds and escape attack, any more than criminals could escape personal responsibility for their crimes; otherwise, those misdeeds – although exposed – would retain powerful supporters. Attention should also be drawn to distressing personal defects such as blindness, deafness or drunkenness 'if the persons suffering from such absolute disqualifications insisted on retaining their places to the injury of the public service.' Warming to his theme, he rejected the argument that it was 'measures, not men' that should be attacked. This was just 'the common cant of affected moderation; a counterfeit language fabricated by knaves for the use of fools.' As for the general charge of 'scurrility' often levelled by malefactors at the righteous satirist, this was nothing but an ingenious device to draw his sting by appealing to the best side of human nature. It was a fact, he concluded, that the language used by the fiercest satirist in the mid-nineteenth century appeared mild by comparison with that accepted as the common currency of the hustings, the House of Commons, and the bar. Libels were inevitable, he admitted, but they were the price to be paid for achieving a much greater good. The model satirist might make mistakes but he must actually be a kind man, 'or how,' he asked, 'should he sympathize with public suffering? He must be a good man, or how should he be able to excite indignation against evil? He must be a man of high aspirings, for he will hardly serve any personal object by satire.'

As satire was the proper weapon against vice, he maintained, so ridicule was the proper weapon against folly. 'It is a fortunate circumstance for mankind,' he wrote – and it is a telling point – 'that those who have no fear of anything else may be reached by it.' Fools cannot be out-argued but they abandon their prejudices quickly enough when they have become 'the object of universal derision.'

Notwithstanding his powerful patron, as a whistleblower dependent on his employment in the diplomatic service Grenville-Murray had little alternative but to write either anonymously or pseudonymously. He had actually discussed the subject in a short essay called 'A Talk With My Public' in *From Mayfair to Marathon* in 1853, but only a few years later it required more urgent and considered attention, for by then his career was at stake (see Chapter 3). Hence this subject was treated in *The Press and the Public Service* as well.

The advantage of anonymity stressed by Grenville-Murray was that it emboldened the widest exposure of abuses in government departments by those best placed to do it; to whit, their own employees. Such a shield for the 'soldiers of truth,' he said, was indispensable, because for some time past the question of the right of civil servants to speak out publicly had been carefully evaded, and those with the courage to do so had been sought out and threatened with dismissal. This was peculiarly wicked because the supposed permanence of their employment was its greatest attraction, and after the age of 30 all comparable careers were virtually closed to them. 'There is no reason,' he concluded, 'why a patriot should always be a martyr,' and without the shield of anonymity liberty would be unlikely to keep many friends.

Anonymity, Grenville-Murray was also keen to stress, had many second order advantages. It preserved the high tone of the press by preventing its use for the gratification of vanity and ambition, and made it more likely that arguments would be judged on their merits rather than on the basis of their authorship. (He neglected the point that they might not be judged at all if they did not attract attention in the first place, the ironic fate of the book in which his arguments for anonymity were advanced.)[151] Writers might also have private motives for adopting it. By this time he had dropped the argument advanced under this head earlier; namely, that since the profession of writing – unless on history, law or divinity – was looked down upon in polite society, anonymity was necessary in order to avoid social disgrace. But he repeated the argument that it might be justly employed in youth in order to avoid being branded for life with immature opinions. And he added that some authors might adopt anonymity from a desire to keep a cool head in reasoning.

But what of the criticism that anonymous writing gave an unfair advantage to its author and was, to boot, cowardly? In answer to the first charge, he replied that it merely levelled the playing field with the powerful; and to the second, that it still required courage because suspicion of authorship remained a real risk, and could be as fatal as certain knowledge of it to any career a writer might have in the public service. In sum, anonymous writing, 'this tower of strength and bulwark of the liberties of the Press may be strenuously defended without a blush or a misgiving.' It had been employed, he observed, by all the great Tory and Whig statesmen, all the bishops and all the lawyers of repute, since the late seventeenth century.

How should an anonymous writer respond if pressed by a person in authority over him to admit or deny authorship? Since anonymous writing was a legal right, the writer was under no obligation to reply, maintained Grenville-Murray. And quite right, too, he maintained. After all, what is the point of it if the writer is required to admit authorship to the first person who challenges him on the point? However, since there is also no law against asking, he might be pressed; in this case, prudence requires good humoured evasion. If pressed still further, there is no alternative to 'self-preservative mendacity,' but the responsibility for this sorry final resort lies with the 'despotic' interrogator

---

[151] Neither the article on G-M in the *DNB* nor in the later *ODNB* (until I was able to re-write it) shows any awareness of *The Press and the Public Service*, despite the fact that it is his most important book.

rather than his weak victim. As we shall see in the following chapter, this was precisely the kind of rearguard the Roving Englishman was himself forced to fight by the Foreign Office. He was fortified in it by constantly having in mind, as he makes clear at some length in *The Press and the Public Service*, the names of many great writers who had denied their writings, among them Swift, Johnson, Scott – and Edmund Burke.

3   Revenge of the 'Cousinocracy'

'It is the popular belief at Constantinople,' wrote Grenville-Murray of the British ambassador Lord Stratford de Redcliffe, 'that his staff live under a rule so stern as to have no choice between the discipline of children and the exile of criminals.'[152] This belief being well founded and Grenville-Murray being no child, it was inevitable that it should be chiefly by means of exile that the cousinocracy had its revenge on him, although the final punishment was to be even rougher: dismissal from the diplomatic service without either a pension or the *exeat* that would have made it possible for him to obtain employment elsewhere in government.

Exiled to Mytilene

As mentioned in the previous chapter, in the autumn of 1853 Lord Stratford banished his insufferable attaché from Constantinople to the British vice-consulate on Lesbos, disingenuously explaining that he wished to offer him 'a wider range of experience.' It was humiliating for any diplomatic officer in that period to be sent to a consular post, although in this case not quite to the degree usually suggested. This is because Grenville-Murray was made *acting* vice-consul, and therefore retained his diplomatic rank as a paid attaché at Constantinople; and he never let anyone forget it, including Lord Stratford. It also enabled him to maintain that at Mytilene he was on 'special service',[153] the important-sounding title given to most extraordinary appointments in the diplomatic service, which also implied the need for extraordinary qualifications.

Apprehensive of his chief's rage, especially after his literary knighting of him as 'Sir Hector Stubble', Grenville-Murray was on his best behaviour at Mytilene. He notified the ambassador promptly of his arrival, and found time

---

152   *Pictures from the Battle Fields*, pp. 39-40.
153   As, for example, in notices he inspired in the *Manchester Times*, 29 April, and the *Daily News*, 13 September 1854.

between writing his Roving Englishman articles to send him 30 numbered despatches and numerous private letters. Some were quite long and showed that he was taking seriously both the economic and political aspects of the work.

Grenville-Murray had arrived at Mytilene on 24 October 1853, the day after Turkish hostilities commenced against the Russian forces that had entered the Ottoman provinces of Moldavia and Wallachia in the summer. The British were apprehensive of an advance of Russian forces on Constantinople, and had tilted to the sultan. As a result, many of the acting vice-consul's despatches dealt with suspected Russian agitation on Lesbos and growing tensions between the Greek islanders and their Turkish rulers. Others reflected his enthusiasm for the tutorial role long adopted by Britain towards the Turks; for example, a proposal for a thoughtful scheme to give 'a few steady lads' a technical education at public expense in various parts of Europe in order to stimulate agricultural production on the island on their return. Exploiting his connections with the press in England, he also took good care to make sure that his benevolent activities on Mytilene received as much publicity as possible.

Stratford had been minded to transform Grenville-Murray's stay at Mytilene into a life sentence when he discovered that it was he who had lampooned him in *Household Words*. But he reckoned without Lord Palmerston. And, as was the exile's custom, he had been scrupulous not only to exempt the more powerful man from his otherwise scattershot attacks on British diplomacy but also to praise him.[154] It was lucky for Grenville-Murray that, although Palmerston was then at the Home Office, he was if anything more popular and thus more influential than ever; as it happened, he also shared Grenville-Murray's dislike of Stratford's personality. It may have helped him, too, that another of Palmerston's protégés, Edmund Hammond, who was a hard driver but kinder to younger men than some and always willing to give credit where credit was due, became permanent under-secretary at the Foreign Office in early April. Once more, therefore, Palmerston came to Grenville-Murray's aid and

---

[154] Palmerston received *four* favourable mentions in 'On Her Majesty's Service', *HW*, 7 January 1854: three times by name, and once – for his sponsorship of an experiment with Englishmen as oriental attachés at Constantinople – in the guise of his earlier incarnation in *Walter Evelyn*, 'Sir Charles Grandison'; see also *Embassies and Foreign Courts*, p. 102.

Stratford's dream of keeping him on Lesbos for ever was foiled. He was relieved at the end of June 1854 and permitted leave until late September on the grounds that he was suffering from severe inflammation of his eyes. This period he spent at Rhodes and Smyrna before finally returning to Constantinople.

Locked out

Back at the embassy in the Ottoman capital, Grenville-Murray found, however, not only that the ambassador was still refusing to consider a mounting claim for expenses but also that he had been locked out of his room. Clearly, his exile was not over after all. Eventually the Foreign Office decided to grant him further leave of absence until either the greatly feared ambassador should drop dead or some other occupation for his troublesome attaché could be hit upon.

This enforced sabbatical at least allowed Grenville-Murray to retain his diplomatic status while permitting him to be a full time journalist. It also put him in just the mood to write *Pictures from the Battle Fields*, which condemned Stratford's role in the Crimean War, a conflict that in the late summer of 1854 was just beginning to hot up.

To gather material for his book, Grenville-Murray visited the British hospital at Scutari on the Asian side of the Bosphorus (where he spoke in German to some Russian officers) and then the French hospital. He next journeyed via Varna to the Crimea itself. Having observed the misery of Balaclava, where he probably stayed for not more than a week or so, he returned to Varna. Then he headed for England by the snow-covered overland route. Posting by horse-drawn carriage and commanding priority treatment because carrying despatches from the seat of war, the Roving Englishman made good speed but on arriving at Bucharest lingered for a while, working on his manuscript and dining daily with the hospitable British agent and consul-general, Robert Colquhoun, with whom he got on famously. He reached England about the end of February 1855.

Grenville-Murray completed *Pictures from the Battle Fields* in the spring of 1855, and in May began to press the foreign secretary, Lord Clarendon, for a new posting. On the face of it, his prospects were favourable because it was on the back of the public outcry against the conduct of the British campaign in the Crimea that his patron, Lord Palmerston, had swept to the premiership in February. But Palmerston had for some time been showing irritation at the fashion for speaking disparagingly of Britain's diplomats,[155] so his protégé was not only getting uncomfortably ahead of but also stirring up troublesome opposition to him.

Indeed, shortly after the appearance of *Pictures from the Battle Fields*, in what is unlikely to have been a coincidence, disquiet in the House of Commons about the diplomatic and consular services once more came to the surface. On 22 May, Liberal members echoed almost all of the themes trumpeted by the Roving Englishman.

In reply, Palmerston assured MPs that his government was fully seized with the question of diplomatic reform, and promised that candidates for the diplomatic service would be examined prior to entry. Nevertheless, he insisted that Britain's diplomatists and consuls were already as good as any in the world. Despite his plea that the House should not divide on the motion, it did – and he lost the vote by a wide margin. This debate clearly placed unwelcome pressure on Palmerston and advertised the wide gap between his views and those of Grenville-Murray. It is likely, therefore, to have steeled Lord Clarendon to take a somewhat rougher line with his *enfant terrible*.

Sure enough, Grenville-Murray failed to get any response from the foreign secretary to his request for a new post. Accordingly, at the beginning of September he informed him of his intention to return to the embassy at Constantinople. Here, Lord Stratford was still ambassador but – having been widely blamed for starting an unpopular war – was not in quite as strong a position as the one to which he had been accustomed.

In the circumstances, the return of the Roving Englishman was hardly going to be that of a penitent, and it seems that the prospect of a major row at the embassy was a further inducement to Clarendon finally to focus on the problem of what to do about him. Still, the foreign secretary did not forbid him

---

[155]   See, for example, his speech in reply to pressure for an examination for budding diplomats in 1853: HCDeb., 8 April 1853, vol. 125, cols. 883-6.

to return; instead, he merely said that, in view of the way he had 'lampooned' his chief, he was sure Lord Stratford would refuse to have him back, and there was nothing the Foreign Office could do about it. Protesting against the charge that he had attacked Lord Stratford in this manner, which had, he told Clarendon, filled him with 'the most painful surprize and concern,' Grenville-Murray added that he remained resolved to return to his post and ultimately win the foreign secretary's approval; he admitted, however, the inadvisability of direct communication with the ambassador. Shortly afterwards, he departed for Turkey.

'Are you, or are you not, the "Roving Englishman"'?

Evidently regretting his indecision, Clarendon caused Grenville-Murray to be interrogated by letter as to his responsibility for the lampoons of Lord Stratford while en route but still to no avail. He belatedly turned up in Constantinople on 22 November, for with neither a warm welcome nor any useful occupation to expect on his arrival, the Roving Englishman had travelled back via the Danube and the delta port of Sulina, and spent the time gathering material for more travel articles for *Household Words*. Four days later the ambassador told Clarendon not only that it was impossible for his attaché to remain at the embassy but also that he believed him to be generally unfit for the Queen's service.

Grenville-Murray set off back to London almost immediately. Once more he carried despatches, including some picked up from the British Embassy at Vienna. Acting as an official messenger had the further advantages of entitling him to relatively generous expenses and privileged passage, and of enabling him to demonstrate still further his usefulness and dedication to the service. He delivered his packages at the Foreign Office shortly before midnight on 13 December, and by 5 January was once more back in Constantinople.

He had not sought Clarendon's approval for the last journey, and yet again was refused residence at the embassy – and yet again was pursued by a letter from the Foreign Office. The agitated foreign secretary now wished for a 'categorical' answer to the question as to whether he was or was not the Roving

6. 22 Brook Street today

Englishman. If he was, he was informed, the Foreign Office would be bound to agree with Lord Stratford that his attachment to the embassy at Constantinople should be formally terminated. This produced a flat denial and left Clarendon still at a loss as to what to do. Two months later, Stratford exploded, emphasising to the foreign secretary that this affair threatened to become 'a public scandal.' Duly galvanized, Clarendon ordered the troublesome attaché to return immediately to England and report at once to the Foreign Office. Assisted by a cheque for his travel expenses which the ambassador provided with unusual alacrity, he was back by the beginning of April.

Meanwhile, the foreign secretary had issued a call for evidence proving beyond doubt that Grenville-Murray was the Roving Englishman, and it was William Grey, secretary of legation at Stockholm, who delivered the goods. Grey had recently joined the Fielding Club, which was not one of the usual places patronised by diplomats on leave but, located in the heart of London Bohemia, chiefly a fraternity for men of letters and thus the ideal place in which to glean intelligence about Grenville-Murray.

Grey was not disappointed in the garrulous members of the Fielding Club. He quickly reported, first, that the well-known authors Albert Smith and William Makepeace Thackeray had confirmed, on the authority of Dickens himself, that Grenville-Murray was indeed the Roving Englishman; and second, that a sub-editor of the *Daily News* had admitted that Grenville-Murray was the author of his newspaper's attacks on the Foreign Office.

With Grey's memorandum in his hands, at the end of May 1856 Clarendon told Grenville-Murray that he now had strong evidence that he was the Roving Englishman, and once more challenged him to prove otherwise or face dismissal. On his 'word of honour as a gentleman', he once more denied the allegation and shortly afterwards gave the same assurance to the Duke of Buckingham, while asking him to pass to Clarendon a supporting document from the publisher George Routledge.

That is where the matter came to rest. It was a desperate lie and everyone knew it. But the Foreign Office was told that he was simply following the etiquette of the press; namely, that anyone writing anonymously did not forfeit their honour by positively denying authorship. Besides, to have called Grenville-Murray a liar and dismissed him from the diplomatic service would have been a serious step for Clarendon to take. This was because – despite their differences – the Roving Englishman still had the support of Palmerston, who, while foreign secretary as well as when in opposition, had denied responsibility for a great many anonymous articles he had himself written for the press. And it was to Palmerston that Clarendon still reflexively looked for instructions. In the circumstances, therefore, there was little the foreign secretary could do but keep Grenville-Murray away from Stratford's embassy, on approved leave, while trying to find him another post.

But Grenville-Murray had received a fright, the more so because a great rise in his family's expenses meant that he could ill afford to jeopardise his income. By this time he was living in Mayfair, London's most fashionable district. At the time of the 1861 Census his household had a coachman, a nurse, and a housemaid, and is hardly likely to have been smaller than this at the height of his publishing fame during the Crimean War. The education of his sons was also bound to become much more expensive. Indeed, in 1857 his eldest, Reginald, would be sent to board at Eton at an annual cost of £200; and he would face similar expense for Wyndham in the following year. The consequence was that the Roving Englishman was never heard of again in *Household Words* after the issue of 29 March 1856; and, with two anonymous exceptions, it was over 15 years before he published another book.

The first and by far the most notable of these exceptions was *The Press and the Public Service*, published in March 1857 and written by Grenville-Murray in the immediate aftermath of his Foreign Office inquisition. Here he not only elaborated his defence of anonymity (see pp. 115 above) but also launched a ferocious attack on the 'low cunning' by which some government officials, encouraged by their masters, sought vengeance on whistleblowers. This suggests that he suspected Grey's motive for joining the Fielding Club and knew that it was by this means that he had been exposed by some of its members – and indirectly by Dickens himself. Indeed, it would be surprising if he had not guessed this or if someone had not whispered it to him. This could have been serious for his relationship with the great novelist. After all, he announced in this book that 'An editor who betrayed a correspondent would render himself peculiarly infamous. He would commit not only a breach of contract but a breach of trust.' But Dickens was too important to him and too much admired in all other respects for him to risk an open breach, and he resumed writing for him – this time anonymously rather than pseudonymously – when *Household Words* was reincarnated as *All the Year Round* in 1859.

The only other book published over the next 15 years by Grenville-Murray was an immensely learned work called *The Oyster*, to which Major Herbert Byng-Hall – a Queen's Messenger he had probably fallen in with on the Constantinople run – might have made a small contribution. Literary co-partnership was one of the devices employed to obscure authorship by anonymous writers; it was also one to which the Roving Englishman had previously drawn attention.

Persian punishment

In 1856 Grenville-Murray was angry and bitter. He had a very high opinion of his own abilities, energy, and passion to serve the public; and there is every reason to believe he did not exaggerate greatly in claiming that he even employed 'his spare hours in the eager study of state questions, instead of going to a ball or a whist-party.'[156] Nevertheless, he thought that he was being persecuted. And why should he not write for money? With salaries in government so low, to deny this to a subordinate officer would be virtually to surrender the whole government service to the rich. But it was 'impious to dare despair,' so he bided his time.[157]

While the Foreign Office was waiting for a suitably uncomfortable post for him to fall vacant, Grenville-Murray seems to have been employed once more in carrying despatches. This was work to which in any case he rightly attached high diplomatic value, evidently liked for the expenses-paid

---

[156] *The Press and the Public Service*, pp. 195-6.
[157] *The Press and the Public Service*, p. 146; see also p. 189.

opportunities it provided for his travel writing, and so wrote about learnedly and at length.

Soon enough, though, in January 1857 an inspired solution for him was triumphantly found. On the same annual salary of £250, he was to be third paid attaché in the legation at Tehran, closed since November 1855 due to an outbreak of fighting between Britain and Persia! Better still, as far as the Foreign Office was concerned, should the mission in due course reappear, he would find himself at a particularly unpopular post. It was not only difficult to reach but – being concerned more with Asiatic than European affairs – was less in the orbit of the Foreign Office than the India Office, which resented having to fund the post and evidently thought that Britain's relations with Persia would be better if its staff had Indian rather than European experience. To cap it all, his new chief was to be the Hon. Charles Augustus Murray, who was among those prominently singled out by the Roving Englishman to illustrate how often patronage worked against the appointment of men with ability and appropriate experience. Never even thought of for Tehran instead of Murray, the Roving Englishman had written, was the soldier-diplomatist of Herat and Candahar, Colonel Rawlinson. Such experience as the colonel's could not compete, he added sardonically, with 'the remarkable proofs of genius' provided by the Hon. Murray; namely, his previous appointments as master of the Queen's household and her extra groom in waiting.[158]

In the event, peace returned to Anglo-Persian relations in the summer of 1857. The Hon. Murray, who had been treading water in Constantinople, duly re-opened his legation in Tehran in July and in anticipation of this Grenville-Murray had set out to join him in the middle of May. But it was 27 October before he finally reached the Persian capital, riding about 1000 miles on horseback and battling snow storms in the mountains. Because of the time wasted and such special factors as war-induced price inflation and the need to hire guards for his retinue in the disturbed state of the Turkish/Persian border region, he had run up the huge bill of £673 for expenses – almost three times his annual salary. And, although his claim was immaculately documented,

---

[158]   *Pictures from the Battlefields*, pp. 256-7.

promptly despatched to Lord Clarendon with a request that it be paid to his wife, and sympathetically endorsed by a British consul in Asiatic Turkey who happened to be on leave in London, the most he ever received from the unremittingly hostile Foreign Office chief clerk, Lenox-Conyngham, was £250 – and that not until August in the following year.

Somehow escaping his Persian purgatory, by late June 1858 Grenville-Murray was back at his Mayfair home. Only a month later, however, he was given another public appointment, and the one that was to prove his last: Consul-General for the Russian Ports in the Black Sea and the Sea of Azof, to reside at the port city of Odessa. The salary was a great increase and he was to leave immediately. In Calais, his mother wrote to the Duke of Buckingham rejoicing at the news of this 'splendid appointment', although her tune soon changed when she learned that she was not to share in the windfall. The 'dear son' of the first letter was to become variously the 'serpent' and the 'scorpion' of those that followed.[159]

The Odessa post had been given to Grenville-Murray by the Earl of Malmesbury, foreign secretary once more since February when Palmerston (and with him Clarendon) had given way to the minority Conservative government of the 14th Earl of Derby. The most likely reason is that Malmesbury had tender feelings for the Duke of Buckingham and thought the post would help the family with its perilous financial difficulties. It may be, as well, that he was less hostile than the Foreign Office to the Roving Englishman's resolute stand on anonymous writing since the new Foreign Secretary was even 'as a minister, capable of satirizing himself and his colleagues, anonymously, in *Punch*.'[160] And he might also have been prompted by a desire to make Grenville-Murray grateful to the Foreign Office while keeping him busy a long way from home. By this means, he effectively neutralized the Office's most dangerous critic at precisely the juncture when the pressure for radical reform both of the diplomatic and consular services was becoming difficult to resist.

---

[159] Her other son, Henry, was no better, she told Buckingham, HL, Emma Murray Mills to 2DBC, October 1858 and 1 April 1859, STG Box 96 (35) and (36) respectively.

[160] Steele, 'Harris, James Howard, third earl of Malmesbury (1807–1889), *ODNB*, January 2016.

Whatever Malmesbury's ulterior motives for appointing Grenville-Murray to Odessa, he must also have been impressed by his qualifications for handling a huge district peopled by different ethnic and language groups, notorious for its bad roads, and politically sensitive in the aftermath of the Crimean War. For he was an outstanding linguist, a hardy and experienced traveller, knowledgeable of parts of the region from his war reporting in 1854–5, and, above all, a man with a keen eye and a gifted pen for describing what he saw. All of this made the appointment defensible, as – initially – it proved. Its announcement in the *London Gazette* caused no comment in parliament, and there was barely a ripple of criticism in the press. On 20 September 1858 Grenville-Murray arrived at what was nevertheless to prove his last post, because it was at Odessa that the revenge of the cousinocracy was most perfectly consummated.

Ordeal at Odessa

The new post certainly carried far more responsibility than the one at Mytilene. Nevertheless, it was another kind of professional exile because on this occasion it meant *formal* demotion to the consular service. On the face of it, this was also the more emphatic because Odessa was one of only two British consulates-general customarily assumed to be a purely commercial post. Despite the high reputation the new consul-general had given to Odessa to save face with Buckingham, the post was unattractive in other ways, too. The town had lost its free port status and the cost of living had risen greatly since the end of the Crimean War. It was also reported to be unpaved, undrained, inefficiently lighted, and poorly supplied with water. The previous consul-general, George Mathew, was only too glad to have escaped.

On the other hand, Grenville-Murray soon enjoyed a great increase in his annual salary. This was not as generous as that proposed by Malmesbury but remained substantial, increasing to £900, with an extra £300 for office expenses. There was also a vice-consul in the office, Frederick Cortazzi, who carried much of the burden of the commercial work, including shipping, and was well thought of by his predecessor. The remoteness of Odessa from the superintending British

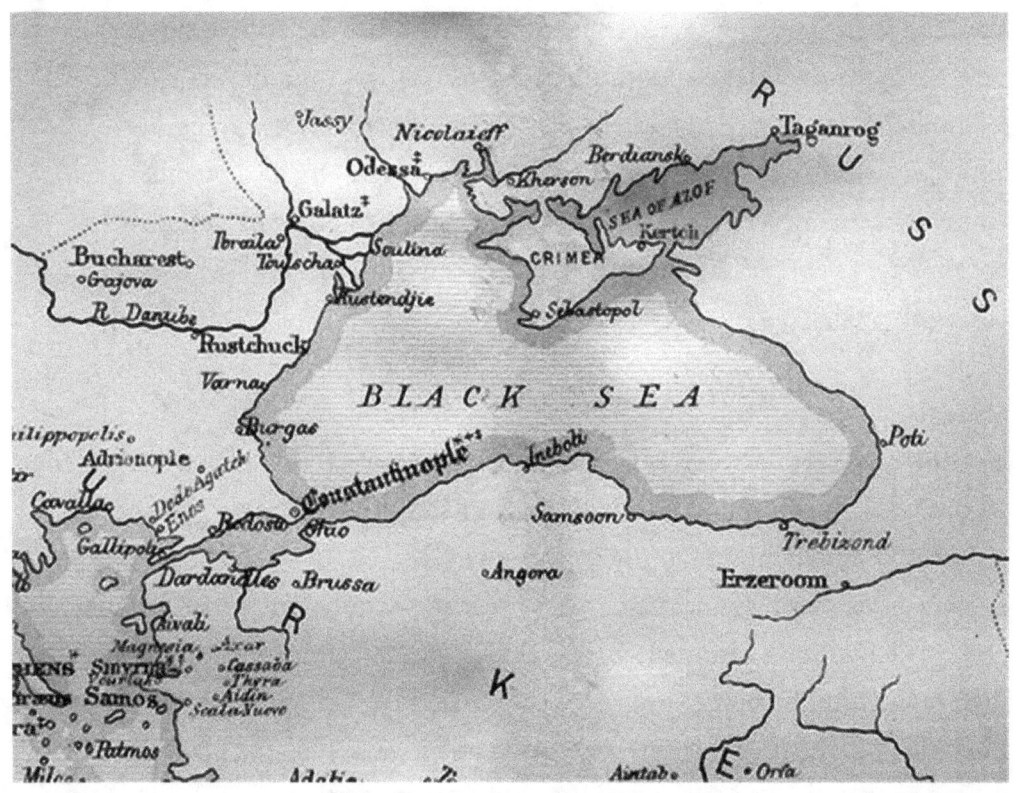

7. The Black Sea and the Sea of Azof, 1879

Embassy in St. Petersburg also meant that the consul-general had considerable independence. Most gratifying to his pride, and in the end most significantly of all, the new consul-general was also expected to give more attention to political and military reporting than had hitherto been customary at Odessa; *in practice*, therefore, it was no longer a purely commercial post. In light of the recent war and the Foreign Office's entrenched mistrust of Russia – particularly of its most influential statesman, Prince Gorchakov – this was hardly surprising.

Nevertheless, Grenville-Murray soon showed that he took commerce as seriously as political reporting. He provided frequent trade and shipping returns between annual reports, and detailed individual communications on such matters as corn prices, the interest of the Russians in British pigs, and the prospects for British companies in the projected gas lighting and paving of Odessa town. His despatches over the winter of 1865–6 on the suspected causes and treatment of cattle plague in Russia, sent at the time of a terrible outbreak of the disease in Britain, were received with particular interest: two were released for publication, to accompanying applause, in *The Times*. In total, five of these despatches were also reprinted in an appendix to the third report of the official commission appointed to investigate the British outbreak, and several were cited as authoritative in both houses of parliament. The commercial reports were also interleaved with long and informed despatches on such miscellaneous subjects as the emancipation of the serfs, the criminal justice system, the Jewish community, and the arrangements he had made for the protection against vandalism of British war graves at Sebastopol, a subject arousing much indignation in parliament at the beginning of the 1860s.

Grenville-Murray believed, however, that the submission of reports was only the beginning of a consul's duty to his country's commerce: his main job was actively to promote it. 'With this view,' he wrote to Sir Henry Bulwer, who had replaced Lord Stratford as ambassador at Constantinople in early 1858, 'it is my intention to fit up a couple of rooms at my office, one with drawings of British machinery, carriages, iron houses, the best breeds of British cattle, and anything and everything that may occur to me as likely to be wanted here; and the other with specimens of Russian produce etc.' He also proposed to post up authentic published lists of prices current during the past year, provided he could get hold of them and the Foreign Office was willing to assist him in establishing contact with British firms. 'In a word,' he said, 'I think a Consulate should be a "Bureau de Renseignments" for trade, a place where really sound information can be obtained, free of suspicion and free of cost.'[161]

Grenville-Murray also lost little time in collecting military and naval intelligence. Reminding the Foreign Office that Odessa was the chief post of observation for detecting any Russian intention to attack Turkey, he persuaded it to provide a modest extra postage allowance to help in eliciting monthly intelligence reports from the consular posts in his huge district. These generally proved fitful in arriving and sparse in their product, but he sought to compensate for this by sending in many highly detailed reports himself. These dealt with any unusual levels of activity at armouries and fortresses and in the transport of weapons; and also with military movements, notably in connection with the serious Polish insurrection in 1863, the perennial fighting in the Caucasus, and the possibility of war with Austria and Turkey. Above all, however, the chief thrust of his military reports (of which there were at least ten in the first two years alone) was evidence that the Russians were 'silently reforming' their fleet in the Black Sea in violation of the Treaty of Paris, which had been feared since 1857; these articles were the most humiliating feature of the Crimean settlement for Russia and chiefly the product of British pressure.

The question of new Russian military activity on and around the Black Sea was one of great sensitivity. Consular reporting on this sort of thing was also common knowledge;[162] and it had long been suspected that the Russian government routinely inspected the contents of all ordinary mail. As a result, Grenville-Murray was asked by the foreign secretary, then Lord John Russell, to send in his military reports by a 'safe hand'. In November 1863, following particularly alarming press reports of Russian violations, he sent a report on the

---

[161] NRO, G-M to Bulwer, 4 June 1860, BUL 1/269/1-44.
[162] For example, in an article in *The Times* of 11 July 1863, its Vienna correspondent cited 'consular sources' as the authority for Russian defence preparations on the Black Sea coast, with Nicolaiev, Yenikale, and Kertch being particularly mentioned.

naval build-up that proved, he said, that it had made even more progress than feared.

In addition to his reporting and his efforts to promote Anglo-Russian trade, Grenville-Murray also grappled effectively with ill-tempered behaviour on the part of British shipmasters and shipowners at a time of uncertainty over whether consular fees imposed on them were to be retained by consuls or sent to the Treasury. In addition, he appears to have shown compassion and attention to detail in arranging the repatriation of British subjects in distress, such as the mentally ill Sarah Mitchell and 18-year old Sunderland boy Thomas Harkus, a pathetic figure who had been imprisoned for theft and then caught dysentery.

Unfortunately, unremitting Foreign Office hostility towards the consul-general led it to acknowledge without praise or simply ignore the many examples of his imaginative, sensitive, and energetic conduct at Odessa. Instead, his office enemies pounced on and exaggerated his misdemeanours, which inevitably multiplied because they deliberately reduced his staff and successfully obstructed most of his efforts to make do by other means.

Despite an increasing pressure of business at Odessa, in September 1861 his number two was transferred to another post. Palmerston himself was on public record as stating that a consul-general should always have the assistance of a vice-consul when there was much British shipping to deal with, and this was also the forthrightly expressed view of Grenville-Murray's eventual successor at Odessa, Keith Abbott. However, this was to reckon without James Murray (no relation), the Foreign Office clerk who had been promoted to the newly created post of assistant under-secretary in 1858 and closely superintended the unpopular and hard-worked Consular Department. Murray was one of Grenville-Murray's most relentless enemies and was regarded by Clarendon himself as at the best of times 'apt to be hard in his decisions, and offensive in style.'[163] He also enjoyed an unusual degree of executive latitude in consular affairs since foreign secretaries never took much interest in them. It was therefore with evident satisfaction, and no fear that his decision would be overturned, that Murray not only told his namesake in Odessa that

---

[163]   Vincent, *Disraeli, Derby and the Conservative Party*, diary 4 July 1866, p. 258.

there was no intention to appoint a new vice-consul but also gave no reason
for his pronouncement. Grenville-Murray struggled on without his former
assistant until the beginning of 1863, but then asked for an *unpaid* vice-consul,
nominating for the post the Lloyd's agent at Odessa, the highly regarded Simon
Horowitz. This request was also denied on Murray's advice, as was another three
years later, on both occasions also without explanation.

Discouraged and increasingly overworked, and because he was not
reconciled to a consular career, Grenville-Murray now needed a new patron.
As a result, he had for some time been cultivating the clever and experienced
Sir Henry Bulwer at Constantinople. Although Bulwer was 20 years his senior,
the ambassador had much in common with the consul-general, including an
extreme dislike of Lord Stratford de Redcliffe

Even while briefly at Tehran, Grenville-Murray had been sending
Bulwer his private views and intelligence on Persian affairs – and impressing the
ambassador. 'The beginning of your despatch … was a masterpiece,' he told him
in one reply. And following his arrival at Odessa a stream of further letters to
Bulwer commenced. Usually lengthy, these contained news of Russian military,
political and economic developments that was often in advance of his reports
on the same subjects to the Foreign Office, and sometimes for the ambassador's
eyes alone. Among other things, his letters also contained high-level gossip,
personal advice on Russian investments, and amusing stories.

The juncture soon arrived for a move on Sir Henry, and it was
Grenville-Murray's resourceful wife, Clara – who had clearly taken over the role
of his London agent – who took the initiative. She begged him to support the
appointment of her husband to the expected vacancy of secretary of embassy
at Constantinople. But although Bulwer probably supported his friend's case,[164]
the Foreign Office appointed another. Undismayed, Grenville-Murray continued
to tell him of his ardent wish to serve under his orders, and lived in hope of
another opening over which he had influence. But the important Cairo agency,

---

[164] Bulwer later said bitterly: '[O]nce or twice when I have written for persons of special qualities which were wanted at the embassy or mission I have had persons sent me who had
none of those qualities,' HCPP (382), 25 July 1870: paras. 4845-6, 4874.

where his old friend of Bucharest days, Robert Colquhoun, was willing to support him as his replacement, had also faded by the middle of 1863.

With his prospects of escaping from Odessa by this time radically diminished and his office still 'usually not unlike a Public house at Election time,'[165] Grenville-Murray continued to ponder the problem of how to make his life more comfortable without a vice-consul. Fortunately, he was able to exploit a windfall. This came in the shape of the extremely able Maltese, James Zohrab, his consul at Berdiansk on the north coast of the Sea of Azof.

Happening to be in Odessa at the time of the suspected robbery and murder in September 1864 of a British shipmaster, Zohrab volunteered to assist its investigation. This was clutched at by Grenville-Murray, who immediately saw that he could use Zohrab for other work as well. Surprisingly, the Foreign Office agreed to bear the cost of Zohrab's stay in Odessa on the risible assurance it had from the consul-general that this would be reimbursed by the Russians.

There were other suspicious deaths of British seamen at Odessa, Zohrab faced local obstruction, and the result was that his investigation stretched to almost a year; meanwhile, Grenville-Murray ignored repeated orders to send him back to Berdiansk. Instead, he made the bill for Zohrab's employment even higher when, for security reasons, he sent him to London to deliver his report in person. Having read it, James Murray contemptuously observed that it could not only have been safely sent by post but also sent 'unsealed.'

The Russians, of course, never met the bill for Zohrab's stay at Odessa, and Grenville-Murray was docked from his salary the whole cost of his consul's round trip to London. At least Clarendon, once more at the Foreign Office, agreed to let him pay it by instalments.

A Russian who took a particularly close and unfriendly interest in these criminal investigations by Grenville-Murray's consulate was the governor of Southern Russia, General Paul Demetrius von Kotzebue, who was close to Prince Gorchakov, chancellor of the empire. Kotzebue also had direct and highly active command of all Russian forces in Southern Russia. He was based at Odessa.

---

[165]   NRO, G-M to Bulwer, 10 June 1864, BUL 1/270/1-30.

8. General von Kotzebue

Kotzebue probably thought that these criminal investigations implied a low opinion of both his justice system and the warmth with which foreigners were received in his town. But there can be little doubt that behind the difficulties he made about them was chiefly his anger over Grenville-Murray's determined attempts to gather military intelligence. The governor would have been only too well aware of these, and it would be astonishing if he was also unaware that Grenville-Murray was very much Palmerston's man; that is, an agent of the chief architect of the humiliating Crimean settlement and outspoken critic of the brutality of Russia's suppression of the the nationalist insurrection in Poland in 1863. All of this must have made Kotzebue regard Grenville-Murray as a dangerous man, and he was determined to be rid of him by blackening his reputation. This made him an invaluable ally of the consul-general's enemies in the Foreign Office, who seem to have been indifferent to the Russian's motives since he had arrived at the right conclusion.

The first opportunity presented to Kotzebue to see the back of Grenville-Murray was provided when a British resident at Odessa, Adelaide Owen, a woman of dubious reputation, complained to him that, during an altercation at her house, the consul-general had struck her with his whip. This affair died a deserved death in March 1865, but was disinterred by the governor in October and drawn to the attention of Gorchakov himself. As a result, Clarendon ordered a full inquiry to be made on the spot.

The person appointed as investigator was the Hon. William Stuart, who held the post that Grenville-Murray had coveted: secretary of embassy at Constantinople. Stuart was an honourable man and, although his opinion of the consul-general had not been improved by what he had seen and heard of him during his visit to Odessa, he found insufficient evidence to believe him guilty of serious misconduct, to Kotzebue's obvious disappointment.

In the Foreign Office, James Murray was equally vexed, the more so after he learned that the highly respected judge and law officer of the crown, Sir Robert Phillimore, had roundly endorsed Stuart's opinion. This did not mean, Murray advised Lord Clarendon, that the Foreign Office could assure the Russian government of Grenville-Murray's innocence. As a result, Prince

Gorchakov was informed that while it would not be removing its consul-general from Odessa, it would not seek to protect him on grounds of his official character should proceedings be launched against him before a Russian tribunal. This never happened, and in April 1866 Clarendon told Grenville-Murray that this cloud had been lifted – more or less. But others were gathering.

Dismissed by 'Count von Quickmarch'

Grenville-Murray had not been in England since 1861, when he was granted three months' leave of absence to attend to private affairs connected with the shortly expected death of his disgraced and penniless half-brother, the 2nd Duke of Buckingham. It was not until November 1866 that he finally got leave.

Back at his London home, Grenville-Murray was re-united with Clara, their continuing marital concord suggested by the fact that only a little earlier she had begged Clarendon to treat her husband sympathetically in the matter of Zohrab's expenses. However, they had been separated by great distances for many years and, in the circumstances, it is perhaps significant that Mrs Margarita Tagliaferro, the widow of a wealthy Maltese shipowner in Odessa alleged to have been an 'inmate' of Grenville-Murray's house at Odessa, had followed him to London and taken up residence in Lower Belgrave Place. Clara might, therefore, have for long been an example of one of the species of 'semi-detached wives' about whom Grenville-Murray later wrote at length; namely, those who led separate lives, doing as they pleased and seeing whom they liked, but – when in the same country – living under the same roof as their husbands, joining them at dinner, and remaining friends. Made possible by money, this kind of relationship, he remarked, was 'passably common in high life.'[166] In the case of Eustace and Clara, their two sons probably provided a bond as well. But even if Grenville-Murray was not in domestic trouble at home, the same could not be said for his position at the Foreign Office. Here, notable among the charges he now encountered was that of responsibility for improper marriage ceremonies at Odessa.

---

[166] *Side-lights*, vol. 1, p. 276. An entire section of this volume is devoted to this subject.

9. The Rich Widow [from *People I Have Met*]

At the time, British subjects could not marry abroad without meeting onerous residence requirements in the consular district where they planned to exchange vows. This presented particular difficulties to any woman going out from England to marry, and in March 1865 a Royal Commission – the work of which Grenville-Murray was himself well aware – had already been appointed to look into this, as well as other peculiarities of British marriage law. It was against this background, and perhaps also because he was something of a romantic, that in the first half of 1866 Grenville-Murray had relaxed application of the residence requirement on two British couples wishing to get married at his consulate.

Unfortunately for the consul-general, both couples lived at Kherson, one of the closest of his out-stations, where the vice-consul, George Stevens, happened to be related to one of the new husbands and nursed a number of grudges against his chief. Grenville-Murray, he believed, had caused him the painful consequences of living for seven years under Russian suspicion of being a spy, given him insufficient assistance when two of his children died from cholera, and failed to support him for promotion. He duly advertised his view that the two couples married by him in 1866 had been joined illegally, and – with Stevens's encouragement – they promptly complained to the Foreign Office. Here Lord Stanley was by this time in charge.

The upshot of Stevens's complaint was Parliament's passage in March 1867 of the so-called 'Odessa Marriage Act', allegedly required to legalize the marriages of these couples because of the 'inadvertence' of the consul-general.[167] In fact, the Act was not strictly necessary and even in the Foreign Office it was privately conceded that the circumstances Grenville-Murray had described excused 'to a great degree' the irregularity he had admitted. That the Act was designed solely to blacken his reputation, therefore, there can be little doubt.

The appetite of George Stevens to undermine his consul-general's position had clearly been whetted by this success, and Grenville-Murray exposed himself to further attacks by prolonging his leave in London while hoping for another post. For in his absence Stevens was made acting consul-

---

[167]   The bill was drafted in the Home Office but the wording was approved by Lord Stanley.

10. Lord Stanley, 15th Earl of Derby ('Count von Quickmarch')

general at Odessa and able to gain access to all of the mission's archives. As a result, by the middle of January 1867, a stream of increasingly poisonous and ominously well informed despatches to the Foreign Office about Grenville-Murray's allegedly sloppy and self-interested conduct of business had begun to flow from his pen. This, he claimed, culminated in collusion in sharp practice over a property sale with Mrs Tagliaferro was 'locally notorious' for her 'imprudent conduct' and lived in Grenville-Murray's house. Poor Grenville-Murray: it was just as Stevens was presenting this case against him that it was confirmed that Zohrab's expenses would not be met by the Russians, so this was added to his charge sheet.[168]

Without access to his own archives Grenville-Murray was hard-pressed to answer some of these accusations, and seems to have been caught in a number of contradictory statements.[169] What was Lord Stanley to do with him? The foreign secretary was sober and unsentimental, and found his clerks to be excellent men. Inevitably, they began to apply relentless pressure for the dismissal of the consul-general.

The Russian government's dislike of Grenville-Murray was sufficient reason to recall him since it greatly reduced his usefulness, James Murray now urged, although he also made sure that the foreign secretary had before him a tendentious list of complaints originating from other sources. If action was not to be quickly taken, the matter would come before parliament and lead to 'a great scandal,' Lord Stanley was warned.

The foreign secretary, however, needed more certainty that he was being counselled to do the right thing, and so fell in with another option suggested by the head of the Consular Department: that another investigator should first be sent to Odessa to examine the charges. He also agreed that this should be J. Edward Wilkins, who had been British consul at Chicago since 1855 and happened to be in London in need of James Murray's patronage because the axe was hovering over his post. Grenville-Murray was informed that until the

---

[168]   G-M/Stanley/Murray corresp. (various), 22-8 February 1867, BB, pp. 94-6; G-M to Stanley, 8 April 1867, BB, pp. 115-16.
[169]   G-M to Stanley, 21 February and 4 March 1867, BB, pp. 77, 78-9; and Murray to G-M, 2 March, BB, pp. 77-8.

result of the Wilkins investigation should be known, he was suspended on half salary but could be present in Odessa for its duration.

News of the imminent investigation must have reached the town as early as the middle of April, for at this juncture five self-appointed representatives of its British community gave a document to General Kotzebue begging him to prevent the consul-general's return. According to the signatories – who had laced their message to the governor with flattering references to his high character and the 'liberal administration of the Imperial Government' – Grenville-Murray's all-round conduct was of such notoriety that his resumption of his post would be a calamity for British interests. As for Kotzebue, rather than saying 'This is nothing to do with me, take it to one of your own representatives,' the Governor of New Russia gobbled up the petition of the Odessa five (whose number later soared to six) and promptly sent it to St. Petersburg. Here it was soon in the hands of Prince Gorchakov, who drew it to the attention of the British ambassador, Sir Andrew Buchanan.

Admitting that the British subjects had not proceeded correctly, the imperial chancellor nevertheless invited the British ambassador to accept their memorial as a strictly private communication. Buchanan, who was one of the 'shire horses' of the Victorian diplomatic service, agreed to this but added his opinion that Kotzebue had also behaved improperly. Furthermore, as he informed Lord Stanley, since the document was vague and 'merely signed by five persons,' he had returned the original to the Russian Foreign Office and not bothered sending a copy home. But the petition had served its purpose; once more, Grenville-Murray's presence had been made an issue in Anglo-Russian relations, while the myth had been created that the whole British community in Odessa was as anxious to be rid of its consul-general as the governor of Southern Russia.[170]

As it happened, Grenville-Murray did not show up in Odessa. He could not afford it, and was also unimpressed by the prospect of having to shuffle around the town in the shadow of his official accuser. Wilkins himself arrived

---

[170] For example, G-M returned to London 'after nearly eleven [sic] years of perpetual discord with the British residents in Odessa', Seccombe, 'Murray', rev. Joseph Coohill.

on 16 May 1867 and remained until the early autumn. He was thoughtfully put up in the house of George Stevens, who no doubt – morning and night – poured into the investigator's ear stories of his chief's delinquencies.

The result of the investigation was a foregone conclusion. The only surprise is that the Wilkins report did not condemn Grenville-Murray more strongly. This was probably in part because the complexity of some of the issues defeated the rather dim investigator. It took Wilkins at least three months to compose his document, and shortly before Christmas the foreign secretary told him in sharp tones that it was neither fair to Grenville-Murray nor in the public interest for it to be any longer delayed. Wilkins also discovered that the consul-general had some energetic supporters among the British community in Odessa after all, among them the Lloyd's agent, Simon Horowitz. This 'native Jew,' Stevens informed Buchanan, was the leader of the pro-Grenville-Murray 'clique', and had so 'bothered' Wilkins that the latter had 'fairly threatened to resign his mission.'[171]

What were the main points of the Wilkins report? It noted the predictable opinion of the fiery registrar-general, George Graham, that there were grave irregularities in the Odessa marriage register.[172] It concluded that the births and deaths' register was unsatisfactory, and that some passports had not been properly issued. But Wilkins had to admit that only inference supported the claim that Grenville-Murray had been levying consular fees improperly; he was also inconclusive on a missing box and silent on the hint of corrupt dealings with a British company. Nor was he able to come to any sensible conclusion on the affair of Margarita Tagliaferro. His report, which was padded out with much recapitulation at the beginning and 40 lengthy enclosures at the end, had no general conclusions: like a lower second class university dissertation, it just fizzled out. The Law Officers of the Crown sang its praises.[173]

---

[171]   UNMSC, Stevens to Buchanan, 4 April 1868, BU23/45.

[172]   Sir Patrick Colquhoun, the barrister who later came to G-M's aid, was particularly scathing about the tone and content of Graham's intervention ('reckless' and 'officially intemperate'), which he believed was more designed to excuse his own negligence than prove that of G-M, TNA, Colquhoun to Stanley, 9 October 1868, FO881/1667.

[173]   TNA, Law Officers to Stanley, 28 January 1868; and min. of James Murray, 10 March 1868, FO65/796.

In order to respond to this report Grenville-Murray appointed solicitors, but was then refused their assistance (as well as access to many of the relevant documents) on the grounds that what was at issue was merely a question of official discipline. He put up a robust defence along predictable lines, but it did no good. A dismissal notice was signed by Lord Stanley and delivered by messenger on 28 May 1868. This was the 'Count von Quickmarch', who had evicted a weak, inoffensive Teuton prince from the fictional state of Pumpernickel in Grenville-Murray's later allegory.[174]

Simultaneously, at the suggestion of the exultant Murray, it was decided to give Wilkins – in addition to his salary and full expenses – a gratuity of £500 in acknowledgement of the way he had so ably conducted his inquiry. Stevens himself was rewarded with promotion to consul, first at Nicolaiev and then, in 1876, to a place with a healthier climate of the sort of which he had always dreamed – the then Danish West Indies (now the US Virgin Islands). As for the important Odessa post, this was left vacant for well over another year.

Grenville-Murray fought a strong rearguard but it was useless. This time there was no powerful figure to save him. Palmerston had died in late 1865 and the new (Third) Duke of Buckingham, who by this time was secretary of state for the colonies, was unable to find a colonial post for him without a clean *exeat* from the Foreign Office, which he was naturally refused. The eminent barrister, Sir Patrick Colquhoun, cousin of his friend Robert Colquhoun, sprang to his defence with great energy and forensic skill, but by the beginning of November he knew he had lost. In mid-January 1869 Grenville-Murray's plea for reconsideration of his predecessor's decision by Lord Clarendon – once more at the Foreign Office – was also rebuffed in mid-January 1869. Shortly after that he was also refused a pension because it could not be confirmed that he had served with 'diligence and fidelity'. His diplomatic career was over.

---

[174] 'Wanted, a King. An Adventure in the Realm of Tobago', *Cornhill Magazine*, August 1870, pp. 239-56.

11. The 3rd Duke of Buckingham ('a safe Duke', *Vanity Fair*, 29 May 1875)

4   *The Queen's Messenger*

By the winter of 1868–9 Grenville-Murray was an angry and bitter man. He was also hard up, and it was probably chiefly for this reason that he had surrendered his Mayfair house in favour of an apartment in the large nearby house owned by the physician Dr David Wilson, although this also enabled the poor mental health of his son Reginald to receive close medical attention. There was now nothing for it but to make his way by full-time journalism, a course of action that also had a secondary advantage: it gave him the means of his revenge.

'Ho, All Ye Who Have Suffered Wrong!'

After his return to England in November 1866, Grenville-Murray had evidently restored his contacts with the Fleet Street dailies, and cultivated them with increasing urgency after falling to half salary. It was the *Morning Post*, the newspaper with which he had been so fatefully associated at the beginning of his career, that also gave him a ready platform from which to resume his anonymous campaign against the agency system in the Foreign Office. This commenced near the end of 1867 with a blistering attack on an unnamed assistant under-secretary at the Foreign Office, obviously James Murray, and was followed only a few days later by an equally savage but more broadly couched assault on the agency system that had Grenville-Murray's fingerprints all over it. Thereafter, barely a month went by until the end of the parliamentary session in the summer of 1868 that did not have one or more articles of the same sort in the *Morning Post*.

Meanwhile, Grenville-Murray was also starting to place longer articles in the periodical press. On 9 November 1867, *All the Year Round* – to which he had probably sent occasional anonymous contributions from Odessa – published anonymously his 'Russian Corn'.[175] This was judged 'very good' by Dickens, and was swiftly followed by three more articles on the same subject.

---

[175]   Storey (ed), *LCD*, vol. 11, p. 506 (mis-transcribed at fn. 4 here as 'Russian Cow').

12. 62 Brook Street today

Among Grenville-Murray's other regular outlets was *Vanity Fair*, the earliest of the serious society journals of the period, which first appeared in November 1868. The proprietor and editor, Thomas Gibson Bowles, has generally received exclusive credit for this. However, his contemporary, H. R. Fox-Bourne, a leading authority on the Victorian press whose work on the subject is still regarded as a valuable source, gave it mainly to Grenville-Murray, while adding that 'as much mystery as possible was maintained as to all the arrangements.'[176] This makes sense, for Grenville-Murray remained doctrinaire on anonymity, while Bowles – who was risking his scarce funds on a new venture pitched at 'high society' – would have wanted no open association with a man under such a dark official cloud.

---

[176]   Fox-Bourne, *English Newspapers*, p. 302.

Vanity Fair became popular for its gentle caricatures of well-known personalities presented as full-page coloured lithographs, a revolutionary combination in Britain at the time. But it struggled in its first months, and would barely have kept Grenville-Murray in cigars; it was also a bit tame for his purposes. As a result, in December 1868 he began to form a plan for his revenge against his enemies in the shape of a more hard-hitting periodical of his own.

On 21 January 1869 this plan was revealed. On this day Grenville-Murray published anonymously the first number of a new weekly, mischievously entitled *The Queen's Messenger: A Weekly Gazette of Politics and Literature*. It was aimed at educated gentlemen of the sort who patronised London's West End clubs, members of the diplomatic corps, and so on. It was published by John Hughes and printed by Peter Ranken at the same premises as *Vanity Fair*. Like all subsequent issues, it appears to have been written more or less entirely by Grenville-Murray himself.

The purpose of *The Queen's Messenger*, as explained in its first leader, was to promote administrative reform in Britain's government, meanwhile serving as the next best thing to the tribunal denied to civil servants in trouble with their departments. 'Ho, All Ye Who Have Suffered Wrong!' rang out the motto emblazoned on its banner; tell us your stories and we'll grab the public's attention with them. It sparkled with mischief. For example, since civil servants could be arbitrarily fined and condemned without trial, those fresh to their ranks were named in a regular column headed 'Proclamation of Outlawry'. The satire of *The Queen's Messenger* was unusually savage, its attacks on named persons open, and its invective more colourful than rivals such as *The Owl*. It was peppered with 'unheard of abuse,' complained the Foreign Office librarian.[177]

Not surprisingly, the chief themes of *The Queen's Messenger* were the supreme power of the senior clerks in all government departments and the abuses to which this led; for they were not only unaccountable to parliament, it reminded its readers, but could also readily deceive its select committees. It was, however, the 'ruling triumvirate' of Hammond, Murray, and Bidwell in the

---

[177]   Hertslet, *Recollections of the Old Foreign Office*, pp. 208-9.

149

Foreign Office who were Grenville-Murray's chief targets. These were old men, he wrote, who had seen little if any service abroad, and were in consequence arrogant and inept in dealing with the representatives of foreign governments in London. By far the main abuse of which *The Queen's Messenger* held them guilty, however, was the one at which he had hammered away in the mid-1850s, and more recently taken up again in the *Morning Post*; namely, their corrupt fleecing of the country's diplomatists and consuls while serving them as agents.

Faced by the attacks on the Foreign Office agencies in the *Post*, which were quickly echoed by radical members in the House of Commons such as Bayley Potter and Henry Labouchere, Lord Stanley had already been placed on the defensive. In February 1868, he was forced to conclude that the agency system was incompatible with the provisions of the Exchequer Audit Act of 1866, announced that its abolition was therefore under serious contemplation, and stated that the only remaining issue was whether the agents should be compensated for their loss of business (he thought they should); and, if so, by how much. However, Grenville-Murray had no faith in the ability of the foreign secretary to push this reform through. Despite a House of Commons vote to supervise diplomatic service expenditure more tightly and Labouchere's description of the agency system as 'abominable', Stanley, he told the *Post*'s readers in an anonymous letter to its editor, remained trapped by 'the spider power of the clerkly web' in the Foreign Office and was simply procrastinating.[178] By the end of 1868 the agency system had still not been abolished, so each of the 30 numbers of *The Queen's Messenger* in the first half of the following year paraded its iniquities on tall stilts.

In the course of this onslaught, Edmund Hammond, the permanent under-secretary, although described as the 'unknown Ruler of the Country … the absolute Sovereign of these Realms,'[179] escaped relatively lightly; after all, he was not an agent. As for James Murray, he appeared in the 'British Curiosities' column, which not only drew attention to the surprising discrepancy between the declared salary of several clerks and the grand houses they maintained in

---

[178] 'The Defeat of the Foreign Office', *Morning Post*, 28 May 1868; see also HCDeb., 26 May 1868, vol. 192, cols. 927-39.
[179] *QM*, 11 March, p. 81.

town and country but also gave their home addresses and encouraged tax-payers to pay them visits and judge for themselves.[180] The clerk who was the chief target of Grenville-Murray's slashing pen, however, was the arch-agent, John Bidwell.

Bidwell was the subject of some of the most prominent columns in each issue of *The Queen's Messenger*. Notable among these was a two-part list that compared the stellar careers of the large number of diplomats and consuls who were his 'customers' with the flatter career trajectories of the smaller tally of those who had declined his services. Another column, soon headed 'The Bidwell Tax', claimed to show how much money Bidwell levied annually on each individual, together with a cumulative total. In general, both columns featured in each issue only diplomats whose surnames began with the same letter ('C's one week, 'D's the next, and so on), so that by this device Grenville-Murray kept constantly in front of his readers compelling detail in support of his campaign. He also had amusement with Bidwell's family names. He claimed to show how, rather than seeking from shame to conceal the extent to which they made their brother officers pay them tolls, they gloried in it: they had not only changed their name to *Bid*well from *Bed*well, but also christened a son in the consular service Charles *Toll* Bidwell![181]

Although it sat a little uncomfortably with its argument that foreign secretaries were just the 'cat's paws' of their all-powerful senior clerks, *The Queen's Messenger* also laid great stress on the serious consequences of weak and deformed political leadership. Lords Stanley and Clarendon, who were attacked at length and with equal venom in almost every issue, were naturally Grenville-Murray's favoured illustrations.

Clarendon, maintained *The Queen's Messenger*, although plausible, had in reality never been anything other than a conventional Whig placeman. He was 'feeble-witted', and had always proceeded by 'concealment, evasion, and denial.' By then old and in poor health, this 'political driveller,' 'effeminate

---

[180] The prototype of this column appeared on 8 April 1869 (col. 1, p. 124), and under the new title a week later.

[181] *QM*, 8 July, p. 280. He did not make this up; see *FO List*, January 1874, p. 61.

nonentity,' and 'artful jobber' only attended to the business of the Foreign Office when the weather was fine – and then arrived at two pm and left at three.[182]

For his part, Stanley was described as shifty, sullen, risibly disposed to self-advertisement, and – *a propos* Britain's commitment to the defence of Belgian neutrality – author of 'the dishonest theory that guarantees cease to be binding the moment they become necessary.'[183] It was, however, Stanley's unfortunate reputation for compulsive stealing, with its alarming implications for the safety of the Foreign Office's Secret Service funds, on which Grenville-Murray's weekly chose especially to dwell.

Lord Stanley's alleged kleptomania was repeatedly highlighted, not only directly but also by means of frequent general discussion of the subject by medical experts in articles and letters to the editor. Extracts were even serialized from a 'prize-winning' essay on kleptomania for which the award and accolade had been granted by none other than Grenville-Murray's Brook Street landlord, Dr David Wilson. This essay was advertised on the back page of every number. Kleptomaniacs were not common thieves, admitted *The Queen's Messenger*, but their condition certainly disqualified them from being placed in positions of authority or trust. At what work would Lord Stanley be better employed? The 'intuitive perceptions' inspired by his kleptomania, wrote Grenville-Murray, qualified him best to be a police detective or an inspector of convicts rather than as 'sole trustee of an immense national property.'[184]

Stanley was by no means the first lunatic to be foreign secretary, Grenville-Murray reminded his readers. Castlereagh had also been mad, as had Viscount Dudley and Ward, the latter having created havoc until the Foreign Office and England were rescued by Palmerston.[185] It therefore behoved parliament to pass legislation (which he suggested might be called 'The Mad Ministers' Act') designed to deal more expeditiously with such situations.[186] Meanwhile, Foreign Office agents and those colluding with them would do well

---

[182] *QM, passim.*
[183] *QM*, 25 March, p. 104.
[184] *QM*, 11 March, p. 74.
[185] *QM*, 18 February, p. 45.
[186] *QM*, 25 February, p. 52.

to remember the retrospective effect of the fiat that pronounced a man insane; for this meant that the acts of a mad minister – the example no doubt at the forefront of Grenville-Murray's mind being the dismissal of a man of genius from the consulate-general at Odessa – were voidable.

Had *The Queen's Messenger* been nothing but a vehicle for Grenville-Murray's campaign for administrative reform in general and his personal vendetta in particular, his readers would soon have lost interest – and the weekly newspaper would not have made him the money that he and Clara badly needed. Nor did he wish to cut himself off from any remaining friends and allies among journalists and editors, or in the London political class more generally. As a result, *The Queen's Messenger* developed features designed to give it broader appeal.

Like today's *Private Eye*, to which it bears such a strong resemblance, *The Queen's Messenger* contained comment – not all satirical – on a whole range of topics. Some of this was a rehearsal of old themes, such as the importance of anonymity and a free press, and the redundancy of resident embassies headed by ambassadors so called. But there were new targets as well. Among these were England's anti-intellectualism, the pollution of the language by 'evasive phraseology' at the expense of plain speaking, and the pusillanimity of much contemporary journalism – notably that of *The Times*, which Grenville-Murray dubbed the 'Ex-Thunderer'. The *Queen's Messenger* was also disposed to censure public institutions that took no account of the difficulties of attending them faced by those who suffered the shameful inconvenience of having to work for a living; the London hospitals, which prohibited sick-visiting on Sundays, were a case in point. However, as befitted the herald of Her Majesty Queen Victoria, *The Queen's Messenger* hastened to emphasise that none of this should be interpreted as a sneaking sympathy for the principles of the French Revolution. Thus its regular royal diary was announced with Talleyrand's family motto, '*Re que Diou re que Lou Rey*' – 'Nothing but God nothing but King Louis.' *The Queen's Messenger* also contained factual reporting of foreign news, chiefly French.

Above all, however, *The Queen's Messenger* sought to add to the number of its readers by titillation and entertainment. It did this by giving them gossip about famous personalities. In the 'Foreign Courts and Cabinets' column, for example, the fortunes of princes and politicians at the gaming tables, and in their affairs with actresses, were recorded with relish. And it sought to achieve the same effect by providing satirical sketches of the hereditary peers, men who were laughably unqualified to be legislators for the greatest empire in the world; blue blood, Grenville-Murray believed, might be a necessary but it was certainly not a sufficient condition for membership of the House of Lords. A series of lampoons, soon to be called 'Our Hereditary Legislators', was started on 4 March 1869, and shortly became the lead in each issue. They had invented names such as 'William Basegreed, Lord Screwham' and the 'Duke of Nothingness' but were easily recognized. As a result, some were in such demand that they had to be re-published in pamphlet form.

Grenville-Murray had made his eldest son, Reginald, the registered proprietor as well as managing editor of *The Queen's Messenger*. The young man needed work and could be trusted to keep secret the real editor's identity; it was perhaps also a device for muddying the issue of responsibility for the paper should any attempt be made to prosecute it for libel. It was the beginning of a long literary collaboration between them. Grenville-Murray installed Reginald in chambers he had taken at the Albany, the most fashionable apartment complex in London, and it was from there that all business connected with the new paper was conducted.

In practice, Grenville-Murray shared the managerial work with his son and seems to have spent more and more time living at the Albany himself, although his wife remained at the Mayfair house. Like the successful novelist and playwright Paul d'Arlay in his later published allegory of married life, no doubt he had hoped to find separate chambers a quieter place in which to write.[187] However, judging by his comments elsewhere on the Albany's 'supposed' reputation for quietness, he was disappointed.[188]

---

[187] 'The Sceptic: a Tale of Married Life', *CM*, July 1875, p. 115.
[188] *The Boudoir Cabal*, vol. 2, p. 104.

Unfortunately for the new father-son collaboration, in early April Reginald's mental health deteriorated. An existing condition had probably been exacerbated when Reginald learned from their publisher, John Hughes, that Bidwell proposed to launch a criminal prosecution against *The Queen's Messenger*. As a result, he was taken by his father to Paris and admitted to a somewhat modest asylum in the Rue Picpus.[189] This was probably the 'large, clean-looking, white painted building with barred and shuttered windows in an otherwise dismal street near the Bois de Vincennes' described by Grenville-Murray in a short article on *maisons de santé* published in the *Cornhill Magazine* just two months later.[190] The Rue Picpus establishment was not 'a common mad-house', its director assured the anxious parent, but a residence suitable to those who wished a quiet retreat in which to convalesce after a period of 'nervous excitement.' Returning hurriedly from Paris, Grenville-Murray then had to take over completely the editorial work on *The Queen's Messenger*, although he received a little help from his other son, Wyndham, then at Christ Church College Oxford. Clara assumed responsibility for the paper's more general management, including relations with Hughes.

A common reaction among the victims, and friends of the victims, of *The Queen's Messenger* was that its editor had 'gone too far' and revived the scurrilous journalism of a best-forgotten age. In the Foreign Office itself, the anger was particularly intense, and James Murray decided to organise a public reply in the form of a bound volume of printed documents, so selected as to present Grenville-Murray's conduct in the worst possible light. A diplomatic 'Blue Book', this was to be a perfect example of a genre of official publicity introduced for propaganda purposes in the early years of the century.

In compiling his own Blue Book, released on 14 June, Murray was assisted by the Odessa investigator, Wilkins, who had been hanging about the Foreign Office for a long time in the hope of further lucrative pickings. To demonstrate that Grenville-Murray's misconduct was nothing new and that the Foreign Office had shown great forbearance towards him, the Blue Book tracked

---

[189] *The Times*, 24 July 1869. Shortly afterwards, he appears to have escaped and returned to England, whereupon he fell foul of the law. He was permitted to return to the asylum in France under police escort, *Birmingham Daily Post*, 30 June 1876.

[190] 'Maisons de santé', *CM*, June 1869.

his alleged misdeeds from the beginning of his appointment at Odessa.[191]
But despite the fact that it was composed of 201 documents (excluding their
numerous enclosures) and stretched to over 300 pages, it omitted Sir Robert
Phillimore's formal dismissal of Adelaide Owen's charge against Grenville-
Murray and, above all, the letters of Sir Patrick Colquhoun, which had provided
such an eloquent indictment of the motives for Grenville-Murray's dismissal
and the procedures by which this was achieved. The Blue Book was, therefore,
not only a weighty headstone on Grenville-Murray's diplomatic grave, but also a
misshapen one.

The Foreign Office's public riposte to Grenville-Murray did not
cause even a ripple in parliament. What did cause a considerable stir, indeed a
sensation, is what happened just a few days later.

The 'Coachington' affair – and jumping bail

On 17 June, in its popular column ridiculing the country's hereditary legislators,
The Queen's Messenger published a savage lampoon called 'Bob Coachington,
Lord Jarvey'. The victim was clearly the 26-year old Charles Robert, 3rd Lord
Carrington: Captain in the Royal Horse Guards, justice of the peace, and
owner of an estate of 26,000 acres. The article mocked his hobby of driving a
four-horse coach; hence 'Coachington'. It also claimed that this was at once an
echo of his family's roots in trade (his grandfather, a 'bargaining bumpkin' and
'Nottinghamshire nobody'[192]), and a symptom of insanity inherited from his
recently deceased father. The latter, it alleged, was 'a harmless lunatic' who was
unwilling 'to sit whenever it was possible by any exercise of ingenuity to stand
up or to lie down' because he believed his backside to be made of 'crockeryware'.
And yet, concluded *The Queen's Messenger*, a Coachman Lawgiver with such
recent ancestry 'may any day chance to have a casting vote for war or peace.'

---

[191]   It was called *Papers relative to the Complaints made against Mr. Grenville-Murray as Her
Majesty's Consul-General at Odessa; and to his Dismissal from Her Majesty's Service. 1858-
69.* It is now formally prefixed with 'HCPP (4163)'.

[192]   Adonis, 'Carington'. The 1st Lord Carrington was a Nottingham banker called Robert
Smith. His peerage was said to have been awarded by Pitt in return for favours, and to have
been 'the only occasion in which the objections of George III to giving British peerages to
tradesmen were overcome.' His successor changed the family name from Smith to Carrington by royal licence, Pollard, 'Smith'.

13. Lord Carrington ('Bob Coachington, Lord Jarvey')

Determined to avenge this slur on himself and his father, on the evening of 22 June Carrington waited for Grenville-Murray outside the Conservative Club in St. James's Street. Even though physically much more than a match for his enemy, he was armed with a stick or riding crop and accompanied by a well-built servant; he also had with him a photograph of the editor to assist in his identification. When Grenville-Murray emerged, shortly after midnight, the fearless young peer accused him of responsibility for the offending article and, despite his denial, struck him with his weapon on the head or shoulders.

Failing to get a formal apology from Lord Carrington, Grenville-Murray reported the incident to the police and the peer was summoned to appear at Marlborough Street Police Court to answer charges of common assault and incitement to a duel. Thus commenced, on 7 July, a series of court cases – the first of which produced a riot in the courtroom – culminating in a jury trial at the Middlesex Sessions a fortnight later. A grand jury had chosen to ignore the charge of incitement to a duel, and the upshot was that Carrington, who had boasted of the assault but gained sympathy by pleading provocation, escaped with nothing more than a rap on the knuckles for taking the law into his own hands. Grenville-Murray, on the other hand, was found guilty of perjury for failing to admit personal responsibility for the lampoon. The hearing on his perjury case was to resume at the Marlborough Street court on 29 July. Facing the certainty of conviction and the heavy punishment attendant on it, he jumped bail and fled to France, where he claimed to be ill. A warrant for his arrest in the event that he should ever return to England was immediately signed.

Exceptional bitterness – tinged with not a little of its near cousin, self-pity – pervaded the pages of the final issues of *The Queen's Messenger*. By this time its editor was bitter not only at his treatment by the Foreign Office, but also by the legal establishment; his fellow writers, whose battle for a free press he saw himself fighting, also disappointed him. He was consoled with the thought that, like Milton, Thomas More and other men of genius punished in their own lifetimes, he would have 'the gratitude of posterity.' Meanwhile, the fight went on.

On 12 August *The Queen's Messenger* was able to give publicity to a widening crack in the Foreign Office's defence of the agency system. It had come under pressure in the House of Commons from Sir Henry Bulwer, who had been elected a Liberal member of parliament in the previous November and had the same attitude to the power and influence of the permanent officials in the Foreign Office as his old friend. But the announcement that the agency system was soon to be reformed by Lord Clarendon occurred shortly before this edition went to press, and the editor was by this time in France. As a result, he could do little more than reproduce a parliamentary report on the subject by the *Pall Mall Gazette* of the previous day, and then re-work its content in a short, separate item.

At this point *The Queen's Messenger*, which was under its third publisher since the beginning of June, announced its closure for the parliamentary recess. It promised, however, to re-appear at the beginning of the next session. The 'storm of anger' that had enveloped it, the editor remarked, was a tribute to the veracity of its reporting, for wilful wrong-doers hated the truth.

After six months' rest, *The Queen's Messenger* promised to renew the fight. It was, therefore, with *au revoir* rather than *adieu* that its editor took his leave of his readers. The last line of this issue added that he was 'still lying seriously ill in Paris.' This was the last line of all; for, while he was to recover, *The Queen's Messenger* was not to be so fortunate.

5   A 'literary manufactory' in Paris

The circumstances of July 1869 in which Grenville-Murray fled to Paris, where he was inclined to described himself as the first political exile since the days of Bolingbroke, were painful indeed. He had been publicly humiliated, deserted by his relative the Duke of Buckingham, shunned by most of his colleagues in the press, and ejected from his club. He had once more had to abandon his wife in London while coping with the continuing mental ill health of Reginald, rebelliously confined, it seems, at the Rue Picpus asylum. As well as all this, he carried debts that were the more difficult to sustain, let alone pay off, because he had forfeited a huge sum in bail money and faced a demand for more fees from Reginald's asylum-keeper. A year later, Grenville-Murray's bankruptcy was recorded in the *London Gazette*.

It was in such circumstances that he was forced to recognise that it had been a mistake to try to combine diplomacy with journalism, as with any attempt to 'drive two trades together.'[193] In France, where the brilliant meteor had fallen to ground burning as brightly as ever, it was the pen alone that could turn round his fortunes. This in the end it did, but in the short run he needed a great deal of money quickly; and for this the earnings of his pen were insufficient.

Even before his flight to France, therefore, and well into 1871, Grenville-Murray once more became a supplicant to the Duke of Buckingham, who by that time had done much to put the affairs of the Grenville family in order. He pressed his claim for family support by many means, most fantastically by sending the duke a stream of post cards quoting biblical texts and warning of the risk of divine retribution should he not do the decent thing. But all that Grenville-Murray ever got out of the 3rd Duke of Buckingham and Chandos was a £50 contribution towards Reginald's asylum fees, with the added stricture that henceforward he should deal with his solicitor. In consequence, the exile

---

[193]   *The Member for Paris*, Tauchnitz edition, vol. 1, p. 184.

remained impoverished, and it was reliably reported that even two years after he had arrived in Paris his brains remained mortgaged to his creditors to such an extent that London editors wanting his articles were required to make payment for them not directly to Grenville-Murray himself but to a solicitor, the latter allowing the author only a portion of his earnings.

A family business

Edmund Yates, the major London literary figure and journalist who was to become a collaborator of Grenville-Murray, regarded him as the ablest journalist in Europe. He also reported a common belief, which he seems to have shared, that the output credited to the former consul-general during his Parisian exile was so immense that it was impossible he could have written it all himself. The exile's chambers in the French capital were conveniently located for journalistic purposes in the Rue de l'Université of the fashionable 7th Arrondissement, close to the National Assembly, government ministries and embassies. And, says his friend, they were thought to be 'a complete literary manufactory, all the work being suggested, supervised, and occasionally retouched by the master hand.'[194]

It would not be surprising if Grenville-Murray had acquired some outside secretarial assistance,[195] but there is no evidence that for the writing itself he had the help of anyone beyond his own family. *The Queen's Messenger* had been a family business, and he seems to have preserved the tradition in Paris. Families, he wrote at the end of his life, had a heavy obligation to give practical encouragement to their young men of genius, while partnerships based on them inspired confidence via intimacy.

Did Clara remain the general manager of the Grenville-Murray family business in Paris? It is invariably assumed that the marriage broke up, and that in Paris Grenville-Murray married a Spanish countess, taking her title and calling himself the Comte de Rethel d'Aragon.[196] At first glance this is plausible

---

[194] Yates, *His Recollections and Experiences*, p. 451.
[195] 'Mr. Murray was so busy that he had to keep three or four secretaries,' according to an untitled press clipping pasted inside a copy of G-M's *People I Have Met* held by the University of Leicester Library. From the internal evidence, this article post-dated his death.
[196] The secondary sources on which this view is based are all recorded in the account of 'Mrs. Eustace Clare Grenville-Murray' in Lohrli, *Household Words*, p. 385.

14. The Promising Son

because the long separations and severe financial blows would have rocked most marriages. Furthermore, his strong interest in widows – not least rich widows – was evident in two of the books he published in his last years,[197] and he *did* use the Spanish title. Nevertheless, the second marriage is almost certainly a myth, and one deliberately cultivated by Grenville-Murray – a legend in his own time for inventing fictitious names – to shelter his family from the opprobrium associated with his real name as well as give him some social standing. It was also a myth easily strengthened by rumour, the potency of which was a constant refrain in his novels.

The strongest evidence that Clara remained 'Mrs Grenville-Murray' after the great family crisis of 1869 and continued to be the family business manager as well, is a plaintive message the Duke of Buckingham wrote hurriedly to his solicitor in June 1875. Obviously recognizing her, he said that

---

[197]   *Side-lights*, vol. 2, pp. 183-286 ('Young Widows'); *People I Have Me*t, pp. 166-75 ('The Rich Widow').

she had got into his house 'under the name of "the Comtesse Rethel Aragon"!' (heavily inscribing this exclamation mark in his letter) and was refusing to leave. This was a little under a year after renewed pressure on the duke by Grenville-Murray to meet his financial claim, accompanied by threats of going public on it.

What role in the literary manufactory was played by the sons of Eustace and Clara? Wyndham, the younger of the two, seems to have been a disappointment and to have made very little contribution. Reginald, however, was a different proposition, even though his own input was probably fitful to begin with because of his youth (he was still only 22 in July 1869) and fragile mental health. In fact, it was probably not until the second half of the 1870s that he began to assist his father substantially with his writing.[198]

The Paris of the Second Empire in which Grenville-Murray began his exile in July 1869 had its consolations. For one thing, the Emperor Louis Napoleon was keen to be thought well of in England and was known to be generous to English journalists who were careful of his reputation; and he had been treated with great respect in the columns of *The Queen's Messenger*. On the other hand, shortly before Grenville-Murray arrived in the emperor's capital, his nimble weekly had cautioned that it might now be as well if the Emperor were permitted to become a constitutional monarch. Clearly, the editor had seen which way the political wind was blowing.

As for Paris itself, this had been rebuilt and its lustre as a centre of fashion and pleasure restored. In politics, resurgent republican sentiment and the growing power of the industrial working class had generated greater influence for representative institutions. And just in the previous year Louis Napoleon had eased a little the empire's repressive press laws, a development particularly close to Grenville-Murray's heart. Furthermore, the spread of literacy and rapid advances in production and distribution methods had brought the French press to the eve of its 'golden age': its organs were multiplying and, for the first time, it was becoming a medium of genuinely mass communication.

---

[198] On Reginald, see my essay on him in the ODNB.

A ghost at the siege

A little over a year after Grenville-Murray's arrival in Paris, in early September 1870, France began to be shaken by momentous events. First, it was humiliated by Prussian arms at Sedan, and Louis Napoleon's Second Empire collapsed in the wake of the defeat. Then a provisional Government of National Defence was formed, and immediately found itself facing a Prussian siege of the capital. This lasted until the end of January 1871, when Paris capitulated. At this juncture, a monarchist-leaning provisional government was formed under Adolphe Thiers – and almost as swiftly provoked the short-lived but immortal Paris commune. The excitement concluded with another siege and the bloody rout of the communards by the army in May, the execution or transportation to New Caledonia of many of the survivors among them, and the reassertion of the authority of the Thiers government. All of this aroused intense interest in England. It might be supposed, therefore, to have been the ultimate consolation to an English journalist exiled to France and as needful of employment, knowledgeable of the country, and fluent in its language as Grenville-Murray.

The turmoil in Paris during these months certainly coloured most of the articles he supplied to the *Cornhill* in 1871 (see Appendix 2), and he might have sent copy impossible to detect to some dailies as well as other periodicals. But the evidence suggests that Grenville-Murray was no more than a ghostly presence in the ranks of the English journalists in Paris during the siege. In his detailed account of their 'daily symposiums' at the Grande Café on the corner of the Rue Scribe, Ernest Vizetelly, the young son of the long-time Paris resident Henry Vizetelly, does not list the exile among the carousers. Nor is there any mention of him in the description of the 'British residuum' in Paris provided by the *Standard*'s John Augustus O'Shea in *An Iron-bound City*, following the departure of many of the colony in early November.

It is not difficult to understand why the exile was neither able nor willing to throw himself into instant reporting of the events of this hectic period. For one thing, the leading English dailies with which he had been connected already had their own correspondents inside the city. But even had Grenville-Murray been able formally to join the ranks of this company, it is unlikely that he would have been comfortable in it. For he had felt deserted, if not betrayed, by the great majority of his English press colleagues at the time of *The Queen's Messenger* affair – and the wounds were still raw. Because he had made no secret of his feelings at the time, as well as for reasons of personal distaste, some members of the English press corps in Paris might also have shunned him anyway.

Without the cooperation of the press corps, Grenville-Murray would also have found operating as a freelance for the dailies to be extremely difficult. Getting information out of the city during the siege was as problematical as obtaining it – and more expensive. Balloons became the main expedient, and it was particularly to exploit them that the members of the English press corps found it necessary to sink their 'home differences'.

Reporting for the dailies was also very risky. There were periodic outbursts of 'spy mania' in the besieged city, and journalists from England – which refused to recognise the provisional government and was not popular – were sometimes accused of supplying information that aided the Prussians, with consequences which threatened their personal safety. Grenville-Murray was accustomed to jotting down detailed observations as he strolled around, and anyone seen doing this was likely to be arrested. In the heat of the moment, even a loud and eloquent claim that he was a political exile from England might not have counted for much. Had he managed to evade a charge of espionage, he might still have feared that his previous reputation as an outspoken supporter of the fallen emperor would make him a special target of the Paris mob.

In such circumstances, Grenville-Murray would have needed the British Embassy to vouch for his credentials as a journalist and provide consular assistance were he indeed to be arrested, as it did for others. However, aside from the fact that the the embassy had been presided over since 1867 by the same Lord Lyons whose first secretary had investigated the Adelaide Owen affair in Odessa and who was on good terms with both Lord Stanley and Lord Clarendon, it was hardly likely to exert itself on behalf of anyone who was a fugitive from British justice. During the siege no British resident of the city could expect much help from the diplomats anyway. This is because – to the outspoken disgust of the English press corps, not to mention kindred spirits in the House of Commons – Lord Lyons followed the French government to Tours in the middle of September, leaving behind only a skeleton staff; and between early December and late January this disappeared as well, to re-emerge only in the shape of a consul appointed from the local banking community.

Two final reasons suggest themselves for Grenville-Murray's ghostly role at the siege of Paris. First, he continued to be consumed by his personal story – and increasingly furious at his own naivety in placing trust in lawyers and his ducal relations. Thus the theme of his first contributions to the *Cornhill* during the siege was the high price of naivety, the higher because of the difficulty of admitting it. Second, he may have been suffering from poor health, exacerbated by miserable living conditions.

The production line

A low profile he might have adopted during the siege, but Grenville-Murray had by no means permitted his production line to stall, as we have seen. Moreover, after stability returned, Paris resumed its importance as a destination for other English journalists and, as time passed and wounds healed, he was able to revive old contacts and make new friends among them; by such means, he obtained the information he needed to keep writing on English as well as French affairs. This contributed to the enormous quantity of press as well as periodical articles, and both fiction and non-fiction books (many profusely illustrated), that Grenville-Murray produced in the French capital over the next decade. As one admirer wrote after his death, the question was rather 'What did he *not* write?' than 'What did he?'[199]

With the ending of the siege, most of the more well-known English journalists – understandably anxious for a square meal – left Paris for home. As a result, Grenville-Murray was soon being pursued by London newspapers to fill their places, and it was not long before he became a more corporeal presence in the press corps. Prominent among his new employers was the *Daily News*, then growing greatly in popularity, which appointed him its Paris correspondent

---

[199] *Sheffield and Rotherham Independent*, 29 December 1881.

15. Henry Labouchere

despite having been charged with cowardice and hypocrisy in *The Queen's Messenger*. He also became Paris correspondent for the *Pall Mall Gazette*, and in his last years wrote for the Saturday newspaper the *Graphic*, the most successful rival of the *Illustrated London News*, to which he also contributed. Grenville-Murray's journalism also reached audiences beyond the British Isles, the more readily because of a marked shift in his political views following consolidation of the Third Republic.

Napoleon III had been an historical blip, he came to believe, a death-twitch of autocracy. He was certainly contemptuous of the naivety and violent predilections of those on republicanism's radical wing, and satirised them hilariously in the *Cornhill*.[200] But a republic, he had nevertheless concluded, was 'the only form of government compatible with the well-being and stability of the country.'[201] This adjustment probably helped Grenville-Murray find work with the French press, and would have been the more advisable since he made no secret of his contempt for the low standards of the great majority of its organs. He wrote for the *Journal des Débats* and, among other Paris newspapers, was an occasional correspondent of the *Figaro*. Several years before his death, he also emerged as one of the principal contributors to a new English-language society journal based in Paris called the *Boulevard*. However, a more notable mark of his international journalistic advance had been registered towards the end of 1873 when he was appointed Paris correspondent for the *New York Herald*.

The *Herald* was one of the most influential pioneers of popular journalism and a highly successful newspaper in its own day. It was owned by the boorish but energetic, innovative, and super-rich James Gordon Bennett Jr., who was French-educated and himself spent much time in Paris, where the *Herald* had its main European headquarters. Every week, Grenville-Murray supplied it with 'seven or eight closely printed columns, dealing with all kinds of subjects.'[202] It was in his capacity as *Herald* correspondent that, on the centenary in 1876 of the American Declaration of Independence, he served with a number of other literary notables on the jury created to award a prize for the play most

---

[200] 'Franklin Bacon's Republic', *CM*, May 1873.
[201] *Men of the Third Republic*, p. 22.
[202] Yates, *His Recollections and Experiences*, p. 451.

powerfully recalling this event; the other jurors included Victor Hugo, to whom he dedicated his third novel, *The Boudoir Cabal*.

As for the British periodicals to which Grenville-Murray supplied abundant copy, these continued to include *Vanity Fair*. On 7 February 1874, this included a cartoon of a rather dazed-looking Lord Carrington ('Charlie'), inevitably enough slumped on the driving seat of a coach, caressing a horse-whip. The accompanying biographical note was, however, too flattering to have been written by the man he assaulted five years earlier. It was also in *Vanity Fair* that *The Boudoir Cabal* was first serialized.

So ubiquitous was Grenville-Murray's copy that he was widely suspected of being one of the firmly anonymous contributors to the subversive editions of *Beeton's Christmas Annual* – hitherto models of political innocence – that began to appear in 1872. These ruffled many stiff feathers in London by satirizing the family of Queen Victoria, particularly her eldest son and heir to the throne, the playboy Prince of Wales; naturally, they sold out in no time and were reprinted in book form.

Other periodicals for which he wrote included the literary monthly, *Temple Bar*, the short-lived satirical weekly, *Pan*, and *The Academy*. The periodicals to which his contributions are, by contrast, well established and particularly worthy of note were *Truth*, the *World*, and the *Cornhill*.

Truth was launched at the beginning of 1877, and for a while edited by the most luminous member of the English press corps in Paris during the siege, Henry Labouchere. Wealthy, witty and iconoclastic, like Grenville-Murray he had been dismissed from the diplomatic service, in his case for agreeing to be second secretary at Buenos Aires only on condition that he might be permitted to fulfil his duties while remaining at Baden Baden. With its determination to expose fraud and hypocrisy, constant diet of gossip and satire, and serial involvement in consequent libel cases, *Truth* was in many ways a more broadly focussed, more professional, and fully illustrated version of *The Queen's Messenger*. It was also highly profitable, and until his death Grenville-Murray supplied most of its 'Queer Stories', a column that appeared with each issue; his own were so popular that after his death many were reprinted in book form in quick succession.[203] It was, however, the *Cornhill Magazine*, a monthly launched in 1860 to cash in on the great appeal of the serialized novel and an immediate success, to which he was most attached.

It is not difficult to understand the *Cornhill*'s attraction to Grenville-Murray. For one thing, it favoured anonymity, even though it was soon common knowledge that he was writing for it. For another, George Smith, the highly successful businessman who was its owner, paid his authors handsomely. Grenville-Murray was less comfortable with the strictures of the *Cornhill* against any serious discussion of politics, morals and religion, and especially with its prudishness: it could not afford to offend the daughters of a country parson, as Thomas Hardy had to be reminded by its editor. But, for the money and the prestige, Grenville-Murray could live with all this and delivered consistently to the *Cornhill* some of his most impressive pieces.

Starting with an article in December 1868, when his hope of reinstatement in the diplomatic service had all but expired, over the next 14 years he published in the *Cornhill* the astonishing total of 67 articles (see Appendix 2); in 1870 there were only four issues in which he did not have one and in 1873 only three. Nor were these short pieces; on the contrary, on average they were 18 pages long or about 11000 words each, an average that would have been significantly higher had their length not tailed off sharply in the last years of his life. This means that by his death Grenville-Murray had contributed over three-quarters of a million words in essays to the *Cornhill* alone.

In the midst of his frenetic journalism, Grenville-Murray also found time to return to novel-writing. Most of his novels were initially published by Smith, Elder in London but, with one exception, were also published more or less simultaneously in Leipzig by the enlightened, fervently Anglophile, and highly successful German publisher, Baron Bernhard von Tauchnitz. The baron's house had long been popular with English-language writers (including Dickens) because it paid them for the reprinting of their works for sale in Europe even before it had been legally obliged to negotiate for this right by

---

[203] The first two series were published in 1886 by Swan, Sonnenschein, and within a year 25,000 copies had been sold. Not surprisingly, by August 1887 the company had issued two more.

conventions on international copyright signed in 1846. Unlike the Americans,[204] the German publisher was no pirate.

Grenville-Murray had only once before written a novel but by the second year of his Paris exile he had brought out another. This was *The Member for Paris: A Tale of the Second Empire*, which introduced some entertaining new characters, notably Mr Drydust, the correspondent of a leading English newspaper, and the sabre-wielding Polish cavalryman, Count Cutandslitski. It sold well and, perhaps to the irritation of General Kotzebue, his enemy in Odessa, it was translated into Russian and was reported to be highly popular in Moscow.

Encouraged by this success, in less than two years Grenville-Murray had produced another novel. Testifying to the recognition he had received, this one, *Young Brown, or the Law of Inheritance* was serialized in the *Cornhill* between July 1873 and February 1874, and published as a book by Smith, Elder later in the year. It was generally believed to be autobiographical, and some critics claimed not only that it had unfairly attacked recognizable noblemen among its fictional characters but even gone so far as to suggest unwitting incest in its leading incident. According to Yates, the *Cornhill* serialization 'caused an immediate sensation.'[205] Naturally, it was at once pirated in the United States, and a century later the Harvard historian and expert on Victorian fiction, Robert Lee Wolff, described it as an 'absolutely brilliant, bitter novel.'[206] Four more were to follow, five including a posthumously published novella.

In the vast output of his production line in Paris, did Grenville-Murray show any continuing interest in diplomatic reform? Save for the extremely funny allegory of his tilts against official abuses, set in the fictional small French town of Touscrétins (All Morons), in which Lord Stratford appears in the new guise of the once brilliant but by then mildly imbecile M. Nul,[207] there was no mention of

---

[204] The Americans did not take the first step to signing up to international copyright until Congress passed the Chace Act in 1891 and at whom, accordingly, Grenville-Murray directed a shaft on the point in one of his most entertaining political burlesques 'Franklin Bacon's Republic: Diary of an Inventor', *CM*, May 1873. At least three of G-M's books were pirated by US publishers. Since then things have only got worse.

[205] Yates, *His Recollections and Experiences*, p. 451.

[206] *Nineteenth-Century Fiction*, p. 188.

[207] 'Consule Julio', *CM*, August 1871.

it in his contributions to the *Cornhill* and hardly any in other periodicals; and, with one exception, no more than faint echoes of it here and there in his books. Then as now, there was little money to be made from writing about diplomacy; and he probably felt there was no more for him to say on the subject, in which in any case he no longer had a professional interest. He was also able to claim – with some justice – that, thanks in some part to his own Roving Englishman campaign of the 1850s and his more recent crusade in *The Queen's Messenger*, the battle for diplomatic reform was now well engaged.[208]

The leader of the reformers was the radical Member of Parliament, Peter Rylands, who thought the diplomatic service too extravagant. He was also irritated that the Foreign Office had taken insufficient notice of earlier select committee reports, and in 1869 had been in the van of those pressing for the new select committee appointed in the following year. And it was Rylands who was believed by the embattled permanent under-secretary, Edmund Hammond, to be so hostile to the Foreign Office that 'in his secret heart' he would like to have been able to summon Grenville-Murray to give evidence. As it was, he told a senior diplomatic colleague, it was the notorious exile 'whose publications he holds in his hand as a brief.'[209]

It is true that it was still to be a long time before patronage ceased to be the route to a career in the Foreign Office and the diplomatic service. However, as a result of pressure for general civil service reform in the early 1850s and the reports of the select committees of 1858 and especially of 1861, some minor reforms had already been introduced by the time that Grenville-Murray fled to France; and in 1870, as foreshadowed in the previous two years, the agency system in the Foreign Office was actually abolished outright. Furthermore, thanks to pressure from Rylands and other reformers, the select committees launched in the same year into the staffing and efficiency of both the diplomatic and consular services lasted until 1872, and prodded the Foreign Office tortoise into inching a little further towards the twentieth century. Among the subsequent changes to which Grenville-Murray contributed, the 'practical

---

[208] The Roving Englishman, *Turkey, being Sketches from Life* (1877), pp. ix-x.
[209] Hammond to Paget (minister at Copenhagen), 1 May 1870, quoted in Jones, *The British Diplomatic Service, 1815-1914*, p. 110.

embassies' he had urged were longer in appearing than some. Nevertheless, there were harbingers of their arrival in the military and commercial attachés to be found in a few major diplomatic missions well before the end of the nineteenth century.

In 1877, Grenville-Murray did bring out a new edition of his 1855 Roving Englishman book on Turkey. Its ferocious attack on the Constantinople embassy in Stratford's time was duly refreshed and, if anything, made even more hard-hitting. In a short, new preface he boasted that it had become a classic, and that Palmerston used to say that it was the best thing on Turkey with which he was acquainted. The one real exception to the silence on diplomacy of the Paris years, however, was the very long and characteristically perceptive section on the different ranks of diplomats and consuls in the first volume of his *Side-lights on English Society*, inserted somewhat incongruously between sections on 'Flirts' and 'Semi-Detached Wives'. In the account of contemporary diplomacy in these pages (also the main theme of the preface to the whole volume) none of his old fire was diminished: reform might be near but nepotism and patronage remained endemic, the result being that the condition of diplomacy was still 'pitiful'.

Such was the high regard for the quality of his writing and the reliability of his delivery that Grenville-Murray's work commanded high prices. Escott wrote that he 'had gained command of a style possessed by no one else and opening to him almost on his own terms the newspaper world.'[210] Coupled with the quantity of his output, therefore, it is hardly a cause for wonder that by the mid-1870s he had put serious money worries behind him. It was also probably around this time that he moved his residence from the Rue de l'Université to an even more fashionable address in the capital: the Avenue du Bois de Boulogne.

Most of Grenville-Murray's books, and the vast majority of his press contributions, remained anonymous or pseudonymous. Like Stendhal and many others, he also muddied the water further by varying the pseudonyms he employed. For *The Member for Paris*, he adopted the pen name of 'Trois-

---

[210]   *Masters of English Journalism*, p. 264.

Étoiles' (also employed for the Tauchnitz edition of *Young Brown* and *The Boudoir Cabal*), for his Chapman and Hall books 'Mark Hope', and for *Vanity Fair* 'Silly Billy'. It hardly needs to be added that, although photography was making striking developments at this time and it was increasingly common to find photographs of authors in the prelims of their books, no photograph of Grenville-Murray was to be found in any of his own. In light of the fact that his identity had been revealed by pirated copies of his books in North America, why did he cling to anonymity for so long?

Anonymity in authorship may have been weakening in the late Victorian era but it was still a strong tradition, and Grenville-Murray remained wedded to it in principle. In France itself it had been outlawed in 1850 but the malign effect of this, he wrote, refreshing the key argument advanced in *The Press and the Public Service* in 1857, was the substitution of 'individualism for combined action and conflict of personalities for polemic of opinions.'[211] In more than one case, he maintained, it had led to violence, as opposing journalists had to work with a pen in one hand and a sword in the other. In *The Member for Paris*, the chief character, Horace Gerold, temporarily on the staff of the opposition organ, the *Sentinelle*, is forced into a duel with a Bonapartist journalist, whom he kills.

In July 1874, Grenville-Murray, together with his friend Edmund Yates, launched a racy weekly spiced with gossip called *The World. A Journal for Men and Women*. It had been Yates's idea, and when – despite a promise of abstinenance – his collaborator could not resist jeopardising sales by using its pages as another outlet for his grievance against the Foreign Office, his friend bought him out only six months later. As it happened, *The World* had been a stunning success and at least Grenville-Murray was able to take with him the sum of £3000, not a bad return on an investment of £350 in such a short time.

Grenville-Murray's usual device for airing his grievance was lengthy allegory. Even in the *Cornhill*, where he had to be particularly restrained, there were numerous examples. And his third novel, the triple-decker called *The Boudoir Cabal*, published in June 1875, invites the sympathy of readers for Mr.

---

[211] *The Member for Paris*, Tauchnitz edition, vol. 1, pp. 201-2.

Engraved by Joseph Brown

Edmund Yates.
1865.

From a photograph by Mons Adolphe Beau

16. Edmund Yates

Job Marvell, a man who owed his government position in one of the Australian colonies to 'mere merit' but had been dismissed via a conspiracy.

After 1875, the allusions to his grievance diminished, but they did not disappear. It flared up again, as we have seen, in *Side-lights*. But in 1881, after publishing a further clutch of novels, many other books, and a fresh library of journalism, the literary manufactory in Paris closed down – or passed briefly to Reginald. It certainly expired altogether when the eldest son changed his name to 'James Brinsley-Richards' and, having understandably concealed his long history of mental illness as well as his scandal-scarred ancestry, went to work for *The Times*. For by the end of 1881, Eustace Clare Grenville-Murray, no doubt to the immense relief of the Foreign Office and the Duke of Buckingham, was dead.

17. The Newspaper Editor

Epilogue

Grenville-Murray died on 20 December 1881. He was 58, the same age at which Dickens died just over a decade earlier. He had finally succumbed to a long and lingering illness: a form of dyspepsia that for more than a year had prevented him from taking any solid food, with the result that he just wasted away. The tone as well as the content of the preface to his *Side-lights on English Society*, dated Paris 1 June 1881, suggest that already he knew he did not have long to live. It was a bitter retrospective on his life, written, he said, 'with all the sad and yearning love which an exile feels towards his country.'

Diplomacy, he recalled in the preface to *Side-lights*, using for the most part exactly the same words he had employed in another book a quarter of a century earlier,[212] was his career of choice. It cost him a great deal of money and he worked at it 'as an ambitious lawyer drudges at the law. I loved it as a soldier loves his sword. In a word,' he said, 'I believed in it.' 'I collected, with laborious care,' he went on, 'whatever seemed to me to bear upon the duties I had, or might have to perform. No fact appeared to me too trifling, no research too minute, that gave me a clearer knowledge of things belonging to my profession.' And what was his reward? 'I was ultimately hustled out of active service by a clerk who had embezzled my salary.'[213]

There is no reason to doubt Grenville-Murray's passion for the diplomatic profession; his *Embassies and Foreign Courts* alone testifies to that. But no-one had embezzled his salary. It also passes all belief that, as he went on to say, he had spent ten years of his life compiling a work on international law, that this was seized (together with other of his private papers) on Foreign Office orders, and that these had disappeared without trace despite an application for their return very kindly supported by Queen Victoria herself. There was no mention of a seized magnum opus, although there was of private papers generally, anywhere

---

[212] *Embassies and Foreign Courts*, pp. 349-53.
[213] *Side-lights*, vol. 1, p. xii.

in his vast correspondence with the Foreign Office following the take-over of his
consulate-general by George Stevens at the end of 1866; and in a private letter
to the Duke of Buckingham written in 1869 the manuscript he claimed had
been seized was of a book on Turkish and Persian history, not international law.
Grenville-Murray lied honourably about his identity as a writer but sometimes
with less justification about other things. Perhaps, however, we should be more
charitable and hazard that, especially as he got older and because economic
necessity required his pen to fly across his paper, he found it increasingly difficult
to observe the boundary between his fictional and his factual writing.

In the preface to *Side-lights* he confessed that he was never completely
satisfied with the books he had written and regretted that he had been unable to
attack abuses without saying some hard things about the individuals who gained
from them. He consoled himself with the thought that his numerous volumes
had found favour with an indulgent public and signed himself off not with *au
revoir* but 'Reader, farewell!'

Grenville-Murray was buried in Paris in the quiet Passy cemetery in
the 16th Arrondissement. The epitaph on his gravestone was his last work of
fiction. Transcribed by Robert Pierpoint following correspondence with the
cemetery's *conservateur*, it reads as follows:

In memoriam
Eustathii Clare Grenville Murray
Comitis de Rethel d'Aragon
Ricardi Plantagenet Ducis de Buckingham
et Chandos
et Henricæ Annæ Marquisæ Strozzi
filii
Natus die Oct. ij[214] 1819. Ob. Dec. xx 1881
Qui seminant in lacrymis in exultatione metent
Viro egregio
Clara Comitissa de Rethel d'Aragon
uxor pia
erexit

---

[214] The *conservateur* told Pierpoint that it was 'ij' that was plainly engraved on the granite but
concluded, surely correctly, that this meant 'II', for 2 October was G-M's date of birth given on
the parish record of his baptism (see p. 5, n. 1 above), *Notes and Queries* (Pierpoint), pp. 292-3.

His father was not Richard Plantagenet, 2nd Duke of Buckingham, but Richard Temple, the first duke. He was born on 2 October 1823 not 2 October 1819, although on the legend that he was the son of Richard Plantagenet (which as we know was widely believed), the second of these myths would have reinforced the claim that he should have inherited the title in 1861, since the Marquis of Chandos, who in the event became the third duke, was born three weeks earlier than Grenville-Murray, on 10 September 1823. His mother was not an Italian marchioness, Henrica Anna Strozzi, entertaining though the notion is;[215] for, as is certain, it was the actress Emma Murray. As to the suggestion in the epitaph that his bereaved wife ('uxor') *Clara* Countess of Rethel d'Aragon was a different 'Clara' from the Sarah *Clara* Lake he had married in 1844 and that it was from this second marriage that he had become a count, this was – as I have argued – almost certainly a fiction too. Clara herself survived Grenville-Murray for another seven years. Upon her death, also in Paris, family representatives decided, probably for legal reasons, to suppress the memoirs of her husband; this was a work to which she was reported to have contributed and which had been repeatedly withheld when its publication was said to be imminent.[216]

Of the two trades he had followed it was as a journalist that Grenville-Murray devoted exclusively his last years and it is only as a journalist that he has been respectfully remembered, indeed remembered at all. Even the nineteenth century *Dictionary of National Biography*, although not going as far in praise of his stature in this profession as Henry Labouchere, whom I quoted in the Prologue, conceded that he was 'certainly one of the most accomplished journalists of his day' and echoed the widespread view that he had done more than any of his professional colleagues to give birth to modern, popular journalism.[217]

---

[215] It was repeated in the press from time to time, with the added twist that it was because his mother was a Roman Catholic and father a Protestant that he was ousted from the ducal succession; see for example the *York Herald*, 15 October 1887.

[216] *Pall Mall Gazette*, 21 March 1889. The manuscript was in the hands of the London publisher Sampson Low & Company, and was first mentioned in the press in the second half of 1886: *Leeds Mercury*, 27 September and *Aberdeen Weekly*, 1 October.

[217] Seccombe, 'Murray'.

But Grenville-Murray spent the greater part of his working life as a diplomatist and he was by no means useless in this role when given serious work to do, which probably for the first time was at Odessa. On the contrary, his reporting, whether on commercial, political or military affairs, was first class and he displayed an interest in the prospects of individual British companies that was well ahead of its time. In addition, he showed a practical concern for British citizens in distress in his vast district and a humane interpretation of the marriage laws found to be at fault only because this was also too advanced. It was just unfortunate that because the Foreign Office knew that he had lied to it about his identity as the Roving Englishman it could not bring itself to place much trust in anything else he said. This, together with institutional conservatism and hostility to his whistleblowing, also led it to receive with cold indifference his eloquent, forceful and generally persuasive arguments for reform. But there were others with whom his campaign found favour; these included radicals in parliament as well as within publishing and the press – and certainly some men in the diplomatic service too, although it would have been more than their careers were worth to own up to it. And it cannot be entirely coincidental that the future shape of British diplomacy was very much that urged by Grenville-Murray. At the least, he had stiffened and helped to shape the direction of a wind already blowing.

Grenville-Murray's ultimate misfortune was that his two great patrons, Dickens and Palmerston, tugged him in opposite directions: the former to the literary exposure of social evils, the latter to the important work of diplomacy. He was no saint but it remains to his credit that, despite the tension between them and the strain that simultaneously plying these two trades imposed on his family, he made such a valuable contribution to both over such a long period. He deserves a better place in history than that pegged on the lazy re-cycling of the myths that he was a 'scurrilous' journalist deservedly 'horsewhipped' by a nobleman he had offended.

Note on Sources

I list here the main primary and secondary sources on which the book draws. First are those that have been of general value; that is, either for the whole book or a substantial part of it. Second are those that – as a rule – have been needed only for one or two chapters. The sources accessible in the Internet Archive, or on some other website, are marked with an *asterisk. Abbreviations used are as follows:

HL, STG: Huntington Library, California, Stowe-Grenville collection

ODNB: *Oxford Dictionary of National Biography*

TNA: The National Archives, Kew

General

Primary sources

British Library Newspapers

The Foreign Office List and Diplomatic and Consular Year Book

Household Words

*Historic Hansard [House of Commons Debates], 1803–2005

House of Commons Parliamentary Papers, especially HCPP (4163), 14 June 1869: *Papers Relative to the Complaints made against Mr. Grenville-Murray as Her Majesty's Consul-General at Odessa; and to his Dismissal from Her Majesty's Service* [A 'Blue Book']

The Times Digital Archive

Secondary sources

Bourne, Kenneth, *Palmerston: The early years, 1784–1841* (London, 1982)

*Fox-Bourne, H. R., *English Newspapers: Chapters in the history of journalism*, vol. 2 (London, 1887)

*Hatton, Joseph, *Journalistic London: Being a series of sketches of famous pens and papers of the day* (London, 1882)

*Hertslet, Sir Edward, *Recollections of the Old Foreign Office* (London, 1901)

Lohrli, Anne, *Household Words: A weekly journal, 1850–1859, conducted by Charles Dickens* (Toronto, 1973)

*Seccombe, Thomas, 'Murray, (Eustace Clare) Grenville (1824–1881)', *Dictionary of National Biography 1885–1900*, vol. 39

Storey, G. et al (eds.), *The Letters of Charles Dickens, vols. Six, Seven, Ten and 11* (Oxford, 1988, 1993, 1998 and 1999 resp.)

*Yates, Edmund, *His Recollections and Experiences* (London, 1885)

1 Powerful Patrons

Primary sources

London Metropolitan Archives, Saint Marylebone, Register of Baptisms, P89/MRY1, Item 024

HL, STG Box 96 (33, 39-47, 49, 50)

TNA: FO65/787, 795; FO881/1647

Secondary sources

Beckett, John, *The Rise and Fall of the Grenvilles: Dukes of Buckingham and Chandos, 1710 to 1921* (Manchester, 1994)

Chamberlain, Muriel E., 'Gower, Granville George Leveson-, second Earl Granville (1815–1891)', *ODNB*, online ed., January 2008

Chambers, James, *Palmerston: 'The People's Darling'* (London, 2004)

*Malmesbury, Earl of, *Memoirs of an Ex-Minister: An autobiography*, new ed. (London, 1885)

Steele, David, 'Temple, Henry John, third Viscount Palmerston (1784–1865)', *ODNB*, online ed., May 2009

*Thomas, Frederick Moy (ed.), *Fifty Years of Fleet Street, being the Life and Recollections of Sir John R. Robinson* (London, 1904)

*Thorold, A. L., *The Life of Henry Labouchere* (London, 1913)

2 'The Roving Englishman'

Primary sources

TNA: FO65/787; FO881/1716, 1717

Secondary sources

*Benson, A. C. and Viscount Esher (eds), *The Letters of Queen Victoria*, vol. 3, 1854–1861 (London, 1908)

Berridge, G. R., *British diplomacy in Turkey, 1583 to the present: a study in the evolution of the resident embassy* (Leiden, 2009)

*Bindoff, S. T. et al, *British Diplomatic Representatives, 1789–1852*, Camden Third Series, vol. L (London, 1934)

Braithwaite, Roderick, *Palmerston and Africa* (London, 1996)

*Cavendish, Francis W. H., *Society, Politics and Diplomacy, 1820–1864: Passages from the journal of Francis W. H. Cavendish* (London, 1913)

Chamberlain, Muriel E., 'Canning, Stratford, Viscount Stratford de Redcliffe (1786–1880)', *ODNB*, online ed., January 2008

*Fitzgerald, Percy, *Memories of Charles Dickens, with an account of 'Household Words' and 'All the Year Round' and of the contributors thereto* (London, 1913)

Hamilton, Keith and Patrick Salmon (eds.), *Slavery, Diplomacy and Empire: Britain and the suppression of the slave trade, 1807–1975* (Eastbourne and Portland, Oregon, 2009)

*Hornby, Sir Edmund, *An Autobiography* (London, 1929)

Jones, Ray, *The Nineteenth-Century Foreign Office: An administrative history* (London, 1971)

Jones, Raymond A., *The British Diplomatic Service, 1815–1914* (Gerrard's Cross, 1983)

Neilson, Keith and T. G. Otte, *The Permanent Under-Secretary for Foreign Affairs, 1854–1946* (London, 2009)

Platt, D. C. M., *The Cinderella Service: British consuls since 1825* (London, 1971)

Steele, David, 'Temple, Henry John, third Viscount Palmerston (1784–1865)', *ODNB*, online ed., May 2009

Tilley, Sir John and Stephen Gaselee, *The Foreign Office* (London, 1933)

3 Revenge of the 'Cousinocracy'

Primary sources

HL, STG: Box 96 (34-6, 52, 54); Box 126 (12-15, 19, 20)

Norfolk Record Office, BUL 1/268/1-6, 269/1-44, 270/1-30

TNA: FO65/589, 647, 667, 711, 720, 787, 789, 793, 794, 796; FO195/477, 597; FO352/46; FO881/1647, 1667, 1718

Univ. Nottingham Manuscripts and Special Collections, BU19/83; BU23/45

Secondary sources

Boase, G. C., 'Buchanan, Sir Andrew (1807–1882)', rev. H. C. G. Matthew, *ODNB*, online ed., January 2008

Boase, Frederick, *Modern English Biography*, vol. II (London, 1965)

*Brinsley-Richards, James [Reginald Grenville-Murray], ed., *Seven Years at Eton, 1857–1864*, 2nd ed (London, 1883)

*Fitzgerald, Percy, *Memories of Charles Dickens, with an account of 'Household Words' and 'All the Year Round' and of the contributors thereto* (Bristol and London, 1913)

*Lane-Poole, Stanley, *The Life of the Right Honourable Stratford Canning. Viscount Stratford de Redcliffe*, vol. II (London, 1888)

Otte, T. G., *The Foreign Office Mind: The making of British foreign policy, 1865–1914* (Cambridge, 2011)

*Redesdale, Lord, *Memories*, Vol. I (New York)

Steele, David, 'Temple, Henry John, third Viscount Palmerston (1784–1865)', *ODNB*, online ed., May 2009

Steele, David 'Harris, James Howard, third earl of Malmesbury (1807–1889) *ODNB*, online ed., January 2016

Vincent, John (ed.), *Disraeli, Derby and the Conservative Party: Journals and memoirs of Edward Henry, Lord Stanley, 1849–1869* (Hassocks, Sussex, 1978)

White, Jerry, *London in the Nineteenth Century* (London, 2008)

4 The Queen's Messenger

Primary sources

The Queen's Messenger

Secondary sources

Boase, Frederick, *Modern English Biography*, vol. II (London, 1965)

Naylor, Leonard E., *The Irrepressible Victorian: The story of Thomas Gibson Bowles, Journalist, Parliamentarian and Founder Editor of the original Vanity Fair* (London, 1965)

*Thomas, Frederick Moy (ed.), *Fifty Years of Fleet Street, being the Life and Recollections of Sir John R. Robinson* (London, 1904)

*Tilley, Sir John and Stephen Gaselee, *The Foreign Office* (London, 1933)

5 A 'Literary Manufactory' in Paris

Primary sources

HL, STG: Box 3 (37); Box 126 (22-4, 26-36); Box 346 (30, 37)

Secondary sources

Beckett, John, *The Rise and Fall of the Grenvilles: Dukes of Buckingham and Chandos, 1710 to 1921* (Manchester, 1994)

Berridge, G. R., 'Richards, James Brinsley- [formerly Reginald Temple Strange Clare Grenville-Murray], 1846–1892', *ODNB*, online ed., July 2024

*Bingham, Cptn. the Hon. D., *Recollections of Paris*, vol. 1 (London, 1896)

*Bowles, Thomas Gibson, *The Defence of Paris; Narrated as it was seen* (London, 1871)

Crouthamel, James L., *Bennett's New York Herald and the Rise of the Popular Press* (New York, 1989)

*Escott, T. H. S., *Masters of English Journalism: A study of personal forces* (London, 1911)

Jones, Raymond A., *The British Diplomatic Service, 1815–1914* (Gerrards Cross, 1983)

Kuhn, Raymond, *The Media in France* (London, 1995)

*[Labouchere, Henry] *Diary of the Besieged Resident in Paris. Reprinted from "The Daily News", with several new letters and preface* (London, 1871)

Nowell-Smith, Simon, *International Copyright Law and the Publisher in the Reign of Queen Victoria* (Oxford, 1968)

*O'Shea, John Augustus, *An Iron-bound City: or, five months of peril and privation*, vol. 1 (London, 1886)

Rae, W. F., 'Rylands, Peter (1820–1887)', rev. Matthew Lee, *ODNB*, online ed., May 2009

Sidebotham, Herbert, 'Labouchere, Henry Du Pré (1831–1912)', rev. H. C. G. Matthew, *ODNB*, online ed., October 2009

*Vizetelly, Ernest Alfred, *My Days of Adventure: The fall of France, 1870–71* (London, 1914)

*Vizetelly, Henry, *Paris in Peril* (London, 1882), vols. 1 and 2

Epilogue

HL, STG: Box 126 (22)

Notes and Queries. Twelfth series, vol. III, 3 March 1917 (Edward Nicholson)

Notes and Queries. Twelfth series, vol. III, August 1917 (Robert Pierpoint)

Bibliography

This list excludes the titles listed in the Note on Sources. An *asterisk indicates available on the web.

Abbreviations in Bibliography:

    ODNB Oxford Dictionary of National Biography

    HCPP House of Commons Parliamentary Papers

Adonis, Andrew, 'Carington, Charles Robert Wynn- , marquess of Lincolnshire (1843–1928)', *ODNB*, online ed., May 2010

*'Albany', *Survey of London: vols. 31 and 32: St James Westminster, Part 2* (1963), pp. 367-89

Baigent, Elizabeth, 'Digby, Jane Elizabeth (1807–1881)', *ODNB*, online ed., September 2004

Beetham, Margaret, 'Beeton, Samuel Orchart (1831–1877)', *ODNB*, online ed., 23 September 2004

Bell, Alan, 'Stephen, Sir Leslie (1832–1904)', *ODNB*, online ed., September 2004

*Bennett, R. A., 'Mr. Labouchere as a Journalist', in A. L. Thorold, *The Life of Henry Labouchere* (London, 1913)

Bergem, Phil, 'Owning an original Beeton's Christmas Annual', *Explorations*, no. 59, Autumn 2009

Berridge, G. R., 'Diplomatic education and training', in Berridge, G. R., *The Counter-Revolution in Diplomacy and Other Essays* (Basingstoke, 2011)

Berwanger, Eugene H., *The British Foreign Service and the American Civil War* (Lexington, 1994)

Blake, Robert, *Disraeli* (London, 1966)

Blakiston, Georgiana, *Lord William Russell and his Wife, 1815–1846* (London, 1972)

Boase, G. C., 'Buchanan, Sir Andrew (1807–1882)', rev. H. C. G. Matthew, *ODNB*, online ed., January 2008

Boase, G. C., 'D'Eyncourt, Charles Tennyson- (1784–1861)', rev. H. C. G. Matthew, *ODNB*, online ed., January 2010

Boase, G. C., 'Richards, James Brinsley (1846–1892)', rev. Joanne Potier, *ODNB*, September 2004

*Boddington, Andy, 'The Dukes of Buckingham and Chandos'

Braithwaite, Roderick, *Palmerston and Africa: The Rio Nunez Affair – Competition, Diplomacy and Justice* (London, 1996)

Bridges, Peter, *Pen of Fire: John Moncure Daniel* (Kent and London, 2002)

Bulwer, The Right Hon. Sir Henry Lytton, *The Life of Henry John Temple, Viscount Palmerston, with Selections from his Diaries and Correspondence*, vol. II, 3rd ed. (London, 1871)

Bury, J. P. T. (ed), *The New Cambridge Modern History*, vol. X (Cambridge, 1964), ch. XVIII ('The Crimean War')

*Byng-Hall, Major Herbert, *The Adventures of a Bric-a-Brac Hunter* (London, 1868)

*Byng-Hall, Major Herbert, *The Queen's Messenger, or travels on the high-ways and bye-ways of Europe* (London, 1865)

Chamberlain, Muriel E., 'Bulwer, (William) Henry Lytton Earle, Baron Dalling and Bulwer (1801–1872)', *ODNB*, online ed., January 2008

Colquhoun, Sir Patrick, *Dismissal of the Ionian Judges* (London, 1864)

Conacher, J. B., *The Aberdeen Coalition, 1852–1855: A study in mid-nineteenth-century party politics* (Cambridge, 1968)

Cook, B. F., 'Newton, Sir Charles Thomas (bap. 1816, d. 1894)', *ODNB*, online ed., January 2008

Cromwell, Valerie, 'Sanderson, Thomas Henry, Baron Sanderson (1841–1923)', *ODNB*, online ed., January 2008

Davenport-Hines, Richard, 'Milnes, Richard Monckton, first Baron Houghton (1809–1885)', *ODNB*, online ed., May 2006

Davies, David, 'Poland, Sir Harry Bodkin (1829–1928)', rev. Eric Metcalfe, *ODNB*, online ed., September 2004

Edwards, P. D., 'Yates, Edmund Hodgson (1831–1894)', *ODNB*, online ed., September 2004

*Emsley, Clive, Tim Hitchcock and Robert Shoemaker, 'Communities – Huguenot and French London', *Old Bailey Proceedings Online*

Feuchtwanger, E. J., 'Grenville, Richard Plantagenet Campbell Temple-Nugent-Brydges-Chandos-, third duke of Buckingham and Chandos (1823–1889)', *ODNB*, online ed., May 2009

*Fitzrovia Neighbourhood Association

*Foster, Joseph, *Men-at-the-Bar: A biographical handlist of the members of the various Inns of Court, including Her Majesty's judges, etc.*, 2nd ed. (London, 1885)

Furniss, Harry, *Paradise in Piccadilly: The story of Albany* (London, 1925)

Garnett, Richard, 'Hunt, Frederick Knight (1814–1854)', rev. C. A. Creffield, *ODNB*, September 2004

Gash, Norman, *Politics in the Age of Peel: A study in the technique of parliamentary representation, 1830–1850* (London, 1953)

Green, F. C., *Stendhal* (Cambridge, 1939)

Griffin, Penny, 'Jones, Henry Arthur (1851–1929)', *ODNB*, online ed., September 2004

Griffiths, Dennis (ed), *The Encyclopedia of the British Press, 1422–1992* (London and Basingstoke, 1992)

Gunning, Lucia Patrizio, *The British Consular Service in the Aegean and the Collection of Antiquities for the British Museum* (Farnham, England, 2009)

Halkett, Samuel and John Laing, rev. ed by James Kennedy, W. A. Smith and A. F. Johnson, *Dictionary of Anonymous and Pseudonymous English Literature* (London, 1928)

*HCPP (162), 1837: *First report of the committee appointed by the Lords Commissioners of His Majesty's Treasury, to inquire into the fees and emoluments of public offices*

*HCPP (611), 25 July 1850: *Report from the Select Committee on Official Salaries; together with the Proceedings of the Committee, Minutes of Evidence, Appendix, and Index*

*HCPP (482), 27 July 1858: *Report from the Select Committee on Consular Service and Appointments; together with the Proceedings of the Committee, Minutes of Evidence, Appendix, and Index*

*HCPP (58 – I. – Sess.2), 4 July 1859: *Estimates, &c. civil services; for the year ending 31 March 1860*

*HCPP (2579), 12 Aug. 1859: *Abstract of reports on the trades of various countries and places, for the years 1857-58-59. Received by the Board of Trade (through the Foreign Office), from Her Majesty's ministers and consuls. No. 7. (Report by Mr Mathew, late British Consul-General for the Russian Ports of the Black Sea and Sea of Azof, on the Trade and Manufacture of those Ports for the year 1857*, pp. 206-11.)

*HCPP (2661), 1860: *Correspondence on the Subject of the Report of the Consular Committee of 1858*

*HCPP (459), 23 July 1861: *Report from the Select Committee on Diplomatic Service; together with the Proceedings of the Committee, Minutes of Evidence, Appendix, and Index*

*HCPP (493), 15 July 1864: *Report from the Select Committee on Trade with Foreign Nations, together with the proceedings of the committee, minutes of evidence, and appendix; and index (493-I)*

*HCPP (3518), June 1865: *Commercial Reports received at the Foreign Office from Her Majesty's Consuls. (Report by Mr. Consul-General Grenville Murray on the Trade and Commerce of Odessa for the Year 1864*, pp. 274-7 [dated 24 Mar 1865].)

*HCPP (3656), 1866: *Third report of the commissioners appointed to inquire into the origin and nature, &c. of the cattle plague; with an appendix*

*HCPP (3669), June 1866: *Commercial Reports received at the Foreign Office from Her Majesty's Consuls, in 1866. (Report by Mr. Consul-General Grenville Murray on the Trade of Odessa for the Year 1865*, pp. 289-90 [dated 2 Apr 1866].)

*HCPP (4059), 1868: *Report of the Royal Commission on the Laws of Marriage. With an Appendix*

*HCPP (3970), 1868: *Foreign Office Agencies. Names of the Persons for whom the Clerks now act as Agents, or have so acted at any time during the last five years; and of the Aggregate Emoluments of the Agents*

*HCPP (3970-III), 1868: *Correspondence respecting the abolition of Foreign Office Agencies*

*HCPP (3970-IV), 1868: *Further Papers respecting Foreign Office Agencies*

*HCPP (C.168), 1870: *Correspondence respecting the grant of Compensation to the Foreign Office Agents*

*HCPP (382), 25 July 1870: *Report from the Select Committee on Diplomatic and Consular Services; together with the proceedings of the Committee, minutes of evidence, and appendix*

*HCPP (C.263), 1871: *Franco-German War. No. 2 (1871). Correspondence with Lord Lyons respecting his Departure from Paris, and Provision made for the Withdrawal of British Subjects*

*HCPP (380), 24 July 1871: *Second Report from the Select Committee on Diplomatic and Consular Services; together with the Proceedings of the Committee, Minutes of Evidence, Appendix, and Index*

*HCPP (314), 16 July 1872: *Report from the Select Committee on Diplomatic and Consular Services; together with the proceedings of the committee, minutes of evidence, appendix, and index*

*HCPP (C.501), 1872: *Reports relative to British consular establishments: 1858 & 1871. Part II*

Healey, R. M., 'Southern, Henry (1799–1853)', *ODNB*, online ed., January 2008

Hollis, H. P., 'Herschel, Alexander Stewart (1836–1907)', rev. A. J. Meadows, *ODNB*, online ed., September 2005

Houghton, Walter E. (ed.), *The Wellesley Index to Victorian Periodicals, 1824–1900*, vol. 1 (London, 1966)

Howarth, Stephen, *Henry Poole. Founders of Savile Row: The Making of a Legend* (Honiton, Devon, 2003)

Jenkins, Brian, *Lord Lyons: A diplomat in an age of nationalism and war* (Montreal and Kingston, 2014)

Keates, Jonathan, *Stendhal* (London, 1994)

*Laughton, John Knox, *Memoirs of the Life and Correspondence of Henry Reeve, C.B., D.C.L.*, vol. 2 (London, 1898)

*Lockhart, R. H. Bruce, *Memoirs of a British Agent* (London, 1932)

Matthews, Roy T. and Peter Mellini, *In 'Vanity Fair'* (London, 1982)

Maxwell, H. E., 'Murray, Sir Charles Augustus (1806–1895)', rev. H. C. G. Matthew, *ODNB*, online ed., January 2008

Melville, Lewis'Vandam, Albert Dresden (1843–1903)', rev. Roger T. Stearn, *ODNB*, online ed., September 2004

Mew, James, 'Bodkin, Sir William Henry (1791–1874)', rev. Nilanjana Banerji, *ODNB*, online ed., September 2004

Middleton, Charles Ronald, *The Administration of British Foreign Policy, 1782–1846* (Durham, N.C., 1977)

Mosse, W. E., *The Rise and Fall of the Crimean System, 1855–71: The story of a peace settlement* (London, 1963)

*National Portrait Gallery, 'Vanity Fair cartoons: drawings by various artists, 1869–1910'

Patten, Robert L., 'Bentley, Richard (1794–1871)', *ODNB*, online ed., September 2004

Pollard, A. F., 'Colquhoun, Sir Patrick Macchombaich (1815–1891)', rev. Catherine Pease-Watkin, *ODNB*, online ed., September 2004

Pollard, A. F., 'Smith, Robert, first Baron Carrington (1752–1838)', rev. Stephen M. Lee, *ODNB*, online ed., May 2009

Pope-Hennessy, James, *Monckton-Milnes: The flight of youth, 1851–1885* (London, 1951)

Rae, W. F., 'Walker, Thomas (1822–1898)', rev. A. J. A. Morris, *ODNB*, online ed., September 2004

Rappaport, Helen, *Beautiful for Ever: Madame Rachel of Bond Street, Cosmetician, Con-artist and Blackmailer* (London, 2012)

Reynolds, K. D., 'Fane, John, eleventh earl of Westmorland (1784–1859)', *ODNB*, online ed., January 2008

*Rolleston, George, *Report on Smyrna* (London, 1856)

Room, Adrian, *Dictionary of Pseudonyms*, 5th ed. (Jefferson, N.C., 2010)

Rubin, G. R., 'Giffard, Hardinge Stanley, first earl of Halsbury (1823–1921)', *ODNB*, online ed., January 2008

*Sala, G. A., *The Life and Adventures of George Augustus Sala*, vol. 1 (London, 1895

*Satow, Sir Ernest, *A Guide to Diplomatic Practice*, vol. 1 (London, 1917)

*Satow, Sir Ernest, *A Diplomat in Japan* (London, 1921)

Scheuerle, William H., 'Appleton, Charles Edward Cutts Birchall (1841–1879)', *ODNB*, online ed., May 2008

Scott, J. W. Robertson, *The Story of the Pall Mall Gazette* (London, 1950)

Seccombe, Thomas, 'Murray, Grenville (1824–1881)', *Dictionary of National Biography*, vol. 39

Seccombe, Thomas, 'Vizetelly, Henry (1820–1894)', *Dictionary of National Biography*, vol. 58

Seccombe, Thomas, 'Yates, Edmund (1831–1894)', *Dictionary of National Biography*, vol. 63

Shattock, Joanne, 'General histories of the press', in J. Don Vann and Rosemary T. Van Arsdel (eds.), *Victorian Periodicals: A guide to research* (New York, 1978)

Sheppard, F. H. W. (ed.), *Survey of London: vol. 40, The Grosvenor Estate in Mayfair, part 2. The Buildings* (London, 1980)

Steele, David, 'Harris, James Howard, third earl of Malmesbury (1807–1889)', *ODNB*, online ed., January 2008

Steele, David, 'Stanley, Edward Henry, fifteenth earl of Derby (1826–1893)', *ODNB*, online ed., January 2008

Steiner, Zara S., *The Foreign Office and Foreign Policy, 1898–1914* (London, 1986), first published by Cambridge University Press in 1969

Sutherland, John, *The Stanford Companion to Victorian Fiction* (Stanford, 1989)

Swaisland, H. C., 'Bourne, Henry Richard Fox (1837–1909)', *ODNB*, online ed., January 2008

Temperley, Harold and Lillian M. Penson, *A Century of Diplomatic Blue Books, 1814–1914* (Cambridge, 1938)

Thompson, F. M. L., 'Grenville, Richard Plantagenet Temple-Nugent-Brydges-Chandos-, second duke of Buckingham and Chandos (1797–1861)', *ODNB*, online ed., May 2009

Todd, William B. and Ann Bowden, *Tauchnitz International Editions in English: A bibliographical history* (New York, 1988)

Vincent, John (ed.), *Disraeli, Derby and the Conservative Party: Journals and memoirs of Edward Henry, Lord Stanley, 1849–1869* (Hassocks, Sussex, 1978)

Vincent, John (ed.), *A Selection from the Diaries of Edward Henry Stanley, 15th Earl of Derby (1826–93), between September 1869 and March 1878*, Camden Fifth Series, vol. 4 (London, 1994)

*Vizetelly, Henry, *Glances Back Through Seventy Years: Autobiographical and other reminiscences*, vol. II (London, 1893)

*Walford, Edward, *Old and New London*, vol. 4: British History Online

Walter, A. F., 'Memorandum on James Brinsley-Richards', Christmas 1888, reprinted in *Etoniana*, no. 128, 1973

Ward, A. W., et al, *The Cambridge History of English and American Literature. volume 14. The Victorian Age, part two. IV, The Growth of Journalism. 9, The Stuarts and The Morning Post* (Putnam's: New York, 1907–21; New York: Bartleby.com, 2000)

*Wellesley, Col. the Hon. F. A. (ed), *The Paris Embassy during the Second Empire: Selections from the papers of Henry Richard Charles Wellesley, 1st Earl Cowley, Ambassador at Paris, 1852–1867* (London, 1928)

Wolff, Robert Lee, *Nineteenth-Century Fiction: A bibliographical catalogue based on the collection formed by Robert Lee Wolff*, vol. III (London, 1984)

*Yates, Edmund (ed.), *Celebrities at Home: First series* (London, 1877)

Appendix 1 Grenville-Murray's books: anonymous, pseudonymous and signed

Most of these books are available free online on the Internet Archive site.

[anon.] *From Mayfair to Marathon* (Bentley: London, 1853)[218]

[anon.] *Walter Evelyn; or, The Long Minority* (Bentley: London, 1853)[219]

Grenville Murray, E. C., *Droits et Devoirs des Envoyés Diplomatiques. Documens recueillis et arrangés par E. C. Grenville-Murray* (Bentley: Londres, 1853)[220]

[anon.] *The Roving Englishman* (Routledge: London, 1854)

Grenville-Murray, E. C., *Doïne; or, The National Songs and Legends of Roumania* (Smith, Elder: London, 1854)[221]

The Roving Englishman [pseudonym], *Pictures from the Battle Fields* (Routledge: London, 1855)

The Roving Englishman in Turkey [pseudonym]. *Sketches from Life* (Routledge: London, 1855)[222]

The Roving Englishman [pseudonym], *Embassies and Foreign Courts: A history of diplomacy* (Routledge: London, 1855)

A Distinguished Writer [pseudonym], *The Press and the Public Service* (Routledge: London, 1857)[223]

---

218 *Indicates that a copyright edition was also published by Bernhard Tauchnitz of Leipzig in the same year, except for *Six Months in the Ranks*, which was not published until the year following the printing of the Smith and Elder edition. The numbers in square brackets are the serial numbers of these books in Tauchnitz's 'Collection of British Authors'.
Attributed to G-M by the BL and Halkett and Laing, vol. 2; internal evidence (numerous chapters were revised versions of articles previously published under the pseudonym of the Roving Englishman in *HW*).

219 G-M identified as author by the Bentley Private Catalogue (Wolff); attributed to G-M by the BL; internal evidence. Published 1 November 1853.

220 Attempting to re-launch this in 1856, its publisher described it as 'Mr Grenville Murray's Manual for the Diplomatic Service', *The Times*, 8 May 1856. It must have had a very limited print-run because it is difficult to obtain. The Bodleian Library in Oxford has a copy, of which the BL itself has a microfilm.

221 The Introduction is dated 12 September 1853, Prince's Island [Sea of Marmora]. The book was reprinted in 1859.

222 Revised in 1877 under the slightly adjusted title *Turkey, Being Sketches from Life*, by The Roving Englishman.

223 No attribution by BL or any other source. Halkett and Laing, however, suspected him (vol. 4: 'Eustace Clare Grenville Murray?'). However, it contains unmistakeable internal evidence in abundance of G-M's authorship; my own copy, obtained from a London second-hand and antiquarian book dealer, also has the following inscribed in pencil on the

[anon.] *The Oyster; where, how, and when to find, breed, cook, and eat it* (Trübner: London, 1861)[224]

*Trois-Étoiles [pseudonym], *The Member for Paris: A Tale of the Second Empire* (Smith, Elder: London, 1871) [1183][225]

[anon.] *Men of the Second Empire* (Smith, Elder: London, 1872)[226]

[anon.] *Men of the Third Republic* (Strahan & Co.: London, 1873)[227]

[anon.] *The Coming K ⊠. A set of idyll lays* (London: 1873)[228]

*[anon.] *Young Brown, or The Law of Inheritance* (Smith, Elder: London, 1874) [1444][229]

*[anon.] *The Boudoir Cabal* (Smith, Elder: London, 1875) [1514][230]

---

title page: 'a bookseller's catalogue attributes it to Eustace C G Murray.' An advertisement in *The Times*, 13 March 1857, announced that it was to be published on 19 March 1857.

[224] Attributed to G-M in Seccombe, 'Murray' and by the Editor of Cassell and Co. Ltd. in a letter to the Editor of the *Royal Cornwall Gazette*, 10 July 1890, in which it was also stated that it was first published by David Bogue; but attributed to Herbert Byng-Hall by the BL and, relying on this, Halkett and Laing, vol. 4. It appeared in a second edition in 1963 with a new chapter, 'The Oyster-Seeker in London.' On the internal evidence as well as the first two sources, there can be little doubt that G-M was the author, although Byng-Hall may have made some contribution. There is no similarity at all between the style of *The Oyster* and Byng-Hall's *The Queen's Messenger* and *The Adventures of a Bric-a-Brac Hunter*.

[225] Attributed to G-M by Halkett and Laing (vol. 4), Wolff and the BL. Published in the same year by James R. Osgood of Boston. Both the pirated US edition and the Tauchnitz edition also appeared under the pseudonym 'Trois-Étoiles'.

[226] 'By the author of *The Member for Paris*'; attributed to G-M by Halkett and Laing (vol. 4) and the BL.

[227] 'Reprinted, with large additions, from "The Daily News"'; attributed to G-M by the BL. Published as *The Men of the Third Republic; or, The Present Leaders of France*, by Porter & Coates of Philadelphia, 1873.

[228] Publisher as well as author anonymous. Attributed to G-M by Halkett and Laing with a query (vol. 1, p. 380), but sometimes attributed to all or several of the following: Samuel Orchart Beeton, Aglen A. Dowty (a regular contributor to the *London Figaro*), George Rose Emerson (biographer and poet) and Evelyn Douglas Jerrold (journalist and poet, son of the more famous Blanchard Jerrold, and a man who – like G-M – lived much in Paris). The other 'scandalous' edition of *Beeton's Christmas Annual* was 'The Siliad; or, The siege of the seats' (1973), which was reprinted under the same title by Ward, Lock, and Tyler of London in 1874. At this point, Ward, Lock, and Tyler lost its nerve and fell out with Beeton, who in consequence broke from them and published the third annual (not under the trade mark name) as *Jon Duan: A twofold journey with manifold purposes*, by The Authors of *The Coming K* – and *The Siliad*' (Weldon: London, 1874), which sold over a quarter of a million copies in three weeks (Bergem, 'Owning'); and the fourth (having missed a year through illness) as *Edward VII: A Play on the Past and Present Times with a View to the Future* (Goubaud: London, 1876). Publicly, *Edward VII* was 'Published for the Proprietors' but there is little doubt that it was the French publisher Goubaud et Fils that brought it out, the *Graphic*, 16 December 1876.

[229] First published serially in the *Cornhill* from July 1873 to February 1874 and attributed to G-M by the *Wellesley Index* (p. 1024) and Wolff. The Tauchnitz edition appeared under the pseudonym 'Trois-Etoiles'. The American edition, published in 1874 by James R., Osgood of Boston, appeared with 'Grenville Murray' as the author's name.

[230] 'By the Author of "The Member for Paris", "Young Brown", etc. In some editions sub-titled *A Novel of Society*. First serialized in *Vanity Fair*. The Tauchnitz edition appeared under

*[anon.] *French Pictures in English Chalk* (Smith, Elder: London, 1876) [1612][231]

The Roving Englishman [pseudonym], *Turkey, being Sketches from Life*, new edition (Routledge: London, 1877)

Grenville-Murray, Eustace Clare, Consul General, *Narrative of an Appeal to the Crown in 1877. An episode of English history* (Laloux, Son & Guillot: Paris, 1877)

Veuve ou Mariée? (Hachette: Paris, 1877)

*[anon.] *The Russians of To-day* (Smith, Elder: London, 1878) [1742][232]

Grenville-Murray, E. C., *Round About France* (Macmillan: London, 1878)

*[anon.] *French Pictures in English Chalk* (Second Series) (Smith, Elder: London, 1878) [1770][233]

*Silly Billy [pseudonym], *Strange Tales. From Vanity Fair* ('Vanity Fair' Office: London, n.d. 1878?) [1793][234]

*[anon.] *That Artful Vicar: The Story of What a Clergyman Tried to Do for Others and Did for Himself* (Smith, Elder: London, 1879) [1820][235]

Mark Hope [pseudonym], *The Prodigal Daughter: A Story of Female Prison Life* (Chapman and Hall: London, 1879)[236]

Mark Hope [pseudonym], *Dark and Light Stories* (Chapman and Hall: London, 1879)[237]

Grenville-Murray, E. C., *Side-lights on English Society, or Sketches from Life, Social & Satirical*, in two volumes (Vizetelly: London, 1881)

*[anon.] *Six Months in the Ranks; or The Gentleman Private* (Smith, Elder: London, 1881) [2064][238]

*Grenville-Murray, E. C., *People I Have Met* (Vizetelly: London, 1883) [2129][239]

---

the pseudonym 'Trois-Etoiles' but a Canadian copyright edition, published by Rogers and Larminie of Toronto in the same year, appeared under the authorship of 'Grenville Murray', as in the case of the earlier US edition of *Young Brown*; not surprisingly, attributed to G-M by Wolff and the BL.

[231] Reprints of articles from the *Cornhill*. The Tauchnitz edition appeared under G-M's own name; attributed to G-M by the BL.

[232] 'By the Author of "The Member for Paris," etc.'; published by Tauchnitz under G-M's own name; attributed to G-M by the BL.

[233] The Tauchnitz edition appeared under G-M's own name

[234] Published by Tauchnitz in 1878 (under G-M's own name and simply as *Strange Tales*), Todd and Bowden, *Tauchnitz International Editions in English*, p. 290, so I am guessing that the British edition appeared in the same year.

[235] 'By the Author of "The Member for Paris", "French Pictures in English Chalk", etc.'; published by Tauchnitz under G-M's own name; attributed to G-M by Halkett and Laing (vol. 6) and Wolff; dedicated to Labouchere.

[236] Attributed to G-M by Halkett and Laing, vol. 4, and by Wolff; also published in the following year in the Routledge Railway Series. The Chapman and Hall imprint (but not that of Routledge) was dedicated to David Wilson Esq, MD, who was G-M's landlord at 62 Brook Street and for some time appears to have had care of his elder son.

[237] Attributed to G-M by Halkett and Laing, vol. 2.

[238] Published under G-M's own name in the Tauchnitz edition and duly attributed to him by Halkett and Laing (vol. 5) and the BL.

[239] Also published by Tauchnitz under G-M's own name.

Grenville-Murray, E. C., *High Life in France under the Republic: Social and Satirical Sketches in Paris and the Provinces* (Vizetelly: London, 1884)[240]

Grenville-Murray, E. C., R. Mounteney Jephson, H. Savile Clarke, etc., *The Social Zoo; being satirical, social, and humorous sketches of our gilded youth, nice girls, noble lords, flirts, and our silvered youth* (Vizetelly: London, 1884)

Grenville-Murray, E. C., *Imprisoned in a Spanish Convent: An English girl's experiences. With other narratives and tales* (Vizetelly: London, 1885)[241]

Grenville-Murray, E. C., *Under the Lens: Social Photographs*, in two vols. (Vizetelly: London, 1885)[242]

Grenville-Murray, E. C., *Spendthrifts, and Other Social Photographs* (Vizetelly: London, 1887)[243]

---

[240] This volume contains revised versions of articles first published mainly in the *Pall Mall Gazette*, and also appeared in at least two later editions, the third in 1887.

[241] This volume of 434 pages contains 15 short stories in addition to the 121-page long novella of its title. The advertisement at the end describes it as 'New Work'.

[242] According to the 'Literature' column of the *Leeds Mercury* of 8 December 1884, this work was completed 'only a few hours before his death.'

[243] This was just a reprint of vol. 2 of *Under the Lens*, published two years earlier.

Appendix 2   Grenville-Murray's articles in the *Cornhill Magazine**

Almost all of these articles are available in the Internet Archive.

1. 'History of the French Silk Trade', December 1868, pp. 730-8
2. 'Our Rough, Red Candidate: The Story of a French Election', February 1869, pp. 159-91
3. 'Maisons de santé', June 1869, pp. 699-710
4. 'The Change in the Cabinet: An Episode under the Second Empire', October 1869, pp. 412-31
5. 'Our Secret Society: A Reminiscence of the "Coup-d'état"', November 1869, pp. 555-87
6. 'Our New Bishop. À Propos of the "Oecumenical"', January 1870, pp. 63-90
7. 'The February Post-Bag. Letters about the Conscription', February 1870, pp. 204-32
8. 'Prince Moleskine's Conspiracy. A Russian Socialist Bubble', May 1870, pp. 544-65
9. 'Yes or No? A Plebiscitum in the Duchy of Gerolstein', June 1870, pp. 677-98
10. 'Our First Success. À Propos of Dramatic Censorship', July 1870, pp. 25-48
11. 'Wanted, a King. An Adventure in the Realm of Tobago', August 1870, pp. 239-56
12. 'L'Empire c'est la Paix. Reminiscences of a Zouave', September 1870, pp. 297-318
13. 'Lieutenant de Chasselay: A Story of 1848', December 1870, pp. 675-99
14. 'L'Ambulance Tricoche: Recollections of the Siege of Paris', May 1871, 537-65
15. 'Consule Julio: An Episode under the Commune de Paris', August 1871, pp. 175-206
16. 'Fleur de Lys: A Story of the Late War', September 1871, pp. 294-321
17. 'Une Pétroleuse: A Souvenir of Versailles', November 1871, pp. 531-52
18. '"Collegers v. Oppidans": A Reminiscence of Eton', December 1871, pp. 688-717
19. 'Le Ministre Malgré lui: A Contemporary Story', April 1872, pp. 423-52
20. 'The Clerk of the Weather: A Chronicle of Nevelundregenstein', May 1872, pp. 551-77
21. '"Regeneration:" A Tale of 1772', June 1872, pp. 674-703
22. 'Diego the Heretic: A Tale of the Carlist Rising', July 1872, pp. 48-69
23. 'Patrick O'Featherhead's Watch: A Dateless Story', August 1872, pp. 188-201

24. 'Mademoiselle Viviane: The Story of a French Marriage', September 1872, pp. 313-40

25. 'Mara; or, the Girl without References', November 1872, pp. 556-83

26. 'An Ugly Dog', January 1873, pp. 55-61

27. 'Le Jour des Morts: A Catholic Custom', January 1873, pp. 73-81

28. 'The Willow Farm: An Artist's Story', February 1873, pp. 191-214

29. 'Aerostatics in France', March 1873, pp. 336-44

30. 'Franklin Bacon's Republic: Diary of an Inventor', May 1873, pp. 562-80

31. 'The French Press. I. First Period. The French Press, from its Foundation to the Death of Mazarin', June 1873, 703-31

32. 'A Scotch Theological College', August 1873, pp. 207-15

33. 'The French Press. II. Second Period. Reigns of Louis XIV and Louis XV', October 1873, pp. 411-30

34. 'Parisian Journalists of To-day', December 1873, pp. 715-32

35. 'The French Press. III. Third Period. The Reign of Louis XVI', February 1874, pp. 154-71

36. 'The Courtier of Misfortune: A Bonapartist Story', March 1874, pp. 308-36

37. 'The French Press. IV. Fourth Period. Newspapers during the Revolution', May 1874, pp. 535-52

38. 'Agathe Marron: The Story of a New Caledonian Déportée', November 1874, pp. 556-81

39. 'The Sceptic: a Tale of Married Life', July 1875, pp. 102-19

40. 'Jacques Girard's Newspaper; or, The Trials of a French Journalist', December 1875, pp. 691-710

41. 'Justin Vitali's Client: a French "Cause Célèbre"', April 1876, pp. 444-67

42. 'Lord Fairland's Secret', June 1876, pp. 709-27

43. 'Forgotten Jokes', November 1876, pp. 595-602

44. 'Anecdotes of an Epicure', January 1877, pp. 56-68

45. 'The Gossip of History', March 1877, pp. 325-39

46. '"Royal and Noble" Gossip', August 1877, pp.185-95

47. 'The Czar's Clemency: A Polish Priest's Story', November 1877, pp. 561-88

48. 'A Romance by Rum-light', April 1878, pp. 438-51

49. 'Rose Cherril: an Exile's Love Story', September 1878, pp. 297-320

50. 'Jérôme Bongrand's Heresy: a Tale about Priests', March 1879, pp. 303-22

51. 'Old Joquelin's Bequest: a Tale about Women', June 1879, pp. 681-711

52. 'Madame de Sainte-Folye's Babies', October 1879, pp. 430-45

53. 'The Regicides of this Century', April 1880, pp. 467-74

54. 'Marius Bougeard's Amnesty: The Story of one Good Turn and Another', May 1880, pp. 571-88

55. 'A Seat in the House', May 1880, pp. 604-11

56. 'Cabinet-Making', June 1880, pp. 735-41
57. 'Foreign Titles', August 1880, pp. 202-11
58. 'Foreign Orders', October 1880, pp. 464-70
59. 'Oxford Honours', February 1881, pp. 183-90
60. 'A Bishop's Confession', May 1881, pp. 555-78
61. 'The French and English Police Systems', October 1881, pp. 421-35
62. 'Political Spies', December 1881, pp. 713-24
63. '"Let Nobody Pass." A Guardsman's Story', February 1882, pp. 171-90
64. 'Cheap Places to Live in', May 1882, pp. 555-66
65. 'A French Assize', June 1882, pp. 662-75
66. 'French Prisons and Convict Establishments', July 1882, pp. 74-86
67. 'Great Men's Relatives', September 1882, pp. 350-9

*Adapted from the *Wellesley Index*, vol. 1; excludes the numerous chapters of Grenville-Murray's novel *Young Brown*, which was serialized in the *Cornhill* between July 1873 and February 1874.

Diplomacy and Secret Service
A Short Introduction

G. R. Berridge

Emeritus Professor of International Politics,
University of Leicester, UK
and
Senior Fellow, DiploFoundation

For Mina

Contents

Preface and Acknowledgements

The ideas in this short introduction have their distant origins in the chapter I wrote on secret intelligence for my textbook, *International Politics*, first published in 1987, but more especially in a stimulating discussion paper called 'Diplomacy and Intelligence' published in March 1998. This was the work of that finest of scholar-intelligence professionals, **Michael Herman**, then retired, for the University of Leicester's Centre for the Study of Diplomacy, of which I was at the time director. (The paper drew on materials from his major work, *Intelligence Power in Peace and War*, published two years earlier, and subsequently appeared in the journal *Diplomacy & Statecraft*.) Michael also visited us and spoke to my students. Raising the question of the relationship between diplomacy and intelligence as he did, albeit rather briefly, sparked my interest but it was not until I was planning the expanded Fifth Edition of my graduate textbook, *Diplomacy: Theory and Practice*, published in 2015, that it belatedly occurred to me to probe the question more fully with a new chapter called simply 'Secret Intelligence'. By this time the academic study of this subject was well-established and a great wealth of revealing material had become available for research, whether in consequence of freedom of information legislation, parliamentary investigations prompted by secret service excesses, or revelations by defectors and disgruntled intelligence officers, among others. This book builds on my textbook chapter on the subject and, as far as I know, is the only extended treatment of what Michael Herman called 'the interface' between diplomacy and intelligence. Such neglect is the more surprising in light of the massive public attention periodically received by the activities of 'spooks' in embassies or, thanks to the Saudi government, in consular missions.

To avoid over-cluttering the text, as a rule I have restricted the footnotes to parenthetical additions not worthy of highlighting in a box, and to sources for quotations as well as occasional statements that might otherwise raise an eyebrow. The list of references at the end of each chapter is designed chiefly as a guide to further reading but also indicates the sources on which it has relied most heavily. A full list of all of the works on which I have drawn is to be found in the 'References' in the endmatter.

I have tried to limit citations of recently published online press articles to those published by the shrinking number of newspapers that do not have a paywall, which as often as not means *The Guardian*. As it happens, this is also the most trusted newspaper in Britain and the most-read quality news outlet, according to figures released by the Publishers' Audience Measurement Company in December 2018. Where possible, and other things being equal, I cite online rather than print sources. With time, some links will inevitably change or disappear altogether but I think the advantages of referencing freely available online resources outweigh these risks.

With the exceptions of the 'Staff of British Embassy Moscow' and 'The Common Cuckoo', which are the author's photographs from works not covered by copyright (*FO List* and Johns's *British Birds in their Haunts*, 1911), and the cover of the Penguin-published *Mitrokhin Archive*, all of the illustrations in this book were obtained via Wikimedia Commons and are therefore in the public domain. The only additional explanations or attributions properly required, are as follows: photographs of Walsingham and Wicquefort portraits – in the public domain in the USA because it was published (or registered with the U.S. Copyright Office) before January 1, 1924; Canaris photo – German Federal Archives, licensed under the **Creative Commons, Attribution-Share Alike 3.0 Germany**; Bandar–Putin meeting – **premier.gov.ru** and licensed under the Creative Commons **Attribution 4.0** + Creative Commons **Attribution 3.0 Unported**; Moussa Koussa – photo by **magharebia** and licensed under the **Creative Commons, Attribution 2.0 Generic**.

I am grateful to Hannah Slavik for supporting this project and to Mina Mudric and her colleagues in the publishing wing of DiploFoundation for their expertise in design and production.

G. R. B., Leicester, January 2019

List of Abbreviations

CIA	Central Intelligence Agency
CREST	CIA Records Search Tool
DNI	Director of National Intelligence [US]
DPRK	Democratic People's Republic of Korea
GCHQ	Government Communications Headquarters [British]
GRU	Glavnoye Razvedyvatelnoye Upravleniye [Russian – formerly Soviet – military intelligence]
Humint	Human intelligence/espionage
ISCP	Intelligence and Security Committee of Parliament [British]
NOC	Non-Official Cover (aka 'illegal')
NSA	National Security Agency [US]
ODNB	*Oxford Dictionary of National Biography*
PCO	Passport Control Officer
PNGing	Declaring a diplomat *persona non grata* – no longer welcome
S&T	Science and Technology
Sigint	Signals intelligence
SIS	Secret Intelligence Service [British; aka MI6]
SVR	Sluzhba Vneshney Razvedki [successor to the foreign wing of the KGB Russian External Intelligence Service]
VCDR	Vienna Convention on Diplomatic Relations, 18 April 1961
WMD	weapons of mass destruction

List of Boxes

List of Illustrations

Introduction

Intelligence officers working under diplomatic protection are rarely out of the news for long, and the last few years have been no exception. In August 2017, the Soviet consulate-general in San Francisco was closed down on Washington's insistence because the eavesdropping on Silicon Valley by its secret intelligence residency (*rezidentura*) had become intolerable. Less than a year later, in March 2018, Britain and other states expelled between them over 150 Russian diplomats alleged to be intelligence officers in retaliation for the attempt by two operatives of Russian military intelligence to murder the defector, Sergei Skripal, with the nerve agent Novichok, in Shrewsbury, England. It can safely be assumed that the equivalent number of diplomats expelled from Moscow in response to these actions also included intelligence officers. And on 2 October 2018 the dissident Saudi journalist, Jamal Khashoggi, was duped into entering the Saudi Consulate-General in Istanbul and there murdered in grisly fashion by a hit squad from Riyadh which included intelligence officers.

Throughout this whole period strong circumstantial evidence also accumulated that Donald Trump, the President of the United States, no less, had become an agent of influence for Russia, whose cultivation began in 1986 and was assisted by intelligence officers in the Soviet/Russian missions in New York and Washington. In the first year of his second administration, Donald Trump did little to discourage this suspicion, not least in his appeasement of the psychotic Russian dictator, Vladimir Putin, over his unprovoked invasion of Ukraine and ingratiating behaviour towards him at the so-called summit in Alaska on 15 August 2025.

The instances in the foregoing paragraphs all show a continuing intimacy between the worlds of traditional diplomacy and secret intelligence in the twenty-first century. But how did the relationship between diplomacy and secret intelligence come about? How did the role of ambassadors in the running of agents evolve? What was the impact on the relationship of the bureaucratization of secret intelligence that began in the late nineteenth century? Is diplomatic immunity, as is sometimes supposed, the only reason why intelligence officers cluster in embassies and consulates? What do their diplomatic landlords think about their secret tenants today, and what if anything can the spooks do to repay the ambassadors for their lodgings? These are among the key questions this work will consider.

1   The Ambassador as Agent-runner

Until well into the nineteenth century, the central figure in secret intelligence was usually the head of a diplomatic mission, whether the ambassador who ran an embassy or the minister in charge of the more lowly ranked – and much more numerous – legation.[244] In the first centuries of the modern state, however, notwithstanding the fact that even then the diplomats' role was significant, the chief responsibility for secret intelligence was sometimes assumed by an individual at home: a 'spymaster'. Therefore, this chapter will begin by examining this species – so loved by television drama-documentaries – before proceeding to look at the role of ambassadors as agent-runners, together with the part played in their schemes by the lowly consul.

The spymaster

Until the eighteenth century, foreign intelligence operations – other than those conducted independently by armies and navies or by post office interceptions – were sometimes directed chiefly by an intimate of a ruler. Such a person created and ran a network of agents with whom his relationship was essentially personal.[245] Among such well-known 'spymasters' were Cardinal Richelieu (1585–1642), first minister of King Louis XIII of France; Axel Oxenstierna (1583–1654), lord high chancellor of Sweden; John Thurloe (1616–68), secretary of state during Cromwell's English protectorate; and, most famous of all in the English-speaking world, Sir Francis Walsingham (Box 1.1), who served the Protestant Queen of England, Elizabeth I, a monarch who faced periodic threats of invasion from Catholic Spain and lived in constant fear of assassination and Catholic rebellion at home. There were national variations but the kinds of agent employed in Walsingham's network were fairly typical of those of other states.

---

[244] For the sake of brevity, I shall henceforward follow the common practice of using the term 'ambassador' for the head of any resident diplomatic mission.

[245] Szechi, *The Dangerous Trade*, p. 3.

Some were employed in 'special' activities such as black propaganda, as well as in the acquisition of secrets by observation, eavesdropping, and theft of letters and other documents.

Box 1.1   Sir Francis Walsingham: Spymaster of Elizabeth I

Sir Francis Walsingham (c.1532–90), previously a successful diplomat, was appointed a principal secretary to Queen Elizabeth I of England in 1573. Building on the secret intelligence work of his master, William Cecil (Lord Burghley after 1571), and in order to supplement the reports he received from English ambassadors, in the early 1570s Walsingham expanded both the number and distribution of intelligence-gatherers in the English network. (His responsibilities also included counter-intelligence at home.) Assisted by the fluency in French and Italian and many foreign contacts acquired in the five years he spent abroad during the reign of the previous English monarch (a Catholic), he is said by his admiring late nineteenth century biographer to have 'had in his pay fifty-three private agents in foreign courts, besides eighteen spies who performed functions that could not be officially defined' (Lee, 'Walsingham'). They were found in France, Germany, Italy, the Netherlands, Spain and even in the Ottoman Empire. His network consisted chiefly of:

- 'intelligencers', freelancers who sold information to the highest bidder
- couriers, whose day job required not only courage and resourcefulness but also some knowledge of foreign lands and languages
- English merchants at home and abroad, who not only supplied intelligence but also served as go-betweens to pay the intelligencers and handle communications with them, and
- disaffected Catholics, including captured priests, who could sometimes be 'turned' as the price of release from imprisonment and torture, and planted in exile communities, Catholic seminaries abroad, and so on

At his London home, Walsingham had a personal secretariat, the members of which helped him to run his agents and were sometimes themselves sent abroad for this purpose. They also helped him to analyse their product, intercept and read correspondence without alerting the addressee, create and break codes, plan what would now be called 'covert actions'; for example, kidnapping the papal legate to France, black propaganda and forged documents. Sometimes, members of his staff also undertook missions of secret reconnaissance abroad and sensitive diplomatic missions.

The costs of Walsingham's operation were met chiefly (but grudgingly) by the Queen and were particularly heavy as the threat increased from Spain, but he had to bear a significant portion of the expenses himself. His network had many successes but his crowning achievement was the advance intelligence it supplied on the size and armaments of the Spanish Armada, which contributed to its defeat in 1588. Dying in 1590, Walsingham predeceased Burghley, whose son Robert subsequently became Elizabeth's chief spymaster.

Some spymasters were very successful but the scheme had serious risks. For one thing, interpretation of the significance of the intelligence obtained was always likely to be weak because the prejudices of the spymaster – who was also a top policy-maker – would go unchallenged, unless a rival for influence at court set up another network, as did the doomed Earl of Essex in competition with Robert Cecil at the court of Elizabeth I.[246] For another, there was the risk that the intelligence would not be usefully distributed because it was regarded as personal property and vital to the spymaster's influence with his sovereign. The most serious limitation of this system, however, was that because the spymaster tended to be focussed on a specific problem as well as holding his agents only by personal loyalty, the risk was always high that the network would dissolve with the abatement of the problem or his death or political eclipse. It was perhaps in part for these reasons – especially the last – that, although the system lingered at least to the end of the eighteenth century,[247] it began to give way to the resident mission after this institution became the fulcrum upon which diplomacy turned in the course of the sixteenth century and the obvious point for the regular, official collection of secret intelligence.

The resident mission

The resident diplomatic mission was established in Italy in the turbulent conditions of the late fifteenth century and before long spread through Europe as far as Moscow and Constantinople. Only through long residence, it was realised, could a diplomat gain sufficient knowledge of his posting and make enough contacts to provide full and reliable reports on political, military and commercial developments of importance, and this was the chief reason for the appearance of this new institution; for the time being, its other functions were secondary. Further evidence of the anxiety for information of those who sent

---

[246] Hammer, 'Essex and Europe'.

[247] There is a strong whiff of Walsingham about the agent-running of Adam de Cardonnel, chief clerk at the British War Office and secretary to the Duke of Marlborough while on campaign in the War of the Spanish Succession, Rule, 'Review of *Espions et Ambassadeurs*', p. 739; as also about the network run in the 1770s by William Eden, under-secretary in the Foreign Office's Northern Department (which included American-born British subjects working as double agents) against the American mission in Paris during the War of American Independence, Bemis, 'British secret service and the French-American alliance'.

them was that ambassadors were also encouraged to mix in the diplomatic corps and engage in periodic correspondence with diplomatic colleagues at neighbouring posts, thereby not only gaining more local knowledge but also learning more of wider affairs. The information-gathering potential of missions was increased further when it had satellite consular posts that were required to report – with some exceptions – not directly to home but to the ambassador.

Because it was known why they were being set up, some states were reluctant to admit resident missions until they realised that it was unflattering not to have their attention and that in any case this was the price of establishing abroad their own envoys. But wariness of their chief purpose was never shaken off and this meant that ambassadors always had to stress that they were not 'spies'; that, unlike such unsavoury individuals, they gathered their information only by open and legitimate means. Nevertheless, in light of the priority usually given to this task – and the urgency added to it at moments of crisis – it was a natural step to seek concealed information as well. Unlike intelligencers, merchants and others, ambassadors were also uniquely well placed to contemplate this with some equanimity: first, because of their ready access to those with power and authority and thus with the secrets most worth penetrating; second, because they had experience of sending information home as quickly and securely as possible; and third, because – should they be caught – the immunity from civil and criminal prosecution they enjoyed under the developing law of nations usually meant that the worst they would suffer would be expulsion. This is why heads of mission became the new agent-runners, developing their own networks to acquire sensitive information by surreptitious means – and supplied with more or less generous funds from home to support the work. This was markedly the case in wartime and in situations such as those prevailing in the United Provinces of the Netherlands in the mid-1780s where external powers were engaged in an intense struggle for influence that could break out into war; and also in peacetime at unfriendly courts, where information was less easy to obtain.

The changing role of the ambassador

From the sixteenth century to the first decades of the nineteenth, some ambassadors were intimately involved not only in launching and directing but also in carrying out secret intelligence work, whether designed to obtain information, recruit agents of influence, undermine foreign enemies or provide material support to foreign friends. With the noun in the phrase loosely construed, many truly were 'honourable spies'.[248] The most effective device for these purposes was money: small payments to minor agents, large 'bribes' to important foreigner ministers and officials, most suitable to the latter purpose being a regular 'pension'.[249] The need to lay out 'gratuities and secret pensions' – albeit 'with artifice' and alertness to the risk of being duped by the beneficiaries – was repeatedly urged by the theorist of the French system of diplomacy, François de Callières, no doubt because he was afraid that most ambassadors spent 'much more willingly in keeping a great number of horses and idle servants.'[250] Among the many examples that could be quoted are those of the Spanish ambassador in Paris, Bernardino de Mendoza, and the British minister in the Hague, Sir James Harris. In the 1580s, Mendoza bought secret information from Queen Elizabeth's ambassador in the French capital, Sir Edward Stafford, who had large gambling debts and a grudge against Sir Francis Walsingham (Box 1.1).[251] As for

---

[248] Wicquefort and Callières, the two most impressive writers on diplomacy of the early modern period, both used this term with approval: Wicquefort, *The Embassador and His Functions*, p. 296. col. 2; Callières, *The Art of Diplomacy*, p. 80. A formidable catalogue of the activities of ambassadors in this regard in the eighteenth century is provided in Horn, *British Diplomatic Service, 1689–1789*, Ch. 14.

[249] As early as 1604, if not before, English ambassadors were being promised fixed allowances to cover this sort of thing, and by the middle of that century a 'Secret Service Fund' had been placed on a reasonably firm basis; beginning in 1797, there was an annual 'Secret Service Vote' in parliament. Although overall only a small proportion of this fund went to the ambassadors, the fund itself was large and in wartime the sums granted to a few of them could be very high indeed, Andrew, *Secret Service*, pp. 1-2; Horn, *British Diplomatic Service, 1689–1789*, p. 282; Cobban, *Ambassadors and Secret Agents*, pp. 110-12; Middleton, *The Administration of British Foreign Policy*, App. VIII. Ambassadors to France, Spain and the Habsburg Empire were each to receive £500 a year for secret intelligence work, and those to Venice, the Spanish Netherlands, and the Dutch Republic, £200, Stone, *An Elizabethan*, p. 233 n. 2.

[250] Callières, *The Art of Diplomacy*, pp. 78-9; see also pp. 113-15.

[251] The only remaining question in this case is the *extent* to which Stafford was responsible for the damaging stream of intelligence obtained by Mendoza. This gave advance warning of the raid on Cadiz by English sea captain Sir Francis Drake, revealed instructions for the concentration of the English fleet, and provided much useful information on English diplomacy in Europe during the Anglo-Spanish war in 1587–8, McDermott, 'Stafford'. Callières held up

Harris, who was determined to win the struggle with the French for influence in the United Provinces in the mid-1780s, he ran a network of agents of the usual sort (which included minor Dutch politicians, the Sardinian consul in Amsterdam, and ship-watchers at Rotterdam) and drew even more heavily on secret service funds to subsidise those actively opposing the 'French party'.[252]

High-level informers would surely have had to be approached by the ambassador in person but in this twilight zone heads of mission had to be careful. After all, the efficient discharge of their other duties depended on the maintenance of satisfactory relations with their hosts, and this could clearly be risked by the exposure of direct encouragement of treachery and other forms of espionage, not to mention covert action.[253] It was even riskier for a head of mission with the *formal* status of 'ambassador' – as opposed to one of lower grade or a mission secretary – because as courts became fussier about ceremonial and diplomatic missions became grander, the idea became fixed that the ambassador had the *full* representative character of his sovereign and thus always a formidable dignity to preserve.[254] It is for these reasons that Abraham de Wicquefort, who was in a position to know (see Box 1.2), believed that diplomats of the 'second order' – who could move and mix more freely – were 'more proper to carry on an intrigue with safety.'

Box 1.2   Abraham de Wicquefort

Abraham de Wicquefort (1598–1682) was an intelligencer, gazetteer and diplomat of the second rank. Born in Holland, nevertheless he served in Paris from 1626 until 1658 as Resident of the Elector of Brandenburg-Prussia, while selling intelligence and producing a weekly newsletter. Eventually falling foul of the French government, he was briefly imprisoned in the Bastille before being expelled. Thereafter, Wicquefort served the States General in his native Holland but – despite having taken an oath of secrecy – continued to sell intelligence to foreign powers, not least England, where the secretary of state's office composed instructions as to the intelligence it needed and received his coded despatches in reply. In 1675, Wicquefort was arrested by the Dutch for espionage and – despite his plea of diplomatic immunity on the grounds that he was

---

Spanish diplomacy as the model to emulate in this regard, *The Art of Diplomacy*, pp. 79-80.

252   Cobban, *Ambassadors and Secret Agents*, esp. pp. 110-16.

253   Prior to going to Paris, Bernardino de Mendoza had been ambassador in London, and notoriously expelled for such activities.

254   Berridge, *Diplomatic Classics*, p. 180 (Vattel ch.).

concurrently the representative at The Hague of the Duke of Luneburg – convicted and sentenced to life imprisonment. In the prison of Loevestein (from which he escaped in 1679), he devoted his time to writing. The most important product of these years was his massive *L'Ambassadeur et Ses Fonctions*, which was written entirely from memory. First published in the year before he died and subsequently reissued many times, this became the greatest manual of diplomacy of the eighteenth century and is now regarded as the first substantial work to deal with what diplomats actually did as opposed to what they were supposed to do. It was ably translated into English in 1716 by John Digby as *The Embassador and His Functions*, and – since it is rare – I have published extracts from it in my *Diplomatic Classics*.

It is, therefore, not surprising that ambassadors were usually minded to detach themselves from direct dealings with the intelligencers and others in the lower ranks of the embassy's network. They did this, where possible, by delegating the responsibility to someone else in the embassy, although this was often difficult because until well into the nineteenth century the 'diplomatic' – as opposed to domestic – staff' of missions still consisted usually of no more than a secretary (possibly two) and some young men of his extended family or that of influential friends attached to the ambassador for the experience. Michel de Castelnau, the French Ambassador to England who was colluding with Mary Queen of Scots in the 1580s, was fortunate. His secretary of embassy, Nicolas Leclerc, seigneur de Courcelles, 'was not just a scribe: he had almost complete charge of Castelnau's operations concerning Mary and English Catholics, in which Castelnau wanted to be personally involved as little as possible,' writes John Bossy.[255] By contrast, in the Hague, two centuries later, Sir James Harris had 'to play a lone hand' because his own secretary of legation, William Gomm, although worthy, lacked the aptitude to be anything other than a scribe.[256] As a rule, nineteenth century ambassadors in the East did not have this problem (see Box 1.3).

Box 1.3 Gerald Fitzmaurice: 'The Wizard of Constantinople'
At embassies in the East, the task was usually transferred to a dragoman, an interpreter, information-gatherer and general 'fixer' in relations between the mission and the mysterious workings of the 'Oriental' bureaucracy. These were usually natives of the country concerned but during the course of the nineteenth century men of the ambassador's own nationality – believed to be more trustworthy – began to be employed in this role. In the British Embassy

---

[255] Unfortunately for the ambassador, Courcelles, had been 'turned' by one of Walsingham's agents, Henry Fagot, who had succeeded in making himself a welcome member of the household – a penetration agent, Bossy, *Giordano Bruno and the Embassy Affair*, p. 20.

[256] Cobban, *Ambassadors and Secret Agents*, pp. 32-3,

in Constantinople, the Armenian, Onik Effendi Parseghian, who was a key figure in the dragomanate but not officially recognized and paid from the mission's secret service fund, was a perfect example of the former; Gerald Fitzmaurice of the latter.

Fitzmaurice (1865–1939) was an unmarried Irish Catholic who spent his working life in the Levant Consular Service, rising in 1907 to one of its top posts: Chief Dragoman at the British Embassy in Constantinople. Fitzmaurice was an outstanding example of a 'minister of the second order' – not just an intelligence-gatherer but also an intriguer, a man of action. He had made his name for 'special service' during the Armenian massacres in 1895–6 and then during the delimitation of the Aden frontier a decade later. Back in Abdul Hamid II's Constantinople, he became the British Embassy's own spy master. He failed to anticipate the sudden Young Turks' revolution in 1908 but then made life difficult for them by encouraging their domestic opponents with advice, black propaganda and hints of British support. The counter-revolution of April 1909, in which he played such a strong hand, narrowly failed – but he remained at his post until shortly before the outbreak of war in 1914. It was he who was then attached to the British Legation at Sofia with a view to using this as a platform for a second attempt to overturn the then German-allied Turkish government and, failing that, to bribe the Bulgarians with an offer of £2.5m to attack the Turks and, by diverting them, guarantee the success of Britain's Dardanelles adventure. Neither of these long shots came off, and 'Fitzmaurice of Constantinople', as he was known in the Levant Service, or 'the Wizard of Constantinople' as he occasionally signed his private letters, ended up in London in Naval Intelligence, the division that not so long afterwards spawned Ian Fleming – and so 'Commander James Bond'.

It was, as it happens, during the course of the nineteenth century that the attitude to secret intelligence of diplomatists as a body – not just those who were heads of mission – seems to have cooled further. This probably had much to do with the professionalization of diplomacy that was beginning to advance during these years, although it had been heralded as far back as the beginning of the eighteenth century in the establishment by the French foreign minister, Jean-Baptiste Colbert de Torcy, of a short-lived school for diplomats in Paris.[257] The consequence was that those who entered diplomacy began to look on it more as a life-long career than as a way of combining public service with a route into a political career, a means of making money by side activities, or pursuit of a hobby such as archaeology or coin-collecting.

Like all professions, diplomacy also acquired its attendant manuals for instruction and reference (see Box 1.2), including works of international law; and its sense of identity was reinforced by regular meetings of heads of mission in the diplomatic corps of each capital city for the purpose of discussing matters

---

[257] Callières, *The Art of Diplomacy*, App. 1.

of common professional concern. The consequence was that a professional credo began to firm up, and central to this was the need for right behaviour. Without this there would be no trust, and without trust negotiations would be difficult and the credibility of information – even from friends – hard to judge. This prudential calculation was fortified not only by religion but also by the code of honour and social prejudices of the European aristocracy that was so strongly represented in the diplomatic service as well as the officer class.[258] This was famously summed up early in the following century when, announcing the closure of the US State Department's Cipher Bureau, Secretary of State Henry Stimson remarked that 'Gentlemen do not read each others' mail.'[259] In any case, it was said, the practitioners of such dark arts were not only expensive and unreliable but also unnecessary; for an able professional diplomat who was liked and respected was perfectly capable of discovering all of the political secrets worth knowing by means of 'a good dinner and pleasant companionship', provided he exerted himself to mix widely and did not overlook the editors of leading newspapers. When secrets 'become serious,' wrote the British mid-Victorian diplomat-journalist, Eustace Clare Grenville-Murray, in his lively and acutely observed work on the profession, 'they become known.'[260] In sum, spies were lower class, untrustworthy, unsavoury in their methods – and dispensable.

To be sure, from time to time ambassadors still received and spent secret service money, some on bribery and influencing the press, but when Sir Ernest Satow published his own – and more famous – manual on diplomacy after the First World War, he was decidedly disapproving of bribery. While seeming to acknowledge the uncertainty on this subject of the 'law of nations' and that it was a 'more or less universal' means of obtaining secret information, Satow thought bribery immoral and only permissible as a last resort. More generally, he quoted Theodor Schmalz, one of two minor early nineteenth century German jurists upon whom he leaned heavily in this passage, that 'nothing is good politics but what is honourable' and that 'An [sic] uniform policy, armed with strength and honesty, has little to apprehend from what is

---

258 Porch, *The French Secret Services*, pp. 21, 43-4.
259 Khazan, 'Gentlemen reading each others' mail'.
260 Grenville-Murray, *Embassies and Foreign Courts*, pp. 260-1.

concealed, and steady attention to what passes around will mostly enable us to divine what is secret.'[261]

Sir Ernest Satow in 1903: British scholar-diplomat

Consuls as 'spies'

In the early modern period, consuls were merchants chosen from the ranks of a local trading settlement by the merchants themselves and, even after most were taken under the control of the state in later centuries, smoothing the path of commerce remained outwardly their sole responsibility. As a result, consular posts tended to be clustered mainly at major ports; but they were also to be found inland, and not just in major cities but also in provinces where their home governments took an interest in the popular mood or adjacent to frontiers of special concern. In many of these places, consuls were in practice encouraged by foreign ministries and war offices to gather and report political and military, as well as commercial intelligence.

---

[261] Satow, *A Guide to Diplomatic Practice*, pp. 142-4. It should, however, be added that Satow's German authorities were still of the view that the 'law of nations' was a system confined to Christian Europe (see Grewe, *The Epochs of International Law*, p. 464), and that he probably believed that a less gentlemanly attitude to intelligence-gathering was more acceptable in the Orient, where his own long diplomatic career had been spent.

Not all of them responded enthusiastically, especially when their 'cover' as commerce-preoccupied consul was thin, as in the case of George Stevens at Kherson, mentioned in the previous book in this omnibus. But some did, especially in war or near-war circumstances. An early instance is provided by Chasteau-Martin, who was consul to the English merchants at La Rochelle in the 1580s and therefore well placed to report on Spanish activities when Spain's threat to England was particularly acute. A key agent in Walsingham's network, he was paid a pension plus expenses and used these to place another agent in Madrid.[262] Harris's reliance on a consul at Amsterdam two centuries later has already been mentioned.

In the late nineteenth century and early twentieth, consuls also played a pivotal role in 'the Great Game': the intense secret intelligence competition for influence in the border regions between the British and Russian Empires in central and south Asia. The British sent 'military consuls' to posts close to Turkey's border with Russia; a very large network of agents was run by Patrick Stevens, British consul at the Russian Black Sea port of Batum; and British and Russian consuls in Persia both ran their own agent networks.[263]

In 1918, while the United States had no secret intelligence agencies, an American vice-consul, Robert Imbrie, set up and ran a short-lived network of agents from Petrograd, the aims of which were to gather intelligence both on the advancing German forces and the Bolsheviks.[264] In peacetime, however, ambassadors and foreign ministries tended to be highly nervous about their consuls being engaged in secret intelligence work.[265]

---

[262]   Stone, *An Elizabethan*, p. 249.
[263]   Hughes, *Diplomacy before the Russian Revolution*, pp. 114-16, 148.
[264]   Langbart, 'Five months in Petrograd in 1918', Doc. II.
[265]   Sir Charles Scott, British ambassador at St. Petersburg (1898–1904), is a recorded case in point, Hughes, *Diplomacy before the Russian Revolution*, p. 114; see also Seligman, *Spies in Uniform*, p. 11.

2   Arrival of the Secret Service

By the end of the nineteenth century, the ambassador had become a reluctant agent-runner. But while foreign ministries might have shared the diplomats' prejudices about secret intelligence personnel and methods, they were less inclined to agree that there was no need for them. Even in the deeply conservative higher commands of armies and navies the need for intelligence on potential enemies – if only for reliable maps of their coastlines and topography – began to be felt with gathering urgency. This was a consequence of developments that made strategic surprise a much greater risk, among them the electric telegraph, which made it possible to transmit military communications more quickly, and the advancing railway networks, which greatly increased the speed with which troops could be mobilized and deployed. The disasters suffered by the French army in the Franco-Prussian War in 1870–1 were only too clearly exacerbated by poor intelligence. It was, therefore, with a collective sigh of relief that, in response to this new situation, diplomats witnessed two innovations that promised to extend even further their arm's length relationship with the 'dirty' world of secret intelligence.

The first innovation was the regular appearance in the embassy of the military attaché, the herald of the military intelligence services; and the second was the emergence of the separate civilian foreign intelligence agency, or secret service, which in its bureaucratic permanence and formal detachment from policy-making was a creature 'far removed' from the spymaster system of earlier centuries.[266] This chapter will examine these changes, glance at the concept of the intelligence community, and reflect briefly on the significance for diplomacy of the secret political power of the secret service.

---

[266]   Herman, *Intelligence Power in Peace and War*, p. 34.

Military attachés

As early as 1680, the great scholar-diplomat Abraham de Wicquefort (Box 1.4) had shown concern at the tendency of some princes to require ambassadors to accompany them on military expeditions, since this implied that the ambassador's own prince endorsed the campaign, which might not have been the case. This would be avoided, he suggested, if embassies were to have a military officer attached to them, for he would not only be a natural substitute for the ambassador but also be more 'capable of judging of martial actions.'[267]

Whether in part for this reason or not, by the end of the eighteenth century army and navy officers began occasionally to make casual appearances in embassies. But it was not until the following century that it became a reflex of the major states formally to provide embassies with military attachés. (Naval and then air attachés were later added and came to be known collectively as service or defense attachés.) Occasionally, too, they were to be found in consulates, including those close to a major naval base such as Kronstadt, the Russian base at the head of the Gulf of Finland.

The military attaché was the most visible and often probably the most important figure in the new military intelligence services (see below) but preceded their appearance by some decades. There were General Staff officers in Prussia's main embassies as early as 1817;[268] military attachés in French embassies from the 1830s;[269] and by the second half of the century they were a regular feature of diplomatic life. In the course of the twentieth century, service attachés became as common in peacetime as in war, although numerous side accreditations were frequent.

The minimum duties of service attachés (who sometimes recruit their own agents[270]) include obtaining intelligence on the armed forces of the country or countries to which they are accredited: the size and equipment of the armed forces in particular but also their morale, training, geographical disposition, tactical and strategic doctrines, defensive fortifications, capacity for

---

[267] Wicquefort, *The Embassador and His Functions*, p. 297, col. 2.
[268] Millotat, 'Understanding the Prussian-German General Staff system', p. 31.
[269] Porch, *The French Secret Services*, p. 21.
[270] Porch, *The French Secret Services*, p. 30.

Foreign military attachés with their German escorts at the Imperial manoeuvres, 1904

swift mobilization, and so on. Service attachés are well placed to do this because it became customary for them to be closely involved in defence collaboration when relations were friendly, and – whether they were or not – to enjoy the hard-drinking intimacy of their 'comrades in arms' at the post to which they were accredited, for eventually these tended to form a well-organized and often convivial sub-division of the diplomatic corps, with its own doyen.

It came to be well understood that the exchange of service attachés, by reducing mutual suspicions, contributes to the stability of the balance of power. Even during tense passages of the Cold War they were tolerated by both sides. However, because of the enduring suspicion of them as 'military spies', the Vienna Convention on Diplomatic Relations 1961 (VCDR) stipulated that, apart from the head of mission (for whom agrément is mandatory), the service attaché is the only member of the staff of a diplomatic mission whose name might, if the receiving state so requires, need to be submitted for approval prior to appointment.[271] In practice, this is something on which receiving states have frequently insisted.

The introduction of service attachés has certainly relieved diplomats of responsibility for the gathering of military intelligence, while their vetting by receiving states has gone some way to reduce the anxiety of ambassadors that the officers appointed are of the sort likely to make trouble. Nevertheless, service attachés have sometimes proved to be a mixed blessing. This is because their primary allegiance is to armed forces' intelligence headquarters at home or to a defence ministry; because they are inclined to adjust imperfectly to the atmosphere and routines of an embassy; and because when a mission's defence section is large it is not unusual to find it housed separately from the building containing the chancery. The consequence of these circumstances is that service attachés are sometimes required by their military masters to engage in activities that are illegal or borderline illegal, and in carrying them out might be insensitive to the embarrassment they are likely to cause a head of mission. This can make for uncomfortable relations in a peacetime mission, and worse relations still if the military establishment and the foreign ministry are tugging in different directions on policy towards the state where the embassy is based. On the other hand, it is true that embarrassing incidents tend soon to be forgotten. For example, improving relations between Israel and Russia suffered nothing more than a temporary hiccup following the expulsion from Moscow in May 2011 of the Israeli military attaché on grounds of espionage. As often as not, too, such expulsions are a symptom rather than a cause of bad relations, as when Venezuela gave two US defense attachés 24 hours to get out of Caracas in March 2013.

Defence intelligence services

Since the avoidance of strategic surprise is usually the top priority of foreign intelligence-gathering, its bureaucratization in the late nineteenth and early twentieth centuries was led by the military; that is, by army high commands and ministries of war. By this time, bureaucracy – pursuit of an objective with the

---

[271]   VCDR, Art. 7.

aid of an impersonal, complex administrative machine – was already emerging as a distinguishing feature of the activities of the modern state, as noted with qualified praise by the German sociologist Max Weber. And for intelligence-gathering, it had at least two advantages. First, it facilitated the analysis, storage, retrieval, and distribution through government of the increasing flow of information that was arriving. Second, it made it possible to build up files on individual agents which contained not only their safe contact details but also their track records of providing reliable information, thereby reducing the risk of paying out large sums to rogues.[272]

Box 2.1 Prussian/German military intelligence

To its twentieth century enemies, the Prussian/German General Staff, which originated in a reorganization of 1803, was the epitome of professional militarism and thus an object of fear and disgust. But it was much admired in the nineteenth century, for it gave form to the idea that military commanders should be required to take the advice of an elite of highly educated and broadly trained officers selected on merit rather than social class; General Carl von Clausewitz, author of the classic work, *Vom Kriege* [*On War*], was one of its earliest members. The General Staff was initially subordinate to the Ministry of War but such was the growth in its prestige that in 1883 it achieved complete independence. Its main budget funded three divisions charged with investigating all matters of military interest in foreign countries, the first being responsible for Sweden, Norway, Turkey and Austria; the second for Germany, Italy and Switzerland; and the third for France, England, Belgium, the Netherlands, Spain, Portugal and America. A fourth division was responsible for military railway transport, while an additional budget provided, among other things, for a war history department and geographical-statistical studies.

Under the Versailles Treaty ending the First World War, defeated Germany was forbidden a General Staff and associated military intelligence service. But the service re-emerged in 1920–1 as the Abwehr, a small section under the Ministry of Defence. 'Abwehr' is the German word for 'fending off' or 'defence' (in this context signifying 'counter-espionage'), and the name was employed to reassure the inter-allied commission that the purpose of the revived service was nothing to be worried about. The Abwehr gradually became a full military intelligence service, especially after the Nazi Party came to power in Germany in 1933 but was generally ineffective. It was also anti-Nazi, and its last chief prior to its merger in 1944 with the notorious SS was Admiral Canaris, who was executed for treason in April 1945. After the war, the residue of German intelligence officers (the Gehlen Organization) was taken under the wing of the CIA, until in 1956 the Bundesnachrichtendienst (Federal Intelligence Service) was formed. The BND gives Germany one agency for both military and civil (political and economic) intelligence.

---

272 Andrew, *Secret Service*, p. 31.

Admiral Wilhelm Canaris: head of the Abwehr, 1940

Notable examples of the nascent defence intelligence services are provided by the intelligence divisions of the Prussian General Staff (Box 2.1) and the services of France and Britain which Prussia's initial achievements helped to inspire.[273]

However, the Prussians apart, military leadership of the bureaucratization of secret intelligence did not move quickly because military establishments everywhere were highly conservative institutions. In France, foreign intelligence – as opposed to domestic surveillance – was not put on a permanent basis until the Section de Statistiques et de Reconnaissances of the Deuxième Bureau of the General Staff was created in 1871. And in Britain, while military intelligence was established in the War Office during the Crimean War, it did little beyond map-making until the 1870s, and it was 1877 before the Naval Intelligence Department appeared. The process of bureaucratization was consolidated only by the emergency of the First World War. When this was over, it was the threat of 'capitalist encirclement' that gave impetus to the organization of military intelligence in the new Soviet Union; hence the Glavnoye Razvedyvatelnoye Upravleniye (GRU), which is still very active today.

---

[273]   Andrew, *Secret Service*, pp. 11, 21, 31; Porch, *The French Secret Services*, p. 28.

Civilian intelligence services

The bureaucratization of military intelligence might have come first but the improvements that came with it were sometimes more appreciated by foreign ministries than the military themselves. Foreign ministries were also keen to secure their own secret services because of the reluctance or inability of military intelligence to seek *political* information; also because, naturally enough, foreign ministries tended to regard foreign affairs as their special preserve. Thus, despite the prestige of the General Staff (Box 2.1), the German foreign ministry established a 'political foreign intelligence service' during the First World War.[274] In Britain, the Secret Intelligence Service (SIS) (Box 2.2) and signals intelligence (given its present name Government Communications Headquarters, GCHQ, in 1942) fell under Foreign Office control after that conflict, and have remained responsible to it ever since. Other civilian intelligence services achieved more independence; notable among these is the American Central Intelligence Agency (CIA) established in 1947, which – like SIS – had its roots in military intelligence, the wartime Office of Strategic Services (OSS).

Sir Mansfield Cumming: first head of SIS

---

[274]   Richter, 'Military and civil intelligence services in Germany', p. 2.

> **Box 2.2 The British Secret Intelligence Service (SIS)**
>
> Also known as MI6, the cover name given to it in the Second World War, SIS began life as the foreign department of the Secret Service Bureau established in 1909 in response to alarm at the possibility of a German invasion. (The Bureau's home department was responsible for counter-espionage and was the forerunner of today's Security Service, also known as MI5.) Its first head was a naval captain, Mansfield Cumming ('C'), and it was initially answerable to the Admiralty. Since Cumming's time, the head of SIS has always been known as 'C' and the service sometimes referred to simply as 'C's organization'.

The full-time members of such services, 'intelligence officers' as opposed to 'spies' or 'agents', work in the guise of diplomats or consular officers but under their own names. They are, therefore, usually described as 'legals'. A much smaller number of intelligence officers are 'illegals' or 'NOCs' (non-official cover). (Legals and illegals are both discussed in the next chapter.)

Operations conducted by a secret service designed to support friends and eliminate enemies abroad sometimes involve violence but more often money, supplies and propaganda. Most secret services engage in this sort of thing from time to time, although some rather more than others. The GRU has a particularly bad reputation for this because of the clumsy attempt by two of its officers to murder a Russian defector, Sergei Skripal, with the nerve agent Novichok in the United Kingdom in March 2018. But during the Cold War, the CIA became legendary for its own covert actions, especially in Central and South America, and – via its Counterterrorism Centre Special Operations branch – revived this reputation, particularly in Afghanistan and Pakistan, during the so-called 'War on Terror' launched in response to the 9/11 attacks on the United States in 2001.[275] Among other secret services with reputations for no-holds-barred political warfare are Israel's Mossad and the secret services of France. In 1985, French intelligence officers blew up and sank in a New Zealand harbour the Greenpeace vessel, *Rainbow Warrior*, which was planning to inconvenience French nuclear testing on Moruroa atoll. For reasons that will be obvious, it is a common view in the secret world that covert action has its role, but that covert action and intelligence-gathering should not be handled by the same agency.

---

[275] Tenet, *At the Center of the Storm*, pp. 211, 225, 251.

The intelligence community

Major powers and middle powers have often had two and sometimes many more secret intelligence agencies, some answering only to the head of government or executive president (as in the USA) and others to different state ministries. In the United States, six separate departments run intelligence services: Defense, Energy, Homeland Security, Justice, State, and Treasury. Moreover, middle powers do not necessarily have fewer agencies (loosely defined) than major powers. Pakistan, for example, has nine intelligence agencies, which is about the same as the United Kingdom.

It is not necessarily a bad thing to have numerous agencies with some overlapping responsibilities, for this reduces the likelihood that an intelligence assessment will go untested and diminishes the risk that one agency will become politically too powerful. What is usefully termed 'tailored intelligence' – giving 'customers' a dedicated agency of their own people (for example, naval intelligence for the navy) – also 'improves communication and trust between them.'[276] But the rivalries between such agencies, which are notorious, can be debilitating, particularly when this results in confusion over responsibility or refusal to share intelligence.[277] The bureaucratization of secret intelligence would not, therefore, have been complete without a move to produce a rational administrative structure that allocated priorities to and harmonised the relations between them, and also distilled their product for the benefit of their busy political masters. Hence the 'intelligence community' – more than an aspirational name, if in practice less than the label implies.

The paradigm case of an intelligence community is that of the United States, which was created by statute in 1992. At the time of writing (August 2025) this formally contains two 'independent agencies' and sixteen 'elements' (Box 2.3). Prompted by the conclusion that poor information-sharing and general lack of coordination between different agencies had contributed to the success of the 9/11 attacks on the USA in 2001 and the false belief in 2003 that Iraq had WMD, the 'elements' were so called to encourage them to think of

---

[276] National Research Council, *Intelligence Analysis for Tomorrow*, p. 8.
[277] Porch, *The French Secret Services*, pp. 44-5.

themselves less as independent bodies and more as essential components of a complex, well-integrated whole. To the same end, in 2005 the office of Director of National Intelligence was created and the DNI made head of the entire body.

Box 2.3   The agencies and 'elements' of the U.S. Intelligence Community
Two independent agencies: the Office of the Director of National Intelligence (ODNI) and the Central Intelligence Agency (CIA). Nine Department of Defense elements: the Defense Intelligence Agency (DIA), the National Security Agency (NSA), the National Geospatial-Intelligence Agency (NGA), the National Reconnaissance Office (NRO), and intelligence elements of the five DoD services; the Army, Navy, Marine Corps, Air Force, and Space Force. Plus seven elements of other departments and agencies: the Department of Energy's Office of Intelligence and Counter-Intelligence, the Department of Homeland Security's Office of Intelligence and Analysis and U.S. Coast Guard Intelligence, the Department of Justice's FBI and the Drug Enforcement Administration's Office of National Security Intelligence, the Department of State's Bureau of Intelligence and Research, and the Department of the Treasury's Office of Intelligence and Analysis.
Source: *Office of the Director of National Intelligence

Secret intelligence as secret power

The risk of secret security and intelligence agencies wielding secret power in the state makes their control an important concern for government in general and – because, as we shall see, they live so closely with them – for diplomats in particular. US president Donald Trump, who complained in his first term about the manoeuvrings against him of the 'deep state' and expressed particular distrust of the CIA and the FBI, is not the first political leader to give voice to views of this sort. An obvious reason for this is that, broadly defined, intelligence communities have domestic as well as foreign responsibilities. Another is their modus operandi, which includes skill in political warfare and control of extensive secret funds. In some states, secret intelligence agencies make a great deal of extra money through criminal activities such as drug-trafficking, a credible charge frequently levelled at Pakistan's Inter-Services Intelligence (ISI), a notorious 'state within a state'.[278] In addition, their knowledge of 'where the bodies are buried', whether metaphorically or, in the case of Saudi Arabia, in reality, always has the potential to give them leverage

---

[278]   Glenny, *McMafia*, pp. 157, 166.

over a political leader – provided that leader is capable of embarrassment. Finally, like most institutions, secret services tend to have deep-rooted political prejudices that might periodically be at odds with the governments they serve. For example, in France the Deuxième Bureau was notoriously anti-semitic, while later the SDECE had a strong pro-colonialists bias;[279] in Germany, as we have already seen, the Abwehr was hostile to its Nazi masters (Box 2.1); and, with its deep attachment to Communism, in 1991 the KGB came close to overthrowing the reformist Soviet leader, Mikhail Gorbachev.

Formally, as already noted, the agencies are answerable either directly to the head of government or to a ministry. In the first case, they are sometimes said to be 'independent' but this only means that they are independent of any ministry; in effect, therefore, they are ministries in their own right. Examples include the CIA, the BND (Box 2.1), Mossad (Israel), the SVR (Russia). And, making the point rather neatly, there is the Chinese *Ministry* of State Security, now judged to be the largest secret service in the world, with over 40,000 officers posted abroad, although many are used to collect unclassified information.[280]

Effective executive oversight of the secret intelligence agencies, meaning well-informed, general direction of their work, is the most potent form of control, and in the liberal-democracies, including those in the post-Communist states, there is now much greater sensitivity to the means by which this should be achieved.[281] But if the executive itself is weak, vicious, or corrupt, what else can be done? One possible solution is to try a different *form* of executive oversight. For example, after the Second World War the French intelligence service, SDECE – today the Direction Générale de la Sécurité Extérieure (DGSE) – reported directly to the prime minister but, following numerous scandals, in 1962 it was placed by President De Gaulle under the Ministry of Defence. Another answer, and now much more common solution, is to subject the secret agencies to oversight by a bipartisan select committee of members of an elected assembly. The lead in such 'parliamentary oversight' was taken by the US Congress in the mid-1970s, following domestic spying scandals

279   Porch, *The French Secret Services*, pp. 9, 275.
280   *ISCP, China Report*, 13 July 2023, p. 27.
281   Born and Leigh, 'Democratic accountability of intelligence services', pp. 6-10.

and revelations concerning CIA covert operations (see Box 2.4), and by 2006 had become 'the norm in democratic states.'[282]

> **Box 2.4 Congressional oversight of the US Intelligence Community**
> Both houses of Congress have a select committee on intelligence. Since they control the funding of the Intelligence Community (Box 2.3), initiate legislation affecting it, have subpoena powers, and are supported by weighty staffs, considerable influence backs up their oversight responsibilities. The Senate Select Committee on Intelligence, which was created in 1976, has 15 members: eight senators from the majority party (one of whom has the chair) and seven from the minority, irrespective of the fluctuating representation of the parties in the Senate as a whole. It meets frequently, usually in closed session. The House 'Permanent Select Committee on Intelligence' (so-called to distinguish it from the temporary creation of the previous two years and now commonly known as the 'House Intelligence Committee') was created in 1977. House rules are silent on the size and party ratios of this committee, as on almost all other House committees, with two consequences: first, they are usually determined by negotiation between the majority and minority leaderships; second, the majority party in the House has a more favourable proportion of committee members than it has of congressmen in the House as a whole. Since the early 1980s, the majority party on the House Intelligence Committee has had on average three more members than the minority party, and holds the chair; at the time of writing (August 2025) the Republicans have fifteen seats and the Democrats twelve.

The provisions for greater accountability will have provided some reassurance to the diplomats of the liberal-democracies that the intelligence officers with whom they work closely are not going to embarrass them. On the other hand, because few of these committees have oversight of operational matters – as opposed to policy, administration and expenditure – they 'can have or give no assurance about the efficiency or the legality of the intelligence services.'[283] Besides, the number of liberal-democracies (always a minority) is shrinking.[284]

---

[282] Born and Leigh, 'Democratic accountability of intelligence services', p. 2; Caparini, M., 'Controlling and overseeing intelligence services in democratic states', pp. 10-14.

[283] Born and Leigh, 'Democratic accountability of intelligence services', p. 12. The American select committees are exceptional in their oversight of operations. The ISCP had such oversight nominally added to its own functions in 2013 but on such restrictive conditions as to make it of little value.

[284] *The Economist Intelligence Unit, 'Democracy Index 2024'.

3 Cuckoos in the Nest?

In 1883 the Czarist secret police, the Okhrana, installed the headquarters of its Foreign Bureau in the consular section of the Russian Embassy in Paris, from which it liaised with *agenturas* in Berlin, Sofia and elsewhere.[285] And in 1919, the British Secret Intelligence Service secured the reluctant agreement of the Foreign Office to give its officers cover as vice-consuls with responsibility for passport control work (Box 3.1). But it was not until after the Second World War, by which time secret services were more well established, that it became the norm for states to give legal cover in diplomatic and consular missions to the greater proportion of their intelligence officers abroad; such cover is now also provided by appointments in permanent missions and secretariats attached to international organizations such as the United Nations. Large numbers of intelligence officers still populate diplomatic missions despite the serious threat posed to human intelligence gathering (Humint) by the dramatic advances made in the technical means of intelligence-gathering since the middle of the last century. For example, if MI5 had correctly identified them, there were at least 23 'undeclared' intelligence officers in the Russian Embassy in London in March 2018 because this was the number expelled in response to the Skripal affair.

> **Box 3.1   SIS and Passport Control Officer cover**
> Prior to the Second World War, the Foreign Office refused to give SIS officers any cover in its overseas posts other than that of Passport Control Officer (PCO). But in addition to the disguise provided, the position had two other advantages: first, it gave immediate access to information on individuals of interest passing through border controls; and second, the pay for the work provided a useful supplement to the parliament-voted Secret Service budget. The trouble was that it tied SIS representation to those countries with which the UK had visa agreements and, because the cover was restricted to one position only, it soon became widely known that all PCOs were in reality SIS officers. This being the case, concluded an official report in 1944, 'little extra harm would have been done by affixing a brass plate "British Secret Service" to the door of their office.' Despite this, when the US State Department agreed in 1946 to give diplomatic cover to operatives of the new Central Intelligence

---

[285] Fischer, 'Okhrana'.

Group (later CIA), it 'sugar coated' the news for chiefs of mission by emphasising not only that the intelligence officers would answer to them but also be concerned chiefly with 'security intelligence' or helping missions by undertaking the clerical work of file-checks on applicants for visas and passports. Either because old habits die hard or because it was thought to be a clever double bluff, when Ruari Chisholm was made chief of the SIS station in the British Embassy in Moscow in 1960 he was given cover as '2nd Secretary (Head of Visa Section)'.

SOVIET UNION.		
Moscow	Ambassador	Sir Frank Roberts, K.C.M.G.
	Minister	W. Barker, C.M.G., O.B.E.
	1st Secretary	K. R. Oakeshott.
	Counsellor (Commercial)	H. W. King, M.B.E.
	1st Secretary (Commercial) ...	K. J. Uffen.
	3rd Secretary (Commercial) ...	L. E. Sturmey.
	1st Secretary and Cultural Attaché ...	C. M. James.
	2nd Secretary	M. J. E. Fretwell.
	" "	T. N. Haining.
	" "	S. W. Martin.
	3rd Secretary	D. C. Thomas.
	1st Secretary and Head of Russian Secretariat	C. R. A. Rae.
	2nd Secretary	M. J. F. Duncan.
	" "	R. A. Longmire.
	3rd Secretary	G. D. G. Murrell.
	2nd Secretary (Head of Visa Section)	R. W. Chisholm.
	Junior Attaché	Miss P. Fletcher.
	" "	Miss J. M. King.
	Naval Attaché	Capt. J. F. R. Dreyer, R.N.
	Assistant Naval Attaché ...	Lt. Cdr. H. M. Ellis, R.N.
	" " " ...	Lt.-Cdr. J. L. Varley, R.N.
	Military Attaché	Brigadier I. R. Burrows, O.B
	Assistant Military Attaché (Technical)	Major J. L. Jealous.
	Air Attaché	Gp. Capt. M. D. Lyne.
	Assistant Air Attaché	Fl.-Lt. R. McQ. Davies.
	" " " (Technical) ...	Sq. Ldr. N. J. Gardner.
	Scientific Attaché	D. A. Senior.
	Honorary Chaplain	Rev. J. B. Roberts.
	1st Secretary and Embassy Medical Officer	Dr. T. R. Austin.
	1st Secretary, Administration Officer and Consul (s)	A. J. V. George.
	2nd Secretary	M. Millar.
	3rd Secretary	C. G. F. James, M.B.E.
	" "	J. R. Neaves.
	Junior Attaché	W. E. Downing.
	" "	A. Riches.
	" "	G. P. Lockton.

Staff of British Embassy Moscow, Foreign Office List 1961

It was certainly technical means – typified by the spy satellite – that was the main reason for the cloud hovering over Humint at the end of the last century but it was not helped by the reputation it had acquired with 'users' for providing information that was not only – in modern conditions – too slow to dig out and deliver but also difficult to judge for reliability when it arrived. On the other hand, aside from the fact that most states either cannot afford or do not have access to the product of advanced technical means of intelligence-gathering, their limitations were highlighted by the failure to understand in 2003 that Saddam Hussein's Iraq did not possess WMD. Technical means cannot hear or see everything; nor cultivate agents of influence; nor – drone strikes apart – carry out more aggressive special operations in the absence of a major contribution by field officers and their agents. This has led to a reappraisal of Humint, which, as well as being cheap compared to other methods of collection, has special advantages of its own. Notable among these are an unrivalled ability to penetrate terrorist groups, procure top secret state documents and also assist Sigint itself; for example, by planting bugging devices and inserting infected flash drives into air-gapped computers or closed computer networks. Humint is, then, still important, and diplomatic cover for its officers is still popular. But why should such cover remain the disguise of choice? How does it work? And – as is sometimes grumbled by ambassadors – do intelligence officers in embassy nests really resemble cuckoos, those parasitic bullies of the bird world?

The Common Cuckoo

The advantages of diplomatic cover

Diplomatic cover has at least four advantages for intelligence officers.

First, it is a good disguise because intelligence officers not only tend to come from the same backgrounds as diplomats but also do much the same sort of thing. Real diplomats also seek information and cultivate friends in high places.

Second, the known presence of intelligence officers in embassies makes these missions magnets for those with secrets to divulge, whether they choose to do this by discreet signalling or openly walking through their doors. Swift assessments of the potential value and credibility of agents presenting in this way can be made and their exfiltration assisted should it become necessary. 'Walk-ins' are sometimes the most valuable of sources although usually difficult to distinguish from deliberate fakes ('dangles'). One of the most remarkable among the genuine sort was the KGB archivist Vasili Mitrokhin, who walked into the British Embassy in Latvia in early 1992 and, after several return journeys to Moscow, was successfully exfiltrated by SIS – together with the massive archive on which this chapter draws heavily – later in the year. Seven years earlier, KGB colonel and double agent Oleg Gordievsky, whose intelligence provided to the UK on the unfounded Soviet fear of an American nuclear attack and preparations for a pre-emptive first strike had greatly helped to avoid a catastrophic war in 1983, had been successfully exfiltrated by the SIS station in the British Embassy in Moscow.[286] Also worth mentioning are Ashraf Marwan, the highly placed Egyptian whose career as a Mossad agent began with an approach to the Israeli Embassy in London in 1970; and Aldrich Ames, the CIA officer whose own double life commenced when he entered the Soviet Embassy in Washington in 1985.

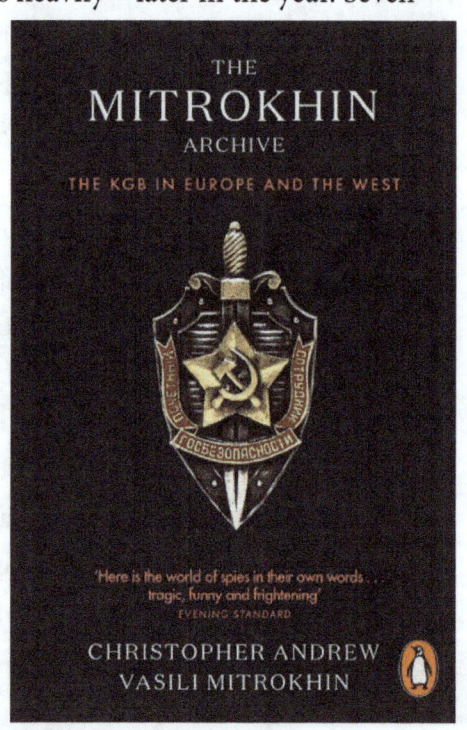

The third and most important advantage of diplomatic cover is the security it gives to intelligence officers. With diplomatic status, they have all of the privileges and immunities of genuine diplomats, whether inside or outside the embassy's walls. The worst that can befall them is to be declared persona non-grata and expelled (PNG-d). By contrast, 'illegals' or – in American usage,

---

[286]   Gordievsky was not a walk-in but had been delicately courted by the SIS station in the British Embassy in Copenhagen following his posting to the Danish capital in 1972, Macintyre, *The Spy and the Traitor*, Chs. 3 and 4.

NOCs (Non-Official Cover) – have no immunity and, if caught, usually face long-term prison sentences, or worse.

> **Box 3.2   The CIA's failed bid for more NOCs**
> Beginning in the mid-1950s, the CIA made efforts to halt the trend to more use of official cover, even setting as a long term goal having more NOCs than officers working legally in embassies. This was prompted partly by reductions in the opportunities for official cover caused by periodic economies in the number of US officials and installations overseas and partly by evidence that diplomatic cover was beginning to provide insufficient protection to officers in turbulent regions. It turned out to be wishful thinking not only because recruiting, training and setting up suitable candidates for NOC work was immensely difficult and took years but also because the constant demand of official customers was for delivery of sound intelligence 'now'. This story leaps out of the pages of the 659 CIA documents brought up by a search for "official cover" using CREST. In addition, in states where counter-intelligence was highly efficient, as in the Soviet Union, the likely arrest of CIA officers without diplomatic immunity would also have served merely to provide the local authority with 'trade bait' – prisoners to be used in swap negotiations.

Furthermore, much time and trouble is required to provide them with the kind of 'legend' that will withstand scrutiny, and as a result their numbers have usually been small (Box 3.2).

US Embassy compound in Somalia, evacuated 1991

Diplomatic status also gives intelligence officers, together with their work stations and accommodation, the physical protection afforded by the walled compounds in which many embassies and staff living quarters are now located in conflict zones. The importance of such protection has also increased further in recent years: first, because the multiplication of threats has led to the hurried expansion of many intelligence agencies, with the consequent need to send untested officers into dangerous operational environments; and second, because 'digital exhaust' fumes now make it so much easier to identify and expose intelligence officers.[287]

Finally, it is important to add that Sigint officers and technicians, as well as Humint officers, benefit from being hidden in diplomatic or consular premises. This is because of the customary proximity of embassies to government buildings, and the occasional nearness of consulates to sites of scientific and technical interest (Box 3.3). However, the increased use of fibre-optic cables for international communications, coupled with the recent use of aerial platforms for Sigint operations, is probably reducing the value of the embassies of the major powers for eavesdropping purposes.

Box 3.3   Sigint bases in Soviet diplomatic and consular posts in the Cold War

During the Cold War, the GRU and the KGB both developed massive Sigint networks based largely in Soviet embassies and consulates, especially in the USA. In 1963 the KGB established a radio intercept post at the Soviet Embassy in Mexico City and more valuable ones swiftly followed – on the top floor of the Washington embassy (only three blocks from the White House) in 1966 and in the New York consulate-general in the year after. By the 1970s, the KGB had five separate intercept posts at different diplomatic facilities in the Washington area and four in the greater New York City region, including one at the 'diplomatic *dacha*' in Glen Cove, Long Island. Since the KGB lacked high-level penetration agents in Washington during these years, these Sigint posts were then its chief sources of intelligence on US foreign and defence policy and in general were probably a good thing because they made it difficult for Moscow to sustain its long-held belief that America was planning a nuclear first strike. In 1976 an intercept post was also established in the KGB residency in the tall building occupied by the Soviet consulate-general in San Francisco, which became a perfect hub for eavesdropping on Silicon Valley until closed down on American insistence in August 2017.

---

287   Corera, 'The spies of tomorrow'. Had he written this piece after the Skripal affair, Corera might have added the vast expansion of CCTV coverage, which helped to identify the GRU officers responsible for this attack.

By the early1980s, the KGB had Sigint stations in 34 diplomatic or consular posts in 27 states. Astonishingly enough, the GRU's network of diplomatic listening posts (which included Soviet trade missions) was by then even bigger than this. The expansion continued remorselessly, so that by 1989 the KGB and the GRU were operating – often competitively – covert listening posts in 62 countries.

Embassy 'stations'

Within the embassies and more important consular posts of larger states, intelligence officers – like other specialist attachés – are to be found organized in sections. The CIA, SIS, Mossad and others refer to these as 'stations' while the Russian agencies call them 'residencies' (*rezidentury*). Such sections are formally subordinate to the ambassador but usually have separate communications and separate budgets, and tend to be generally semi-detached. The legendary Soviet ambassador to the United States, Anatoly Dobrynin, says that the KGB officers rarely made any contribution to discussion at general staff meetings in his embassy;[288] and in London, as was probably the case in some other capitals, the GRU residency was based in a separate building.

Anatoly Dobrynin, Soviet Ambassador to the United States, 1962–86

As to the typical diplomatic ranks that disguise intelligence officers, it is impossible to pronounce on this with any certainty without knowing who they are, although the pattern favoured by SIS after the Second World War is

---

[288] Dobrynin, *In Confidence*, p. 356.

probably still not unusual. With the bad experience of the PCO disguise in mind (Box 3.1), an influential official report in 1944 on the future organization of SIS advised that it was important to 'ring the changes' among diplomatic titles for its officers.[289] At first, therefore, they were concealed in a variety of relatively minor positions, among them assistant commercial secretary, press attaché, and vice-consul. Outside recruitment to such positions was in any case quite common, so new arrivals without career pedigrees in the diplomatic or consular service were unlikely to arouse much suspicion. It was not long, however, before more senior positions were also used as cover, as claimed by the SIS officer and KGB double agent, Kim Philby.[290] Philby himself had cover as a first secretary at the British Embassy in Turkey while head of the SIS station in that country in the late 1940s; the same rank was customarily held by the chief of the important SIS station in the Beirut embassy in the 1950s and 1960s; while at Paris and Washington the chief of station was usually a counsellor.[291] The more junior David Cornwell, better known as the master of the spy novel, John le Carré, had cover as a second secretary in the British Embassy in Bonn in the early 1960s and then briefly as a consul in Hamburg. SIS officers appear, however, only in exceptional circumstances to have been heads of mission (Box 3.4) and only rarely to have led important embassy sections. The highly regarded veteran BBC world affairs reporter, John Simpson, says that 'If you want to see who's in the British intelligence game, look at their titles. They're always a couple of steps below the level you'd expect for their age and seniority.'[292]

Box 3.4 British Consulate-General, Hanoi, during the Vietnam War
At least two SIS officers were head of mission (Consul-General) at this post during the Vietnam War: Gordon Philo (aka the novelist 'Charles Forsyte') and Daphne Park. This was an exceptional case because it was the hardest of 'hardship posts' and the consul-general was the only consular officer in the mission; fortunately for them, tours only lasted for six months.

[289] Jeffery, *MI6*, p. 603.
[290] Philby, *My Silent War*, p. 124.
[291] Bower, *The Perfect English Spy*, pp. 232-4, 327, 351; Andrew and Mitrokhin, *The Mitrokhin Archive*, p. 442.
[292] 'Our Friends in Beijing', p. 111.

A close cousin of the secret service station in the embassies and consular posts of some states is the science and technology section. This is because S&T intelligence – acquiring industrial secrets by more or less innocent methods – has been of huge importance for many decades. Espionage with this end in view is most commonly practised by states such as Russia, China, France and North Korea that have extensive direct or indirect control of key industries. However, Washington also began to give more attention to S&T intelligence in the late 1970s because by then the USA was contributing less than one-third of S&T advances, whereas in the 1950s it had originated three-quarters.[293]

Under the cover of responsibility for publicizing outstanding research and innovation in its own country and promoting international collaboration in research for the common good, the less innocent S&T section cultivates an agent network, often enough relying chiefly on post-doctoral students, academics and company chief executives in its diaspora community, as well as on local scientists and engineers with whom their own researchers have struck up personal relationships. S&T officers might well be intelligence officers, as they certainly were in Soviet missions in the days of the KGB and probably still are in those of its successor, the SVR.[294] China, for long notorious as a leader in S&T intelligence, is believed to have Ministry of State Security officers in its missions devoted to this work; if they are not intelligence officers, it would be surprising if they did not liaise closely with them. The fact that Donald Trump constantly alleges Chinese culpability in this area does not make the allegation groundless. A sizeable consular post adjacent to a concentration of leading universities and research institutes, as in New England in the United States, or high tech industries, as in Silicon Valley (Box 3.3), is very likely to have an S&T section. The French consulates-general in Boston and San Francisco both have such sections.

---

[293] CIA Science and Technology Advisory Panel, 'S&T Intelligence'.
[294] Run by Directorate T of the foreign wing of the KGB, they were called 'Line X officers' and were usually part of the residency, Andrew and Mitrokhin, *The Mitrokhin Archive*, pp. 280, 282-3, 456, 539, 548.

Modus operandi

Intelligence officers are often required to take an active hand in shaping events. Variously known as covert action, active measures, special operations or political warfare, this covers a spectrum from the modest to the murderous. As a rule, the contribution of those intelligence officers with diplomatic cover tends to be at the modest end, and they serve instead chiefly as agent recruiters and handlers – 'case officers'; where their own 'illegals' are present, they might also be required to give them support. Furthermore, they do not usually take serious risks to obtain intelligence from protected sources themselves, except when receiving it from their agents, and this is a process in which various devices of 'tradecraft' are designed to minimise the risk of detection; for example, cut-outs and dead drops. Such discretion does not prevent them from actively seeking information from open sources, and to this end – like any genuine diplomat – perhaps travelling widely; in some circumstances and in some degree, this will also provide a check on the veracity of the intelligence supplied by locally recruited agents.

The most sought-after agents are 'agents in place'; that is, persons occupying positions of trust in sensitive targets who are persuaded to divulge the secrets that come to them in the course of their work. The means of persuasion are well-known: money, the threat to expose embarrassing private behaviour, and the arousing of known or suspected ideological, religious or ethnic sympathies.

In principle a less valuable asset, acquired by the same means, is the 'agent of influence'. However, if highly placed, that influence might be used to steer important policy in a favourable direction, while such an agent might also pass over secrets without realizing it. The twice president of the United States, Donald Trump, is widely suspected of being an agent of this sort in the Russian interest, *kompromat* having been obtained on him not only through his shadowy business dealings with Russian oligarchs but also because of off-stage activities during the Miss Universe beauty pageant in Moscow in 2013.

Intelligence officers with diplomatic cover in unfriendly states are usually well-known to or strongly suspected by the local security services.

This is because embassies tend to be the object of careful surveillance and diplomatic lists sometimes make it relatively easy to form a shrewd idea of the officers' identities. Anatoly Dobrynin added other reasons why, in his embassy in Washington, KGB officers were easily identified by the FBI. Compared to the genuine diplomats, they had more expensive apartments, private cars, and more money for restaurant entertaining. They also spent far more time 'around town' and showed interest in everything, whereas genuine diplomats were known to the State Department 'through routine working contacts on specific problems.'[295]

While identification of intelligence officers cramps their style, this is normally less serious than might at first be thought. For one thing, being case officers rather than field agents, it is unlikely they will be caught doing anything illegal. It is also difficult for a counter-intelligence agency to keep track of them all if it is under-resourced and the number of intelligence officers in an embassy is swollen deliberately, which was a popular tactic of the former KGB.[296] And such 'legals' are usually tolerated on the basis of reciprocity ('we'll permit yours in reasonable numbers on the tacit understanding that you'll permit a similar number of ours'). This is why in 1978 the CIA opposed a request that the Justice Department deny entry visas to known Soviet bloc intelligence officers; to do so, it pointed out, would merely result in retaliation in kind, thereby drastically reducing, if not eliminating, its operational capability in those states.[297] The matter is different if legals are indeed detected in criminal activity themselves or are present in thoroughly alarming numbers; but even then, their fate is only to be PNG-d and sent home.

When posted in an embassy to a friendly and particularly an allied country, however, the balance of intelligence officers' work is often quite different. States spy on their friends as well as their enemies, so they might still be engaged in agent recruitment and handling. But it is common practice for them to give more weight to liaison with one or more elements of the local intelligence community; and, to this end, to 'declare' their true role.

---

[295] Dobrynin, *In Confidence*, p. 356.
[296] Andrew and Mitrokhin, *The Mitrokhin Archive*, pp. 538-9.
[297] Memorandum for the Record.

Cooperation between friendly intelligence agencies in the struggle against common enemies has long been valued; for example, between the Okhrana and the Sûreté against revolutionaries in Paris before 1917.[298] And today examples are plentiful. The most well-known is the Five Eyes' alliance (see Box 4.4).

Intelligence officers with diplomatic cover who are undeclared but strongly suspected are tolerated not only on the basis of specific reciprocity but also on condition that two other unwritten rules of the game are observed. These are that espionage is never admitted, and that its operatives – whether case officers and their agents or covert action personnel – do not act so clumsily as to attract public attention.

The diplomatic price of diplomatic cover

The invention and growth of secret services might have relieved ambassadors of all practical responsibility for running agents themselves, but only at the cost of giving house room to the thinly disguised personnel of these services, sometimes in large numbers. This often causes tension – sometimes acute – between the diplomats and the intelligence officers. Why should this be so? After all, intelligence officers do work regarded as vital to national security and which sometimes invites personal danger despite their diplomatic protection.

The most common source of the tension between intelligence officers and real diplomats is the duty of the former to take at least some risks with good relations with the host government; this also applies to defence attachés, as noted in the previous chapter. This is a strong temptation for intelligence officers when they populate an embassy in strength, their funds are lavish, their political support powerful, and their communications with home direct; in short, when they are 'cuckoos in the nest'.[299] In such circumstances, heads of mission might find that the chief of station is the real ambassador. It is notorious that KGB residents were often the de facto heads of Soviet embassies but the phenomenon appears also to have been common in those of the United

---

[298] Porch, *The French Secret Services*, p. 26.
[299] The cuckoo is a brood parasite that lays eggs in the nest of another species; these incubate faster than those of the host bird and produce beefy chicks which frequently kick out the other eggs they find.

States (especially in developing countries), and no doubt also in those of many other states.[300] Whether chiefs of station rule the embassy kingdom or are only powerful barons within it, the activities they direct often pose a risk to good relations because all states dislike being spied on and object even more strongly to foreign secret services meddling in their internal affairs. Moreover, receiving states usually have diplomatic and domestic law on their side. When, therefore, the association of a diplomatic or consular mission with espionage or covert action is exposed, trouble is bound to ensue. In hostile states, ambassadors will have to face the 'visceral feelings about the enemy within' it has stimulated, possibly expulsions of their staff;[301] and perhaps greater fury when an important ally is the victim and heads of mission have had no warning.[302] The last was no more eloquently demonstrated than by events in Pakistan in the first half of 2011 (Box 3.6) and in Germany in October 2013, when it was revealed by the German press that the Americans had been tapping the mobile phone calls of German chancellor, Angela Merkel, almost certainly from a Sigint post in their Berlin embassy. It seems to have been the US diplomats' demand for no more unpleasant surprises that led to the signing of what DCI Admiral Stansfield Turner described only half in jest as the 'treaty of friendship' between the CIA and the State Department in 1977 (Box 3.6).

Box 3.5   The Raymond Davis affair, Pakistan 2011
On 27 January 2011, Raymond Davis, a private security contractor employed by the CIA with cover as a member of the administrative and technical staff of the US Embassy in Islamabad, shot to death on a busy Lahore street two young (armed) Pakistanis shadowing him on motorbikes; a third (wholly innocent) Pakistani was accidentally run down and killed by a CIA vehicle speeding to their colleague's assistance. Davis was arrested by the police, charged with double murder, and imprisoned for almost 10 weeks until Washington – which insisted he had diplomatic immunity – secured his release. Anti-American

---

[300]   Stockwell, *In Search of Enemies*, p. 63; Church Committee, Ch. 14; National Commission on Terrorist Attacks, p. 94; Mazzetti, 'How a single spy helped turn Pakistan'.

[301]   Herman, *Intelligence Power in Peace and War*, p. 191. On the diplomatic downside of 'intrusive' intelligence-gathering – including 'close-range technical collection' – see also pp. 371, 372 and 385.

[302]   However, in discussing close international cooperation between intelligence services, Herman revealed 'a tacit professional recognition that cooperation is not necessarily a bar to continued targeting of each other's government, defence forces and the like,' *Intelligence Power in Peace and War*, p. 211; see also Pearce, *Spymaster*, pp. 137, 272, for the penchant of SIS officer and later chief, Maurice Oldfield, for spying on Britain's European allies.

sentiment, which was already inflamed by drone strikes against Al-Qaeda and Taliban militants near the frontier with Afghanistan, rose further, and US-Pakistan relations, as the US ambassador Cameron Munter said later, went 'straight to hell'. Neither were they rescued from its fires by the CIA-managed mission that killed Osama bin Laden at Abbottabad, not far north of Islamabad, only a few months later. Munter, who had serious misgivings about the drone campaign and was at loggerheads with the CIA station chief, resigned only half way through his posting.

When intelligence officers with diplomatic cover are expelled, this is usually justified publicly by the accusation of action 'inconsistent with their diplomatic status.' Even the station chief of a friendly state can fall victim to this fate, as in the case of the head of the Mossad station in Israel's embassy in London when it was learned that some of the Mossad officers responsible for assassinating a leading Hamas militant in Dubai in 2010 had travelled on the forged passports of 12 British-Israeli citizens.[303] If breaking the rule of the game against attracting public attention can result in this sort of reaction, so can breaking the rule against cramming too many intelligence officers into an embassy. This is why in 1971 the British government terminated the London posting of 105 Soviet intelligence officers with diplomatic cover.

Box 3.6 The State-CIA 'treaty of friendship', 1977
The 'State-CIA treaty' was signed in the spring of 1977 by Secretary of State Cyrus Vance and CIA Director Adm. Stansfield Turner. The CIA refused to allow their station chiefs to divulge the operational mechanics or the identity of agents to ambassadors because this would increase the risk of exposure and – if such a procedure were to be public knowledge – possibly be a fatal blow to its ability to recruit foreign nationals willing to commit treason against their own government. This is no doubt why, in discussing the treaty at the Cosmos Club on 25 January 1978, Adm. Turner admitted that the treaty required station chiefs to reveal more to ambassadors – 'but not everything.'
Sources: *Message from Director of Central Intelligence Turner to Chiefs of Station, Washington, October 4, 1977 and *CIA-RDP80B01554R002700420001-0

Expelling intelligence officers usually leads to a 'tit-for-tat' reaction by the second state – expulsion of the identical number of diplomats of the first. Insulation of the dispute in this way minimizes the chances of broader damage to relations but can have serious drawbacks for both embassies. First, via guilt by association, it brings them into bad odour. Second, it is quite possible that

---

[303] *The Telegraph*, 25 December 2010.

country specialists with local language skills who are not intelligence officers will be swept up in the exchange; for example, in 1971 the Soviet government's retaliatory expulsions from the British Embassy in Moscow included the remaining members of the mission's Russian Secretariat.

Even in the absence of expulsions, in-house intelligence officers might cause difficulties for a mission. Unwelcome attention by the security agencies of receiving states, especially when unfriendly, will probably be invited. This might well happen anyway but the presence of the spooks tends to make it more aggressive. Diplomatic premises are bugged, phone calls tapped, staff followed and sometimes physically harassed, and local citizens actively discouraged from having contact with them. Such actions all became routine in states locked directly in the Cold War, and remain a regular feature of some international relationships today. The known or simply suspected presence of intelligence officers can even stimulate or at least provide a ready pretext for popular hostility and mob attacks on embassies. This was the notorious fate of the US Embassy in Tehran, which housed a major CIA station, in late 1979.

Matters might not be much better in friendly states, particularly if the mission represents a state sensitive to human rights and the local security service has a well-earned reputation for brutality. As well as attracting criticism at home, liaison between the embassy's intelligence officers and such an agency will complicate the embassy's relations with the local authorities since it will be required to draw attention to human rights abuses, and present an obstacle to any attempt to maintain discreet contact with the opposition.

The knowledge that large numbers of intelligence officers are likely to inhabit the embassies of major powers is also likely to complicate – perhaps even sabotage – plans for the expansion of an embassy, or building of a completely new one at a different location. Suspicion of why the Russian government wanted an enlargement of their embassy premises in south Dublin, Ireland, to include a vast and comfortably equipped underground complex certainly complicated this project, for there remained ample space on its 5.5 acre mission site for cheaper above-ground building.[304] Similarly, at the time of writing

---

[304] *Berridge, 'The embassy that planned 13 toilets underground', 11 February 2024.

(August 2025), a long-awaited decision by the British government on China's project to build an entirely new embassy in London has been held up again by worry about why parts of its plans have been redacted.[305]

Finally, there is also unlikely to be a relaxed relationship between intelligence officers and genuine diplomats when the former are also required to keep a close eye on the latter for any sign of political unreliability, as is unfortunately the case in some states.

In sum, whether in unfriendly states or friendly ones with different attitudes to human rights, the effect of giving diplomatic cover to intelligence officers is usually to generate some degree of tension between the real and the fake diplomats, and occasionally to impair – and in extreme cases terminate – pursuit of the legitimate functions of the diplomatic or consular mission.

Repaying the diplomats

With all of these risks to hosting intelligence officers in their missions abroad, why do foreign ministries tolerate the practice? Patriotic sensitivity to the needs of a vital service is obviously an important factor and, where this is absent or weak, crude political pressure from a secret service powerful at home will be sufficient. But there is another very important reason: secret services can repay the diplomats for the favours they receive.

First and foremost, intelligence officers can provide 'diplomatic support', sometimes also known as 'policy support'. This means supplying information – including that obtained by decrypts of top secret, intercepted messages – that can furnish valuable tactical assistance in negotiations on any important subject, especially if it reveals the fall-back position of the other side or some point of personal weakness on the part of one or more of its key officials that can be exploited.[306] Herman, who was in a position to know, guesses that in the early 1990s Western intelligence agencies allocated about ten per cent of their resources to 'tactical support to diplomacy'.[307] To mention just two

---

[305] *Ben Macintyre, 'Embassies are always hotbeds of espionage', *The Times*, 9 August 2025.

[306] Herman, *Intelligence Power in Peace and War*, pp. 51, 97, 153-4; Pearce, *Spymaster*, pp. 283-4.

[307] Herman, *Intelligence Power in Peace and War*, p. 54.

examples, it is, therefore, credible that the CIA has 'aided and abetted plenty of negotiations' between Israel and the Palestinians, as claimed by George Tenet,[308] and that successful Sigint attacks on the computers and smartphones of delegates attending G8 and G20 summits are said to have provided welcome real-time information to their 'customers'.[309] Most negotiations of great importance by-pass embassies today but even if their diplomatic staff are not direct beneficiaries of diplomatic support, they are well aware of its value and of the contribution that from time to time is made to it by the intelligence officers in their midst.

Closer to the embassies' immediate needs, intelligence officers can also provide them with valuable practical assistance in critical circumstances; for example, by helping with communications and giving warning of attacks, as in the case of the planned Al Qaeda assaults on US embassies in Albania and Uganda in 1998 probably forestalled by the CIA.[310] Generally skilled at operating in the shadows, intelligence officers can also take the strain from the diplomats by serving as paradiplomats in sensitive relationships. (This is the subject of the final chapter.) Last but not least, the 'platform' provided by embassies and consulates for the conduct of operations by intelligence officers, as well as kindred spirits such as drugs and immigration liaison officers, helps greatly to justify their continued existence: no cuckoos, then fewer, smaller, and less well feathered nests. Some secret intelligence agencies even pay rent to their diplomatic landlords; SIS certainly does so.[311]

With incentives on the part of both diplomats and intelligence officers to live in harmony, peaceful coexistence between them has been reinforced in the liberal democracies by the oversight measures introduced in recent years to curb the occasional excesses of the intelligence agencies, as described at the end of the previous chapter. Elsewhere, there is probably still more of a downside to this relationship for the diplomats than for the spooks. In light of the grisly

---

[308]   Tenet, *At the Center of the Storm*, p. 55.
[309]   'GCHQ intercepted foreign politicians' communications at G20 summits', *The Guardian*, 17 June 2013.
[310]   National Commission on Terrorist Attacks, p. 127.
[311]   ISCP, *Annual Report, 2010–2011*, p. 32.

killing of the Saudi journalist, Jamal Khashoggi, in the Saudi consulate-general in Istanbul in early October 2018 by a hit squad in which intelligence officers are reported to have had a hand, this observation is probably well taken by members of the Saudi diplomatic service.

4 Spooks as 'Diplomats'

Intelligence officers in the higher ranks of their organizations frequently serve as 'diplomats' in two capacities: first, as special envoys to hostile states; and second, as builders and managers of international secret service alliances, together with less formal and more numerous 'liaison' relationships. As for the first role, why might they be given such tasks when it surely means 'blowing' their cover and there are usually so many other officials to choose from, among them senior political advisers and even seasoned diplomats themselves? As for the second, at first glance it might be assumed that this role is accepted solely for the obvious advantages it carries for the secret services; so what, if any, are its broader diplomatic benefits, whether intended or not?

Intelligence officers as special envoys

Special envoys, otherwise known as the leaders of 'special missions', are sent abroad to conduct diplomacy with a limited purpose for a limited time, and are recognised in diplomatic law.[312] They are a feature of normal diplomatic relationships but are particularly valuable to the diplomacy between states which are so hostile that they do not enjoy the exchange of permanent missions. In such circumstances, special envoys are the next-best alternative. They also provide great security for the secrecy of a message, which, in the circumstances, might be of considerable sensitivity. And their use to bear a message – especially if they are high-ranking – underlines the importance attached to it, thereby making it more likely that it will receive serious attention.

When special missions are employed in diplomacy between hostile states, they are often despatched in secret, and almost always when contacts are at an early stage. The first reason for this is the need to minimise the risk of political sabotage. Public knowledge that a special mission to a hostile state is planned, especially if it is a high-level one rumoured to be seeking a

---

[312] *Convention on Special Missions, 1969.

253

DNI James Clapper briefing President Obama on N. Korea, 23 November 2010

rapprochement, is likely to spread alarm among factions at home and allied governments abroad whose interests are locked into the *status quo*. Advance warning of what is afoot permits them time to marshal their forces and nip it in the bud. The second reason for secrecy is the need to guard prestige, which is seriously threatened by appearing as a supplicant at the seat of the rival's power, especially if the mission is a failure. These were the main reasons for the intense secrecy cloaking the highly significant first mission to Beijing in July 1971 of US National Security Advisor, Henry Kissinger.

Box 4.1 James Clapper's secret mission to North Korea, November 2014
At the beginning of November 2014, Washington received strong indications that two Americans serving long prison sentences in North Korea would be released. The only conditions were that the United States should send to fetch them a high-level official bearing a personal letter from President Obama, presumably to demonstrate respect for the DPRK's young leader, Kim Jong Un, and help to confirm his authority at home. The Americans quickly chose James Clapper, a former USAF general, career intelligence officer and DNI since 2010. Together with a small team, he flew secretly to Pyongyang on a US military aircraft a few days' later; some members of Congress were briefed in advance and the governments of Japan, South Korea and China were also notified. Although he had gone with no guarantees of success, Clapper swiftly returned with the released prisoners, this

time in public. In light of his later public interviews, he was probably chosen for this mission for the following reasons, in roughly descending order of importance: (i) he was certainly, as requested, a high-level official (ii) as America's 'top spy', it was natural that his North Korean counterparts, General Kim Won Hong, minister of state security and General Kim Young Chol, director of the Reconnaissance General Bureau, would wish to be his interlocutors – as proved to be the case – and that as men in the same business they would more readily come to an understanding on the technicalities (iii) since Clapper was neither a diplomat nor a politician, his selection served to underline the Obama administration's keenness to show the North Koreans that he was not being sent to negotiate wider issues (iv) as an intelligence officer he was nevertheless well qualified to watch and listen for pointers on such matters (v) he was further qualified to do this because in the early 1980s he had served as a director of intelligence for U.S. forces in Korea, and followed developments on the peninsula afterwards, and (vi) seeing the North close up had for long been on his 'bucket list'.

Prince Bandar bin Sultan meeting Russian president, Vladimir Putin, 14 July 2008

In light of the above, it is hardly surprising that the use of intelligence officers as special envoys has a history as long as that of secret services. The first of their qualifications for the role is that almost all will have had more or less intimate acquaintance with the world of diplomacy by virtue of serving in embassies under diplomatic cover. A few might even have been genuine diplomats earlier in their careers, a case in point being that of Prince Bandar bin

Sultan. Bandar served as Saudi ambassador to the United States from 1983 until 2005, then became a much-travelling secretary-general of his country's National Security Council, before finally – from 2012 until 2014 – adding to this the position of head of Saudi intelligence.[313] Another is Moussa Koussa (Box 4.3).

The employment of senior intelligence officers as special envoys has two further advantages that are obvious and one that is perhaps less so. First, on secret missions, their experience makes them the best qualified not only to avoid the danger of exposure to the international press but also to remain composed in what might well be an intimidating environment. It is interesting in this context that at one tense point during James Clapper's secret mission to North Korea (Box 4.1) he was told by his hosts that he had been 'demoted' from his status as President Obama's envoy since he was unable to discuss wider issues and that – 'the people' being in consequence 'agitated' – his security could no longer be guaranteed.[314]

Second, intelligence officers should have a special knowledge of the latest intelligence on their destination, and might well be familiar with the local language. These were the chief reasons why SIS officers were used in secret contacts with Iraqi officials in the run-up to the war against Saddam Hussein's regime in 2003 (Box 4.2).

Box 4.2   SIS contacts with Iraq in the run-up to the war in 2003
In evidence to the Iraq Inquiry (the official British post-mortem on the 2003 war), SIS contacts with Iraqi officials in the pre-conflict period were confirmed but all details redacted. Nevertheless, Sir Richard Dearlove ('C') made clear that SIS knew much more than the Foreign Office (which had no embassy in Baghdad) both about Weapons of Mass Destruction (WMD) proliferation matters and Iraq in general – and so implicitly explained why SIS was chosen to send the envoy to meet the Iraqis. Gordon Corera, the leading British writer on SIS, says that the envoy in question was the SIS Controller for the Middle East. Because of the government priority attached to knowing whether or not Iraq possessed WMD, a related factor was that Dearlove was in regular contact and got on well with the prime minister, Tony Blair. In the event, the SIS controller was unable to vouch for the credibility of his Iraqi contact's information, although it turned out to be true; namely, that Iraq had no WMD.

---

[313]   *Reuters*, 15 April 2014; *The Guardian*, 16 April 2014.
[314]   Gorman and Entous, 'U.S. Spy Chief Gives Inside Look at North Korea Prisoner Deal'.

Sir Richard Dearlove: head of SIS, 1999–2004

The third and less obvious advantage of choosing intelligence officers for sensitive special missions is that there is always a good chance it will stimulate the appearance of intelligence officers among those they find themselves negotiating with on their arrival. This is probably because of the fit of the proposed agenda with the remit of the local intelligence services and the keenness of the locals to take the measure of their foreign counterparts. The point is, though, that this means that, as well as being on the same professional wavelength as their interlocutors, the visitors will be holding discussions with individuals who are potentially among the most powerful in the country (see section 'Secret intelligence as secret power' in Chapter 2) and thus those with the power to conclude an agreement. These at any rate are among the most important points to emerge from the episodes described in Boxes 4.1 and 4.3, both of which were successful.

Box 4.3 CIA/SIS team negotiates Libya's agreement to abandon WMD, March–December 2003
Assisted by secret intelligence contacts, Colonel Muammar Gaddafi's 'rogue state' of Libya had been inching towards a rapprochement of sorts with the NATO powers since 1999. But in March 2003, when a US-led attack on Iraq was clearly imminent, the pace quickened.

Seeming to fear that he might be next, the Libyan leader sent his son, Saif, to London to inform SIS that he wanted to talk about his own WMD. Shortly afterwards, two SIS officers flew to Libya, where they met Gaddafi himself. This was the start of a lengthy negotiation between a joint CIA-SIS team and a Libyan team led by Moussa Koussa, many years earlier head of the notorious People's Bureau in London but then the head of Gaddafi's own 'External Security Organization'. There were several meetings in a European capital, one in Tripoli attended by Gaddafi himself, two visits to weapons sites and a final negotiating session in London on 16 December at the Travellers' Club, a well-known haunt of diplomats and intelligence officers. Encouraged by a phone call from Tony Blair, on 19 December the

Moussa Koussa

Libyan leader publicly announced that he was to abandon his programme to develop nuclear weapons. The quid pro quo was that if this were verified, US sanctions on Libya would be lifted. In the event, most US sanctions had been lifted by September 2004.

By way of a footnote to this episode, in October 2008 and January 2009 Moussa Koussa was himself a special envoy to the UK, the upshot of which was the release from a term of life imprisonment in Scotland of Abdelbaset Ali Mohmed al-Megrahi, the Libyan intelligence officer who had been convicted in 2001 for the bombing of Pan Am Flight 103 over Lockerbie in 1988.

Tradecraft and special knowledge of the proposed negotiating partner are qualities that are particularly appropriate where contact needs to be made with hostile non-state groups, the more so if they have been labelled as 'terrorists'. And it is noteworthy that many of the known instances of 'clandestine diplomacy' have taken place with groups of this sort rather than with states. Instances that are now well known include the contacts of the CIA with the PLO, and of SIS with the Provisional IRA in Northern Island, the Taliban in Afghanistan, and the Palestinian organization, Hamas. The New York Convention on Special Missions 1969 is silent on contacts with such entities. More importantly, because of state reluctance to confer any respectability – let alone formal recognition – on them, the maximum secrecy that only intelligence officers can provide is the more essential.

The final point to be made on this subject is that there is an excellent chance that – especially if they are senior figures in their services – the identity of intelligence officers sent on special missions will already be known to the other side, so the argument that using them 'blows their cover' falls away. In any case, intelligence officers are sometimes headquarters-based precisely because their cover has been blown already and they are, as a result, no longer of use in the field.

Secret service alliances and liaisons

Fruitful relationships between the secret intelligence services of different states – whether formal alliances or less formal liaisons – were slow to develop but increased greatly following the end of the Cold War in 1991, as international relationships became more fluid and common threats such as terrorism and climate change accelerated. Already in 1996, Herman revealed that at that time Britain had 'relationships of some kind with the intelligence and security organizations of some 120 countries.'[315] For his part, CIA Director George Tenet, in memoirs published in 2007, emphasised how the CIA's 'War on Terror' was highly dependent on 'scores of other intelligence services', many of which were in the Islamic world and could infiltrate terrorist sanctuaries to a degree well beyond the capability of his own organization.[316] And in 2018, Rana Banerji, a long-serving Indian intelligence officer, recorded that India had 'constructive ongoing intelligence-sharing arrangements with Afghanistan, Bangladesh, Bhutan, Myanmar, Nepal and Sri Lanka', and, beyond its chief focus on South Asia, also with Israel.[317] Intelligence liaisons as well as alliances are usually strengthened by the presence in embassies of 'declared' intelligence officers with formal responsibility for liaising with the local intelligence community.[318]

Secret service alliances tend to be founded on shared political values, common ethnic roots, the same language, intimate military co-operation and a similar professional culture. The only intelligence alliance that is well-known, exceptionally integrated and very long-lived is the so-called 'Five Eyes' alliance (Box 4.4). Burden sharing with a common goal in view can also extend to covert action, as provided for in the Four Square Agreement of 1954 between SIS and

---

[315]   Herman, *Intelligence Power in Peace and War*, p. 208.

[316]   In return, the Americans provided them with technical assistance, 'analytic training', and a great deal of cash, Tenet, *At the Center of the Storm*, pp. 121, 127, 129, 149-50, 253.

[317]   Banerji, 'South Asian allies …'.

[318]   Interestingly, the embassies of 'strategic adversaries' might also house some 'declared' intelligence officers, *ISC, *International Partnerships*, 5 December 2023, p. 18, para. 74. Such embassies must see some advantage in making a virtue of a likely necessity.

the CIA, in which the former was to have responsibility for anti-Communist operations in Burma, Singapore and Malaya, the latter to take the lead in the Philippines, with operations to be run jointly elsewhere in the Far East.[319]

Box 4.4 The Five Eyes' alliance

Originally composed only of the UK and the USA, this developed during the Second World War, was formalised by an international agreement in 1946, and afterwards was joined by what used to be called 'white dominions' of the British Empire – Canada (1948), Australia and New Zealand (1956). It was initially an agreement to cooperate only in the gathering of Sigint, with a division of labour and the product shared, but over time the alliance came to embrace cooperation over all types of intelligence gathering. It also provides that no member shall collect intelligence on the others, although this has not been taken seriously for many years. A number of 'third parties' from Western Europe were added much later but cooperation with them is more limited and the core of the relationship probably remains that between America's NSA and Britain's GCHQ. The Five Eyes' alliance was not formally acknowledged until 2010 and much more about it was revealed in 2013 by the whistle-blower, Edward Snowden, an employee of an NSA private sector contractor. In its valuable report on 'International Partnerships' published just under a year prior to the success of Donald Trump in the November 2024 US elections, the Intelligence and Security Committee of [the UK] Parliament was predictably high in its praise for the unique value of the Five Eyes' alliance – but emphasised the importance of <u>trust</u> to any such relationship. That must now be at an all time low. For Trump swiftly resumed his flirtation with the war criminal and sworn enemy of NATO, Vladimir Putin; his vice-president, J. D. Vance, openly aligned Washington with the extreme right-wing AfD in Germany; former Fox News host Pete Hegseth was made Defense Secretary (with NSA in his intelligence empire) and is regarded as a joke by the US military; Tulsi Gabbard – another notorious Putin apologist – was made Director of National Intelligence, no less; US relations with Canada plunged spectacularly; and news that the president's national security team was using an insecure commercial app for a group chat hit the headlines in March. What could possibly go wrong with the Five Eyes' alliance?

By contrast, 'liaisons' tend to be just marriages of convenience in the face of common enemies. They are especially productive when fortified by good personal relations between the heads (and other senior officers) of the intelligence services concerned, especially when they are powerful figures at home and remain in office for many years, as in the case of B. N. Mullick of India's Intelligence Bureau and R. N. Kao of its Research and Analysis Wing.[320] Since Russia's invasion of Ukraine in February 2022 and subsequent pressure from Western economic sanctions, it has also been badly in need of intelligence

---

[319] Pearce, *Spymaster*, pp. 148-9; Jones, "'Maximum Disavowable Aid'", p. 1194.
[320] Banerji', 'Access to political leadership …'.

sharing wherever it can find it. Whether this search has benefited from the personal charm of bosses in its own intelligence community is an open question. Nevertheless, SVR chief Sergey Naryshkin, who has also maintained arms length contact with the US Director of Central Intelligence, has publicly boasted of Russia's close intelligence relations with Iran and especially China.[321]

The intelligence value of such arrangements is obvious, but what is their diplomatic importance?

First, because they are out of sight, secret services can continue to collaborate as usual and thereby help to underpin important diplomatic relationships when these are strained by wide differences over one or more high profile issues. This was certainly true of the Five Eyes' intelligence relationship between Britain and the United States at the time of the Anglo-American tensions over the Suez Canal in 1956 and – during Donald Trump's first administration – the Paris Agreement on climate change, the Iran nuclear deal, tariff policy, and the Middle East.[322] It remains to be seen whether the Five Eyes' itself will even survive the second Trump administration and, if so, whether it will have the same beneficial effect in preserving at least reasonably good diplomatic relations between the United States and the other four parties..

Second, intelligence officers might also have a soothing effect when a foreign government believes that the diplomats of a sending state have a prejudice against it. Thus the British Foreign Office for long had the reputation of being pro-Arab and it was for this reason that, after the Suez fighting in 1956, preceding which there was secret Anglo-French collusion with Israel to attack Egypt, the new British prime minister, Harold Macmillan, employed SIS to communicate with the Israelis.[323]

Third, close intelligence relationships discourage the targeting of each other's normally well guarded secrets, which could otherwise jeopardise friendly

---

[321] Teslova, *Anadolu Agency* [Turkish], 17 January 2023; Faulconbridge and Davis, *Reuters*, 17 January 2023.
[322] Bower, *The Perfect English Spy*, p. 197; House of Lords International Relations Committee, 'UK foreign policy in a shifting world order', p. 10.
[323] Bower, *The Perfect English Spy*, p. 240.

diplomatic relations. This is true despite the fact that there is 'tacit professional recognition' that it is not completely forbidden.[324]

Fourth, a close relationship can be used discreetly to offer or imply a diplomatic quid pro quo in return for intelligence assistance. For example, it seems highly likely that this was anticipated by the Indian government in using one or other of its agencies – probably naval intelligence and the coastguard – to kidnap and return Sheikha Latifa to her brutal father, the prime minister of its close ally, the UEA, in early 2018.[325]

---

[324] Herman, *Intelligence Power in Peace and War*, p. 211.
[325] *The Guardian*, 4 and 6 December 2018. On the close and valuable ties between India and the UAE at the time, see 'India, UAE sign currency swap deal to boost trade ties', *Gulf News*, 4 December 2018.

5 Conclusion

By the time that the resident embassy was well established in the sixteenth century, the ambassador was an important figure in the creation and running of secret agent networks, although in some states he played second fiddle to a home-based 'spymaster'. The relationship of the spymaster to his own agents was, however, essentially personal and, partly for this reason, his networks were fragile. Gradually, therefore, ambassadors were given 'secret service' money and largely left to get on with it. Unlike intelligencers, merchants and others, they were uniquely well suited to the task. They had ready access to those with the secrets most worth penetrating; experience of sending information home as quickly and securely as possible; and, under the developing law of nations, growing immunity from prosecution in the event they should be caught receiving stolen secrets or fomenting rebellion. By the nineteenth century, however, ambassadors had begun to cool to espionage and political warfare; not only to direct involvement in it but also to the need for it at all. At this juncture on the threshold of becoming members of a self-confident profession of high social status, with its own code of right conduct, diplomats had come to regard themselves as perfectly capable, via charm and good dinners, of gleaning all of those secrets worth obtaining. In extremis, any grubby business needed could be handled at arms' length by a lower ranking officer or consul.

In the last decades of the nineteenth century, which saw intense great power rivalries, technological developments increased the risk of strategic surprise. The result was that military high commands and foreign ministries (if not so much their diplomatic services) began to think that special efforts should be made to obtain intelligence on potential enemies. This in turn led to the regular appearance in the embassy of the military attaché, shortly followed by the creation of military intelligence services, and then to the emergence of separate civilian foreign intelligence services as well. The distinguishing feature of these new services, which set them apart from the spymaster system of earlier centuries and culminated in the idea of the intelligence community, was their bureaucratization. This facilitated the storage, retrieval, analysis, and distribution through government of the increasing flow of information, and also made it easier to manage agent networks. There is no evidence that these developments were at first greeted with anything but a 'whatever next!' scepticism by the all-seeing diplomats but at the least they promised the opportunity to extend even further their arm's length relationship with the 'dirty' world of secret intelligence. In some states, secret services came to wield great political influence.

The demonstrable limitations of technical means of intelligence-gathering have led to a re-discovery of the value of Humint in recent years and thus arrested what might otherwise have been a slow decline in the numbers of intelligence officers sheltering in diplomatic missions, where they have all of the privileges and immunities of genuine diplomats. The diplomatic price of this is sometimes high: like cuckoos in a nest, intelligence officers sometimes throw their weight around inside the mission and create embarrassing disturbances outside. But they can be a diplomatic asset as well, not least by providing tactical support in important negotiations and a valuable argument for maintaining large embassy networks in order to provide 'platforms' for their work. In some circumstances, high-ranking intelligence officers are also well suited to serve as special envoys, while the alliances and looser liaisons they forge help to underpin important diplomatic relationships when these are seriously strained. In the liberal-democracies, parliamentary oversight of the intelligence community now provides some reassurance to diplomats – along with everyone else – that abuses will not be tolerated.

The relationship between diplomacy and secret service is one of mutual dependence. And, since both are vital to global stability – the one concentrating on the settlement of differences and the other on removing the ignorance that breeds fear and false alarms – it is important that this relationship should be well understood. A serious corollary of this for public policy is that governments should be wary of expelling intelligence officers from embassies in droves simply to make a political gesture or because they are unwilling to spend the money on keeping watch over them. In this regard it is important to remember that the intelligence on US foreign and defence policy gathered by the large Sigint posts inside the Soviet missions established in the United States in the 1970s made it more difficult for the ideologically blinkered, desk-bound KGB chiefs in Moscow to sustain their long-held belief that America was gearing up for a nuclear first strike; and that it was embassy-based intelligence officers who enabled KGB defector Oleg Gordievsky to warn Western leaders in time, in the early 1980s, that Soviet paranoia was driving Moscow to the catastrophic conclusion that their country's only chance of survival was a futile attempt to pre-empt NATO aggression with a nuclear first strike of its own.

References

An *asterisk preceding a reference indicates online availability at the time of writing, usually without a paywall. Here and there the same system has been employed in footnotes.

Adams, S.; Bryson, A.; Leimon, M.,'Walsingham, Sir Francis (c.1532–1590)', *Oxford Dictionary of National Biography*, 21 May 2009

Aid, M., 'Eavesdroppers of the Kremlin: KGB Sigint during the Cold War', in Leeuw, Karl de and Jan Bergstra (eds), *The History of Information Security: A comprehensive handbook* (Amsterdam, 2007)

Allen, E. John B., *Post and Courier Service in the Diplomacy of Early Modern Europe* (The Hague, 1972)

Andrew, Christopher, *Secret Service: The making of the British intelligence community* (London, 1985)

Andrew, Christopher, *The Defence of the Realm: The authorized history of MI5* (London, 2009)

Andrew, Christopher and Oleg Gordievsky (eds.), *Instructions from the Centre: Top secret files on KGB foreign operations, 1975–85* (London, 1991)

Andrew, Christopher and David Dilks (eds.), *The Missing Dimension: Governments and intelligence communities in the twentieth century* (London, 1984)

Andrew, Christopher and Vasili Mitrokhin, *The Mitrokhin Archive: The KGB in Europe and the West* (Harmondsworth, 1999)

*Banerji, Rana, 'South Asian allies essential for Indian intelligence', *Asia Times*, 11 October 2018

* Banerji, Rana, 'Access to political leadership key to India's success in intelligence cooperation', *Asia Times*, 12 October 2018

Barkin, Noah, 'Five Eyes intelligence alliance builds coalition to counter China', *Reuters*, 12 October 2018

Bemis, Samuel Flagg, 'British secret service and the French-American alliance', *The American Historical Review*, vol. 29 (3), April 1924

Berridge, G. R., 'The ethnic "agent in place": English-speaking civil servants and Nationalist South Africa', *Intelligence and National Security*, vol. 4 (2), April 1989

Berridge, G. R., *Gerald Fitzmaurice (1865–1939): Chief Dragoman of the British Embassy in Turkey* (Leiden, 2007)

Berridge, G. R., 'Fitzmaurice, Gerald Henry (1865–1939)', *Oxford Dictionary of National Biography*, 19 May 2011

Berridge, G. R. (ed.), *Diplomatic Classics: Selected texts from Commynes to Vattel* (London and Basingstoke, 2004)

Berridge, G. R., *British Diplomacy in Turkey, 1583 to the present: A study in the evolution of the resident embassy* (Leiden, 2009)

Berridge, G. R., *The Counter-Revolution in Diplomacy and other essays* (London and Basingstoke, 2011)

Berridge, G. R., *Embassies in Armed Conflict* (New York, 2012)

*Berridge, G. R., 'The Trump-Russia dossier cannot be dismissed lightly' (12 January, 2017)

*Berridge, G. R., 'Trump and Putin: that 'secret meeting' at the G20 dinner (19 July, 2017).

Born, Hans and Ian Leigh, 'Democratic accountability of intelligence services', *Policy Paper 19* (Geneva Centre for the Democratic Control of Armed Forces, 2007)

Bossy, John, *Giordano Bruno and the Embassy Affair* (London, 1991)

Bower, Tom, *The Perfect English Spy: Sir Dick White and the secret war, 1935–90* (London, 1995)

Budiansky, Stephen, *Her Majesty's Spymaster: Elizabeth I, Sir Francis Walsingham, and the birth of modern espionage* (New York, 2005)

Callières, François de, *The Art of Diplomacy*, ed. H. M. A. Keens-Soper and Karl W. Schweizer (New York, 1983), Chs. 3 and 8 and App. 1

Caparini, M., 'Controlling and overseeing intelligence services in democratic states', in H. Born (ed.), *Democratic Control of Intelligence Services: Containing rogue elephants* (London, 2007)

*Chesterman, S., 'The spy who came in from the Cold War: intelligence and international law', *Michigan Journal of International Law*, 2005–6, vol. 27

*'Church Committee': *Foreign and Military Intelligence. Book I. Final Report of the Select Committee to Study Governmental Operations with respect to Intelligence Activities. United States Senate* (Washington, 1976)

*CIA Science and Technology Advisory Panel, 'S&T Intelligence: The Intelligence Community's capability to meet new and evolving needs of national policy-makers', 17 September, 1980

*CIA Scientific and Technical Intelligence Committee, 'The Overt Collection of S&T Intelligence', December 1978

Clinton, Hillary Rodham, *What Happened* (London, 2018)

Cobban, Alfred, *Ambassadors and Secret Agents: The diplomacy of the First Earl of Malmesbury at The Hague* (London, 1954)

*Convention on Special Missions, 1969

Corera, Gordon, *MI6: Life and Death in the British Secret Service* (London, 2012)

*Corera, Gordon, 'The spies of tomorrow will need to love data', *Wired*, May 2016

Croft, Pauline, 'Cecil, Robert, first earl of Salisbury (1563–1612)', *Oxford Dictionary of National Biography*, 23 September, 2004

*DeVine, Michael E. and Heidi M. Peters, 'U.S. Intelligence Community Elements: Establishment provisions', *Congressional Research Service*, 27 June 2018, available **here** Dobrynin, Anatoly, *In Confidence: Moscow's Ambassador to Six Cold War Presidents* (New York, 1995)

*Federation of American Scientists (n.d.), 'Pakistan Intelligence Agencies'

Faulconbridge, Guy and Caleb Davis, 'Kremlin says U.S.-Russian spy chief meeting would make sense, *Reuters*, 17 January, 2023

*Fischer, B. B., 'Okhrana: The Paris Operations of the Russian Imperial Police' (CIA History Staff Center for the Study of Intelligence, 1997)

*Glassman, Matthew Eric and Sarah J. Eckman, 'House Committee party ratios: 98th-114th Congresses', *Congressional Research Service*, 7 December, 2015

Glenny, Misha, *McMafia: Seriously organised crime* (London, 2008)

Gorman, S. and A. Entous, 'U.S. Spy Chief Gives Inside Look at North Korea Prisoner Deal', *The Wall Street Journal*, 14 November, 2014

*Graham, David A. (2018) 'Is Money-Laundering the Real Trump Kompromat?' *The Atlantic*, 19 January, 2018

Grenville-Murray, E. C. (The Roving Englishman), *Embassies and Foreign Courts: A history of diplomacy* (London, 1855)

Grewe, Wilhelm G. H., *The Epochs of International Law.*, trsl. and rev. Michel Byers (Berlin, 2000)

Hammer, Paul E. J., 'Essex and Europe: Evidence from confidential instructions by the Earl of Essex, 1595–6', *The English Historical Review.* vol. 111 (441), April 1996

Haynes, Alan, *Walsingham: Elizabethan spymaster & statesman* (Stroud, Glos., 2004)

Herman, Michael, *Intelligence Power in Peace and War* (Cambridge, 1996)

Herman, Michael, 'Diplomacy and Intelligence', *Diplomacy & Statecraft*, vol. 9 (2), July 1998

Horn, D. B., *The British Diplomatic Service, 1689–1789* (Oxford, 1961)

*House of Lords, Select Committee on International Relations, 'UK foreign policy in a shifting world order', HL Paper 250, 5 December 2018

Hughes, Michael, *Diplomacy before the Russian Revolution: Britain, Russia and the Old Diplomacy, 1894–1917* (London and Basingstoke, 2000)

Hutchinson, Robert, *Elizabeth's Spy Master: Francis Walsingham and the secret war that saved England* (London, 2007)

*ISCP, *Annual Report, 2010–2011*, July 2011, Cm 8114

*ISCP, *Annual Report, 2016–17*, December 2017, HC 655

*ISCP, *China*, 13 July 2023, HC1605

*ISCP, *International Partnerships*, 5 December 2023, HC288

*The Iraq Inquiry, Private Evidence

Jeffery, Keith, *MI6: The history of the Secret Intelligence Service, 1909–11949* (London, 2010)

*Jervis, R., 'Reports, Politics, and Intelligence Failures: The Case of Iraq', *The Journal of Strategic Studies* 29 (1), February 2006

*Johnson, Charles W. et al, *House Practice: A guide to the rules, precedents, and procedures of the House* (Washington, 2017)

Jones, Matthew, '"Maximum Disavowable Aid": Britain, the United States and the Indonesian Rebellion, 1957–8', *The English Historical Review*, vol. 114 (459), November 1999

*Khazan, Olga, 'Gentlemen reading each others' mail: a brief history of diplomatic spying', *The Atlantic*, 17 June 2013

Kynaston, David, *The Secretary of State* (Lavenham, 1978)

*Langbart, David A., 'Five months in Petrograd in 1918: Robert W. Imbrie and the US Search for information in Russia', *Studies in Intelligence* (CIA),vol. 52 (1), March 2008, Web Supplement

*Lee, Sidney, 'Walsingham, Francis (1530?-1590)', *Dictionary of National Biography*, vol. 59

Leimon, M. and G. Parker, 'Treason and plot in Elizabethan diplomacy: the "fame of Sir Edward Stafford" reconsidered', *English Historical Review*, vol. 111 (444), November 1996

*MacAskill, E. et al, 'GCHQ taps fibre-optic cables for secret access to world's communications', *The Guardian*, 21 June 2013

MacCaffrey, Wallace T., 'Cecil, William, first Baron Burghley (1520/21–1598)', *Oxford Dictionary of National Biography*, 23 September 2004

Macintyre, Ben, *The Spy and the Traitor: The greatest espionage story of the Cold War* (New York, 2018)

Matthews, Owen and Matthew Cooper, 'Spy or Diplomat? Meet Russian Ambassador Sergey Kislyak, the Most Radioactive Man in Washington', *Newsweek*, 22 June 2017

Mazzetti, Mark, 'How a single spy helped turn Pakistan against the United States', *The New York Times Magazine*, 9 April 2013

McDermott, James, 'Stafford, Sir Edward (1552–1605)', *Oxford Dictionary of National Biography*, 24 May 2012

Memorandum for the Record, Justice Department Appropriations Report Language, 8 August 1978 (CREST)

Middleton, C. R., *The Administration of British Foreign Policy, 1782–1846* (Durham N.C., 1977)

*Millotat, C. O. E., 'Understanding the Prussian-German General Staff system', 20 March 1992, Strategic Studies Institute: U.S. Army War College

*Moore, Richard [formerly British Ambassador at Ankara, later Chief of the Secret Intelligence Service (MI6) 2020-2025], interviewed on The Mishal Hosain Show, Nov. 2025

*National Commission on Terrorist Attacks Upon the United States, *The 9/11 Commission Report: Final Report of the National Commission on Terrorist Attacks Upon the United States* (U.S. Government Printing Office: Washington D.C., 2004), Chs. 3 and 13.

National Research Council, *Intelligence Analysis for Tomorrow* (Washington DC, 2011)

*Office of the Director of National Intelligence, Intelligence Community Assessment: 'Assessing Russian Activities and Intentions in Recent US Elections', 6 January, 2017

Pearce, Martin, *Spymaster: The life of Britain's most decorated Cold War spy and head of MI6, Sir Maurice Oldfield* (London, 2016)

Philby, Kim, *My Silent War* (St. Albans, Herts, 1969)

Porch, D., *The French Secret Services: From the Dreyfus Affair to the Gulf War* (London and Basingstoke, 1996)

Potter, David (ed), *Foreign Intelligence and Information in Elizabethan England* (Cambridge, 2004)

Radsan, A. John, 'The unresolved equation of espionage and international law', *Michigan Journal of International Law*, vol. 28 (3), 2007

*Read, Conyers, 'Walsingham and Burghley in Queen Elizabeth's Privy Council". *The English Historical Review*, vol. 28 (109), January 1913

Read, Conyers, *Mr Secretary Walsingham and the Policy of Queen Elizabeth* (Oxford, 1925)

Richter, L., 'Military and Civil Intelligence Services in Germany from World War I to the end of the Weimar Republic', in H. Bungert, J. G. Heitmann and Michael Wala (eds), *Secret Intelligence in the Twentieth Century* (London, 2003)

*Rohde, David, 'Digitizing the CIA', *Reuters*, 2 November 2016

*Roth, Andrew, 'The man who drives Trump's Russia connection', *Washington Post*, 22 July, 2017

Rule, John C., 'Review of *Espions et Ambassadeurs au Temps de Louis XIV* by Lucien Bély', *The International History Review*, vol. 14 (4), November 1992

Satow, Rt. Hon. Sir Ernest, *A Guide to Diplomatic Practice*, 2nd. rev. ed., vol. 1 (London, 1922)

Seligman, Matthew S., *Spies in Uniform: British military and naval intelligence on the eve of the First World War* (Oxford, 2006)

*Senate Judiciary Committee, Interview of: Glenn Simpson, 22 August, 2017

Simpson, John, *Our Friends in Beijing* (London, 2021)

*Smallteacher, R., 'Egypt-U.S. intelligence collaboration with Omar Suleiman "most successful"', *Wikileaks*, 1 February, 2011

*Smith, David and Spencer Ackerman, 'Who is Sergey Kislyak, the Russian ambassador rattling Trump's presidency?', *The Guardian,* 3 March, 2017

**Spiegel* Staff, 'Embassy Espionage: The NSA's Secret Spy Hub in Berlin', *Spiegel Online International*, 27 October, 2013

*Steele Dossier

Steele, J., 'Vitaly Churkin obituary', *The Guardian*, 21 February, 2017

Stockwell, John, *In Search of Enemies: A CIA story* (London, 1979)

Stone, Lawrence, *An Elizabethan: Sir Horatio Palavicino* (Oxford, 1956)

Swaine, Jon and Shaun Walker, 'Trump in Moscow: what happened at Miss Universe in 2013', *The Guardian*, 18 September, 2017

Szechi, Daniel (ed), *The Dangerous Trade: Spies, spymasters and the making of Europe* (Dundee, 2010)

Tanikawa, K. and K. Ikeida, 'Japan in Depth / Satellite to keep tabs on N. Korea', *Japan News*, 28 February, 2018

*Taylor, P., 'Iraq war: the greatest intelligence failure in living memory', 18 March, 2013, *The Telegraph*

Tenet, G., *At the Center of the Storm: My years at the CIA* (New York, 2007)

Teslova, Elena, 'Intelligence ties with China at 'unprecedented' level, says Russian spy chief', *Anadolu Agency*, 17 January, 2023

Trump, Donald J. with Tony Schwartz, *Trump: The art of the deal* (London, 1988)

*U.S. House of Representatives, Permanent Select Committee on Intelligence, *Interview of: Glenn Simpson*, 14 November, 2017

*US Senate Select Committee on Intelligence Rules of Procedure

*Vienna Convention on Diplomatic Relations, 1961, United Nations, *Treaty Series*, vol. 500

Wicquefort, Abraham de, *The Embassador and His Functions*, trsl. Mr Digby (London, 1716)

Wikipedia, 'Agent of Influence'

Wikipedia (n.d.) 'Francis Walsingham'

Wilson, Derek, *Sir Francis Walsingham: A courtier in an age of terror* (New York, 2007)

INDEX

www.ingramcontent.com/pod-product-compliance
Lightning Source LLC
Chambersburg PA
CBHW082247120626
46555CB00009B/2988